The Structure and Function of European Integration

JAMES A. CAPORASO
Northwestern University

GOODYEAR PUBLISHING COMPANY
Pacific Palisades, California

75-1334

Y-8472-6
ISBN: 0-87620-847-2
Library of Congress Catalog Card Number: 73-83391

Current printing (last digit):
10 9 8 7 6 5 4 3 2 1

Printed in the United States of America

to Jeanne

Preface

In writing this book I had a twofold goal. On the one hand, I wanted to write a book that could serve as a general introduction to the political processes characteristic of the European Community, an introduction that was not completely descriptive but was instead cast within an explicit conceptual framework. On the other hand, I wanted to write a book of interest to the specialist in regional integration. To this end I have attempted to rework the basic materials of European integration into a coherent framework. Specifically, it involves the identification of the key structures, both formal and informal, in the integration process and the evaluation of their functional significance. At times I may bore the specialist and at other times frustrate the beginner. If so, these are the risks of pursuing a middle course.

Given these goals it follows that this book does not attempt to fashion a new theory or approach nor does it primarily attempt to test hypotheses. Rather the focus is in assembling our knowledge of politics in the European Community and examining it in a structural and functional context. By doing this I hoped to impart some general significance to the bits and pieces of the integrative process which we observe. In terms of its place in the process of scientific inquiry, this book has to do with providing the language of a theory, its key concepts, and suggestions of how the concepts may be related.

Although a book of this nature is inevitably the result of a dialogue between the author and many other individuals, there are several people who distinctly deserve mention. Robert Mahoney of Northwestern University patiently read the entire manuscript and gave helpful comments on the overall organization of the book. Kenneth Janda, also of Northwestern, read and gave helpful comments on Chapter Six. Other individuals were especially helpful. The librarians at the various libraries of the Commission of the European Communities were always ready to assist me. I owe a special debt of gratitude to Mme. Jacqueline Lastenouse-Bury and to Mme. Lakdar, both of the University Information section of the European Community. I spent four virtually uninterrupted months at their library and during this time they put me in touch with countless documents that were otherwise inaccessible to me. I would also like to extend my gratitude to Northwestern University for facilitating my research in many ways and in particular, for providing funds and released time in the spring and summer of 1970 to return to Europe. Last, I thank my wife, Jeanne, for her encouragement and support, and my children, Jeanice and Jody, for whatever patience and restraint they managed to show during the several years of my writing of this book. I thank them also for their distractions, for while no doubt they slowed the book down, they are also responsible for whatever good humor remains in me.

Contents

Abbreviations

CAP	Common Agricultural Policy
CET	Common External Tariff
CGIL	Confederazione Generale Italiana del Lavoro (General Confederation of Italian Workers)
CIBE	Confédération Internationale des Betteraviers Européenne (International Confederation of European Sugarbeet Growers)
CIRAI	Comitati Italiano per le Relazioni Agricole Internazionali (Italian Committee for International Agricultural Relations)
CISL	Confédération Internationale des Syndicats Libres (International Confederation of Free Trade Unions)
CNPF	Conseil National du Patronat Français (National Council of French Employers)
COCCEE	Comité des Organisations Commerciales des Pays de la CEE (Committee of Commercial Organizations of the Countries of the European Economic Community)
COMECON	Council of Mutual Economic Assistance
COPA	Comité des Organisations Professionelles Agricoles des Six Pays de la Communauté Economique Européenne (Committee of Professional Agricultural Organizations of the Six Countries of the European Economic Community)
CPR	Committee of Permanent Representatives
DBV	Deutscher Bauernverband (German Farmers' Union)
EC	European Community
ECSC	European Coal and Steel Community
EDF	European Development Fund
EEC	European Economic Community

EFTA	European Free Trade Association
EPA	European Parliamentary Assembly
ESC	Economic and Social Committee
EURATOM	European Atomic Energy Commission
FEOGA	Fonds Européen d'Orientation et de Garantie Agricoles (European Agricultural Guidance and Guaranty Fund)
GATT	General Agreement on Tariffs and Trade
IPS	International Processes Simulation
NATO	North Atlantic Treaty Organization
OEEC	Organization for European Economic Cooperation
PEP	Political and Economic Planning
UACEE	Union de l'Artisanat de la CEE (Union of the Craftsmen of the EEC)
UNICE	Union des Industries de la Communauté Européenne (Union of Industries of the European Community)

CHAPTER ONE

Political Development and the Study of International Integration

CONVERGENCES BETWEEN THE STUDY OF NATIONAL AND INTERNATIONAL POLITICS

Since the end of World War II, two striking developments have characterized the national and international arenas. On the national scene, there has been a tremendous upsurge of social change, most of which has been labeled development or modernization but which in fact has also included breakdown and decay.[1] This has given rise to a renewed interest in non-Western areas and a burgeoning literature on political and economic development. At the same time the international system has undergone changes of its own. The nearly three decades that have elapsed since World War II have witnessed the proliferation of a variety of international organizations that are attempting to cope with problems previously under the exclusive jurisdiction of the nation-state. There have been military pacts (North Atlantic Treaty Organization), free trade areas (European Free Trade Association) and customs unions (the European Economic Community). This development has in turned impelled a mushrooming literature on international integration.[2] One beneficial upshot of both trends has been a marked interest in general theories of social change.[3] In this regard, integration and development have been treated not in distinct fashions but as species of the more generic theory of social change along with theories of sociocultural evolution and theories of economic growth.

But the rapid pace of social change has produced yet another convergence in our scholarly efforts, that between the study of national and international politics. In part, the tendency for the distinctiveness of these two fields to break down is a result of the demise of the unqualified and undifferentiated "state as actor" approach, as in the classical billiard ball analogy of international politics.[4] It is also partly attributable to the growing awareness, however, that perhaps our entities (e.g., nation-states, international systems, local communities) do not provide the most theoretically persuasive way to organize our subject matter and that helpful insights can be gained by applying the same conceptual frameworks to national and international systems.[5] Thus Chadwick Alger, in his article "Comparison of Intranational and International Politics," illustrates the benefits

1

to be obtained by applying a conceptual framework formulated for nation-states to the international political arena. Such transference of knowledge could serve at least two purposes. One, if knowledge is more advanced in one area than in the other and if one is a valid analogy for the other, then insights culled from one field may aid the other. Two, if two units are related to each other so that the one may evolve into or change to become more like the other then it may aid us in understanding social change by viewing both units as differentiated on a continuum. In the latter sense it has been helpful to compare international political systems with underdeveloped national ones or with primitive political systems as Alger has done. This indulgence in analogical reasoning may be permitted as long as we recognize that analogies are sources of hypotheses and not of confirmation. Any insight garnered by analogical reasoning must stand the muster of empirical test and be judged on its own terms.

The unusual flux at the national level has presented some intriguing questions as well as some vexing problems. First, do the rapid change, turmoil, and attendant dislocations indicate an "eclipse of community" as some have suggested, or do these things only intimate a new kind of community, one that has lost its territorial moorings?[6] If new communities are being formed, will we be able to characterize them in the same manner as nation-states?

The process of integration in Western Europe provides a convenient laboratory for an examination of these processes and forces us to take a hard look at our conceptual equipment for dealing with the study of these changes. It is an unfortunate fact that the theory of political and social change is one of the most impoverished areas within the social sciences. In addition, at a time when the world seems insistent on protracted change, some social theorists have turned to approaches that they openly recognize as static.[7] This inadequacy in our theories of change, and integration in particular, is evidenced by the inability of scholars of international integration to agree on even the simplest descriptive claims. For example, Karl Deutsch, Ronald Inglehart, Leon Lindberg, and Ernst Haas come to widely different conclusions as to the present level of European integration compared with that which existed in 1958.[8] Some feel that the European Economic Community (EEC) came to a grinding halt with the crisis precipitated by the French walkout in June 1965.[9] Others talk about the EEC as having "passed the point of no return,"[10] of deepening the level of *engrenage,* or irreversible involvement.[11]

The controversy above does not appear resolvable in its present form since different authors utilize different conceptual categories. Thomas Kuhn has convincingly argued that in the absence of a common conceptual language, or of a theoretically neutral one, it is difficult to resolve disputes because they spring from different conceptual bases, possess different definitions, and differ as to what constitutes evidence. Criteria for success and standards for progress vary in each case.[12]

FUNCTIONALISM AND INTERNATIONAL INTEGRATION

The problem is not that we lack factual information about the process of regional integration in Europe. The difficulties stem from inadequate organization of such information. How should these facts be organized, into what categories ought they to be funneled, and what are the ways in which these categories can be linked to one another? In short, the fundamental problem is to find a suitable conceptual framework. This will guide us to what is relevant, suggest ways in which the data must be organized, and aid in the task of interpreting research results.

One approach that recommends itself to this particular problem is the functional approach, as developed by Gabriel Almond in his Introduction to *The Politics of the Developing Areas* and later amended by Gabriel Almond and G. Bingham Powell, Jr.[13] This approach is appropriate for several reasons. First, the functional approach has a general appeal across all political systems in that a given set of political functions is present in all polities, although the content of the structures through which these functions are performed is left open. This method makes for standardization and increased ease of comparison, facilitates deductive transitions from one field situation to another, augments the communicability of results, and consequently has wider cross-national appeal. Application of the functional approach would help to overcome ad hoc empiricism by providing for some stability of meaning between research settings. It would also enhance contextual meaning by suggesting how partial research findings relate to the larger system. For example, a study of interest groups would be important not only in terms of the internal structure of socioeconomic groups, their various activities, and how these groups attempt to influence the political process, but also in terms of how the form and function of these groups relate to other political institutions, for example, parties, elections, and so on. A second advantage of this approach is that problems of political development and problems of international integration can be treated within a common conceptual apparatus. It should help to diffuse insights and understanding culled from one area to the other and at the same time aid the consolidation of our research efforts in the most parsimonious fashion.

The approach here is somewhat novel in that it attempts to apply Almond's framework to an emerging supranational system (the EEC), not to a domestic one. My reading of the functional approach, however, is that it applies to political systems in general and not just to those polities organized at the nation-state level. In addition, it is my conviction that the process of integration, with some important exceptions, is not very different from the process of development. For example, one way of ascertaining how integrated Europe is would be to examine how well developed the structures for performing political functions at the European level are. To what extent do interest groups, political parties, and the like operate in a supranational environment, making demands of a "European" political system? To what extent do structures exist for the formulation and execution of regulations with binding force? What kinds of capabilities characterize the European political system? One could ask these same questions about every political function. This view of integration asks to what extent an emerging unit has acquired or is acquiring the structural and functional characteristics of a political system. In this sense it differs from development only in that the unit in question is emerging out of a set of component units that were previously independent.

I proceeed in the following fashion: First, I spell out my conception of integration and show its relationships both with developmental theories as well as with other theories of integration; second, I attempt to link my view of integration more fully with the functional approach and to develop their points of articulation more clearly.

DEVELOPMENT, INTERNATION INTEGRATION, AND SYSTEMS BUILDING

The literatures of political development and political integration have rarely confronted one another. Despite this, they are surprisingly related. One view (and it seems to me the most common one) of integration is that of systems building.[14] In related manner, one often looks upon political development as the acquisition by the system of the capacity to allocate values, respond to system demands, and command the legitimacy of the members of the political system. The difference between the two approaches is in terms of the unit or focus of reference. In political development, one takes the unit as given (e.g., India) and examines the growth and development of structures and functions around that unit. The unit is a constant. It is variation in structural characteristics (e.g., the degree of structural differentiation or the extent of subsystem autonomy) that is of interest. Political integration does not assume the existence of a crystallized unit. It is precisely the emergence and development of this unit which is of interest. There is, however, a relationship to political development in terms of our interest in the emergence and growth of political structures around a new focus which is larger, more comprehensive, and more intensive than the former. By "more comprehensive" we may mean geographically more comprehensive as evidenced by the formation of the European Coal and Steel Community (ECSC) or by the addition of England, Denmark, and Ireland to the European Community. We could also mean by "more comprehensive" that a particular unit was increasing its scope, for example, in terms of the number of issue areas it comprehended. The transition from the European Coal and Steel Community to the European Economic Community involved the shift from limited cooperation in the production and marketing of coal and steel to cooperative endeavors in agriculture, social policy, transport, tariff policy, parts of external relations policies, and many others. Finally, a unit could become functionally more comprehensive by multiplying the number of functions performed within an issue area. Here we are talking not so much about mere tasks or items of business of which the Community must dispose as about functions in the meaning of that term derived from structural-functional requisite analysis. In these terms a function becomes a pattern of activity necessary for the maintenance of the system, at least within certain limits. An example of this kind of integration would be the gradual politicization of European agriculture since the EEC came into operation. All of these indexes of increases in the scope of integration should be distinguished from the vertical integration that comes with the intensification of integration in any given sector. This may involve some measure of increase of frequency, such as a higher rate of meetings of the Council of Ministers devoted to resolving problems in the transport sphere; or it may involve some measure of output, such as the number of decisions agreed upon by the Council of Ministers.

This view of integration is not so different from that taken by several scholars. Morton Kaplan defines integration in terms of "regulatory processes which join systems or organizations with separate institutions and goals within a common framework providing for the common pursuit of at least some policies."[15] Ernst Haas looks upon integration in similar terms. Integration refers to "the process whereby actors in several distinct national settings are persuaded to shift their loyalties, expectations and political activities toward a new and larger center, whose institutions possess or demand jurisdiction over the pre-existing national states."[16]

The definitions of both Kaplan and Haas stress the shifting of attitudes and behavior to new units whose jurisdiction is increasing. Haas includes attitudinal reorganization along with the transference of patterns of political activity. Kaplan lays particular emphasis on the pursuit of common objectives within a shared institutional framework. The crucial element is the acquisition on the part of the new system of a generalized capacity to mobilize resources to achieve common political objectives.

The other dominant approach to integration views it in terms of harmonizing the operation of different system parts. Since components of systems have at least some measure of autonomy and since increased differentiation generally increases this autonomy,[17] the problem arises as to how to mesh or coordinate behavior among various parts of the system. The focus here is on some unit already in existence. The question of how this unit emerged and acquired its functions is not treated as problematic. Rather concern is with differentiation of these functions into more specialized structures. This viewpoint is voiced by Talcott Parsons and Neil Smelser: "solidarity is the generalized capacity of agencies in the society to 'bring into line' the behavior of system units in accordance with the integrative needs of the system, to check or reverse disruptive tendencies to deviant behavior, and to promote the conditions of harmonious cooperation."[18]

A third view of integrative processes, provided by Karl Deutsch, highlights the development of processes of orderly change and security-community. Deutsch defines integration as "the attainment within a territory, of a sense of community, and of institutions and practices strong enough and widespread enough to assure, for a long time, dependable expectations of peaceful change among its population."[19]

The definitions supplied by Parsons, Smelser, and Deutsch are inadequate for our purposes. Parsons and Smelser, by focusing primarily on the problem of interunit relationships, divorce themselves from what is of primary theoretical interest for us, viz., how those units came into existence. Deutsch, on the other hand, by defining integration in terms of progress toward a security-community, disassociates himself from what is certainly a common feature of many processes of rapid change, viz., a certain amount of dislocation, turmoil, strain, and violence. Integration is after all a process of systemic transformation and we would hardly expect the demise of the nation-state with only a whimper. In addition, by focusing on "peaceful" communities regardless of the number of issues being processed and without respect to the extent of mobilization of societal resources for the attainment of system goals, we can be led into the paradoxical situation where a community is perfectly integrated but where little politics exists. I would expect that the higher the number of collective goals pursued by a society, the heavier the strain in the system.

THE PLACE OF POWER

To view international integration in terms of the gradual acquisition of system capabilities by new political units immediately demands an introduction of the concept of power. The concept of power arises in the context of our discussion of politics as involving the mobilization of societal resources for the attainment of collective goals. This will become clear through our discussion.

The definition of power provided by Talcott Parsons is appropriate for our theoretical purposes: "Power then is generalized capacity to secure the performance of binding obligations by units in a system of collective organization when the obligations are legitimized with reference to their bearing on collective goals and where in case of recalcitrance there is a presumption of enforcement by negative situational sanctions. . . ."[20] This definition includes two components: one, it stresses the capability aspect and, two, it raises the possibility of invoking sanctions should societal resources not be capable of being mobilized voluntarily. It should be clear that the view of power here is in nonzero-sum terms, in accord with the Parsonian formulation.[21] Thus the acquisition of power and capabilities by an emerging supranational system need not detract from the power and capabilities of the nation-states that make it up. A gain in power for the new unit does not imply a corresponding loss of power for the older units. The total power capacity for a set of systems may so increase that none of the systems suffers a diminution of power. The appropriate metaphor here is the expanding pie in which everyone gains even where the number of receivers increases, rather than the fixed pie where, if the number of actors increases, each actor will be distributed less. Total growth characteristics are emphasized rather than just reallocations and changes of existing patterns of behavior. This distinction is particularly important for the study of integration since much confusion has been generated concerning whether the growing strength of the EEC augurs the demise of the nation-state or whether the EEC is only an organizational adaptation on the part of the nation-state to prolong its existence and strengthen its position. In line with the nonscarcity assumptions built into our notion of power, we may view both forms of organization as growing in strength and viability.

The relationship among power, development, and integration should now be clear. Both development and integration are processes that involve the acquisition of capabilities to effectively pursue societal goals. Power becomes the medium used in the pursuit of these goals. Development has been conceived by Almond in terms of capabilities (the performance of a political system in its environment), conversion functions (how demands and supports are translated into policy outputs), and system maintenance and adaptation functions.[22] Manfred Halpern sees development as the growing capacity of a society to "generate and absorb continuing transformation."[23] Finally Karl von Vorys views development as "a process which includes social and economic changes, but whose focus is on the development of the governmental capacity to direct the course and the rate of social and economic change."[24] All these definitions revolve around growth patterns that are of note in the study of international integration.

There is a threefold interest in the process of integration: first, how does a given international system come into being, that is, what are the processes that characterize an emerging system; second, how does it evolve into a set of more differentiated structures after it comes into being; and third, how do the components of the emerging system fit together in some coherent ensemble? Posing these priorities in a sequential fashion does not suggest that one must precede the other. There may be some rough phasing involved but it clearly must take a back seat to the reciprocal influences of all three processes operating simultaneously. All these processes are crucial to integration. We must ask how specialized components of a political system came into existence just as we must identify the processes that hold the system together. The next question involves examining the process of gradual differentiation of functions into a set of specialized structures. Such specialization of functions should serve to increase the capabilities and effectiveness of the new political system. The initial focus is on boundary processes where older systems mingle with their environments, blur their boundaries, and evolve into new systems. A new system may be said to have come into existence when the new unit acquires capabilities for mobilizing societal resources in the pursuit of collective goals.[25] When this threshold is crossed the focus shifts from the emergence of functions to their increasing or decreasing differentiation. This does not necessitate our focusing entirely on internal processes. Almond's notion of capabilities provides us with a crucial theoretical link with the environment.[26]

APPLICATION OF ALMOND'S FUNCTIONAL APPROACH TO THE EUROPEAN COMMUNITY

The theoretical context for the application of the functional approach is that of systems analysis. A system is defined minimally as a set of elements (in this case political structures) with determinate patterns of interaction and maintaining some sort of boundary with respect to its environment, that is, a system must possess some negative feedback loops to preserve its distinctive organization. A set of elements may be called a system if variations in one part affect variations in other parts in such a way that these variations can be predicted better by the substantive model than by a null one.

The functional approach may be viewed in this context as an attempt to (1) delineate the elements (i.e., structures) of the system; (2) suggest how these categories of elements fit together, that is, find out what their interrelationships are; and (3) suggest what some of the more significant processes might be which transpire *through* these structures. It is argued that the categories proposed are neither ad hoc nor purely descriptive but in fact are a carefully worked out set of concepts that provide a potential ordering matrix for theory building. The principal purpose of this strategy is of course one of mapping developments of events concerning European integration into a functional framework. If meaningful theory is to emerge, we need to know the categories and variables in terms of which it will be constructed. In some ways then an emphasis on political morphology precedes an emphasis on political process.[27]

The approach developed by Almond and his associates is general, although originally applied to polities at the nation-state level.[28] Alger has already demonstrated the utility of viewing emerging, supranational polities in terms of this framework.[29] Here I try to set out the general applicability of this framework to the study of international integration in the EEC. As mentioned, one way to approach the question of integration in the EEC would be to examine how well developed the structures for performing political functions at the European level are. To what extent do interest groups, political parties, and the like operate in a supranational environment, making demands of a European political system? When and under what conditions will European elites act through supranational as opposed to national channels? To what extent does a supranational bureaucracy exist which administers European policy and has this bureaucracy acquired autonomy? To what extent can Europe be characterized as possessing a set of structures for socializing and recruiting new members into European political roles and for communicating political information? In what ways can Europe be characterized as possessing structures for making binding policy, implementing it, and adjudicating conflicting claims with respect to it?

THREE KINDS OF FUNCTIONS: CAPABILITIES, CONVERSIONS, AND SYSTEM MAINTENANCE AND ADAPTATION

In *Comparative Politics: A Developmental Approach*, Almond and Powell elaborate the original functional scheme by presenting a threefold typology of functions. These are conversions, capabilities, and system maintenance and adaptation functions.[30] Conversion functions may be thought of in terms of those functions which are concerned with the translation of political inputs into outputs. Demands are made of the political system, they are articulated and aggregated, and communicated from one part of the system to another. The final product is a set of binding policies, implementation of these policies, and adjudication of them should conflict over their interpretation arise.[31] System capabilities, on the other hand, describe the political system as it operates in its environment and can be thought of in terms of the performance or effectiveness of a political system. Five kinds of functions are suggested: extractive, regulative, distributive, symbolic, and responsive.[32] These functions are discussed shortly. Finally, a political system has to provide a set of structures to reproduce its basic patterns of behavior and to induct new members into political roles. The system maintenance functions are those of political socialization and recruitment. These functions are not directly a part of the conversion process; yet they impinge upon this process and the effectiveness of the system by socializing members into new roles and providing them with appropriate role expectations.[33] These functions are crucial if we are to understand the relationship between individual level accounts of political phenomena and macropolitics. An understanding of socialization processes should sensitize us to some of the special problems of human behavior in social situations as well as provide a linchpin between motivational and systemic explanations. It is through the socialization process that a true integration of motivations and role expectations takes place, where psychological orientations dovetail with systemic needs. Thus, the traditional problem of order, or for that matter the problem of society in general, is not explained in terms of a happy occurrence or some "harmony of interests." If order is achieved and if society is successful in harnessing the motivations of its members to its goals, it is at least partly because of the process of socialization.[34]

Each of these functions is examined individually to show how it might be relevant to the study of integration in an emerging community, the EEC.

Conversion Functions

Interest articulation refers to the way demands are initially formulated and placed on the political system. The question of how many issue areas there are in which groups place demands on the EEC would be one kind of indicator of its integration. Between 1952 and 1957, when the Six (Belgium, Federal Republic of Germany, France, Italy, Luxembourg, and the Netherlands) cooperated under the ECSC, the scope of cooperation was very narrow. Since January 1958, when the EEC was put into operation, this scope has been broadened to include other issue areas such as commercial policy, transport, and agricultural policy. The important matter for interest articulation is the question of the extent to which interest groups and other articulating structures do in fact place their demands on Community elites or whether they choose to operate through national channels. Werner Feld, in a survey of European interest-group elites, found that 70 percent of his respondents indicated that demands made through national governments were more likely to succeed than those placed directly on Community institutions.[35] There are also strong indications that for these sectors in which important policy decisions are being taken, this figure is even higher. For example, Feld notes that when only industrial and agricultural interest groups are taken into account, the percentage in favor of channeling demands through national government goes up to 90 percent.[36] Thus the more salient the issue area the less autonomy the political structures of the EEC have. One might expect that as long as the Council of Ministers of the EEC is the important policy-making body, interest groups will continue to look to national institutions. The Council includes one representative from each member state. Often this representative is the foreign minister. These representatives are carefully instructed spokesmen of their national governments whose full-time job is with their own domestic government. Since the final authority resides with the Council, and since the Council is seen as the faithful purveyor of domestic interest, elites see little need for the reorganization and shifting of present patterns of interest group activity.

Despite the general tendency to work through national channels, the impression should not be given that a considerable amount of activity does not transpire through European institutions, as is indicated by the 250 or so umbrella organizations at the Community level.[37] These umbrella organizations may be thought of as general, peak organizations that include a variety of more specific interest groups. The Commission, because of its supranational proclivities, has been one of the favorite targets for interest groups. The Committee of Permanent Representatives (CPR), composed of one representative from each member state, is becoming an increasingly attractive target,[38] especially since the agricultural crisis of June 1965-January 1966 in which the French representatives boycotted the EEC. This Committee is charged with much of the day-to-day responsibility of the Council of Ministers, since Council members are too preoccupied with their full-time domestic jobs. As such one might expect to see it grow in strength and yet not to share all the strong nationalistic viewpoints of Council members.

Not all demands are articulated through formal, associational interest group structures. Many demands and issues are formulated by internal elites. Occasionally demands originate in national bureaucracies, and quite often in the Commission itself. In fact, technically, as one author has pointed out, with few exceptions, proposals for substantive policy can originate from no source other than the Commission.[39] While this is true the Commission takes into account a variety of viewpoints before proposals are made.

Who or what structures perform the function of interest articulation is a very important and interesting question in itself. Whatever the answer to that question it seems fruitful to view the progress of European integration partly in terms of the development of this function. As Clark aptly put it: "A good gauge of the progress of the European Community is the degree to which the politics of Europe have reoriented from their traditional national framework to a broader framework of the Common Market. There is no fooling politicians or lobbyists, who are quick to discover where decisions are really being made and where political power is shifting."[40]

Although there are some disturbing aspects of the development of interest group activity at the Community level, one should nevertheless note that interest groups may be very important in bridging the elite-mass gap. The Community has been severely criticized for its undemocratic, elitist nature. The Dutch in particular have been worried over the fact that increasing areas of performance are passing outside control of national parliaments while there has been no corresponding growth of control institutions at the supranational level. Interest groups are no substitute for representative institutions, but they could act as a kind of vertical cement. The activity of interest groups, however, has also a negative aspect. Despite the steady growth of organized groups at the European level to the present number of more than 350, some serious questions must be confronted. First the question arises whether Europe has become a huge welfare agency indulging the interests of all-powerful organized groups and requiring sacrifices from no one. Adrian Zeller, in a book widely read in Europe, launches a devastating critique of the excessive influence of interest groups in the EEC. He documents at length how Europe has become a haven for sugar beet farmers, tomato growers, dairy farmers, and so on.[41] More often than not, the agreement to establish common price levels has meant adjusting individual national prices upward toward the highest price with the result that the consumer pays more for the product. These inequities are made possible and aggravated by the fact that interest groups operate in a truncated political environment. The additional web of political factors and of forces responsible for tempering the role of interest groups is nonexistent. Public opinion is inchoate and ineffective as a check. The role of political parties is minimal and of course there are no elections where the general populace can register its discontents and preferences. If, as Schattschneider has argued, the "function of public authority [is] to modify private power relations by enlarging the scope of conflict,"[42] then very little government exists in the EEC. If interest groups have played an important role in the domestic politics of many Western countries it is because (partly) their activity has occurred within a political matrix overlaid with and circumscribed by other political structures: for example, political parties, legislatures, regulatory agencies, electoral systems. These political structures have not only acted as countervailing forces to interest groups but also aided the more unorganized publics (e.g., consumers) by expanding the scope of public conflict.

Interest aggregation refers to the process whereby individual demands are compromised, sifted, and packaged into a viable set of policy alternatives from which decision makers can choose. If this function is being performed effectively policies will tend to include positions from a variety of interest groups, at least in some watered-down version. If interest groups are ideological, there is an attempt to maintain the purity of alternative positions with the result that differing viewpoints are not easily compromised, and programs are often little more than conglomerates of specific positions which may be in conflict with one another. Almond has demonstrated how immobilism can be an upshot of this type of system.[43]

The most striking thing is that political parties have very little to do with the performance of this function in the EEC. One must look elsewhere for the appropriate structures. Upon close examination no one structure seems to be responsible for discharging this function; rather it seems to reside in a variety of procedures that are vaguely referred to as the Community Method. This method involves the continuous interplay among national experts, the Committee of Permanent Representatives, the Commission, and the European Parliament, a legislative body consisting of 142 members drawn from the original six member states. To take an example of how the Community Method works, let us briefly look at the development of a common agricultural policy in the EEC. The first major decisions in agriculture were not taken until January 1962. Yet as Leon Lindberg notes: "Throughout the preparation period (1958-1960), the Commission was in contact with the Agricultural Committee of the EPA (European Parliamentary Assembly), with the specialized Agricultural section of the ESC, and with representatives of interest groups."[44]

Lindberg develops this line of thought more fully:

> Throughout 1958 and 1959 the Commission's General Direc-
> torate for Agriculture, under the leadership of Commission Vice-
> President Sicco Mansholt (former Dutch Minister of Agriculture),
> was engaged in preparing the Commission's proposals. Throughout
> this period, close working relationships were maintained with govern-
> mental and non-governmental experts drawn from the Member
> States, in addition to which Mansholt and the six Ministers of Agri-
> culture held meetings at intervals of two to four weeks. Of special
> importance from the Commission's point of view were the close
> contacts maintained with interest groups.[45]

Compromises are thus worked out not by any one structure but by a complex process of interaction among a variety of structures. The centrality of the Commission's role here is evidenced by the fact that the Commission inter- acts with most of the other institutions. The function of this process is to narrow the range of possibilities that the Council will have to consider and to screen away as much of the unimportant detail as possible. The Committee of Permanent Representatives plays a crucial role in this screening process, crucial especially because Council members are only part-time European politicians who want to avoid as much detail as possible. The Committee's role is twofold here. First, it seeks to approve uncontroversial matters so that they need not occupy the Council. Second, it seeks to screen out the controversial issues so that they can be dealt with in more depth. As a result by the time a proposal reaches the Council it is both a pared-down and compromised version of what initially went into it. The Council's role is greatly facilitated in that the members have to choose among a set of proposals that have been shorn of detail and which represent at least partial compromises based on painstaking collaboration among many interests. The Council is at once freed from suffocating detail and keyed into genuine problem areas.

One specific manifestation of the function of aggregation has become almost commonplace in the field of agricultural policy. Here the so-called package deal has become the primary vehicle of progress in the agricultural sector. Often what cannot be accomplished in bits and pieces has to be dovetailed into general or package proposals. That the package deal has become a recog- nized part of the Community's decision-making apparatus is evidenced in the following quote: "One cannot help concluding that by and large the progress accomplished during this past session has been extremely modest. The Ministers clashed on all the important problems still unsettled in the draft regulations. As far as the 'rice' and 'beef' regulations are concerned, this failure may be ex- plained by the common desire to reserve a good bargaining position for the package deal next week."[46]

Political communication refers to the process by which political informa- tion is disseminated throughout the political system. The development of the communication function focuses not only on the emergence of structures to spread information but also on the autonomy and specialization of these struc- tures. In the EEC a great deal of the political communication function is per- formed by political structures whose primary focus is on something other than communication. Press releases and press conferences by the Council of Ministers or speeches by Commission members are examples. It indicates that political communication has up to this time not succeeded in becoming differentiated from other societal sectors. It makes it difficult for communication to operate as an effective, neutral instrument in imparting information to the citizenry. One would hardly expect information emitted by the Council or the Commission to be neutral or objective. In addition, since there is no independent news media, there is very little autonomy to political communication. National administrations hold a tight rein on the content and flow of communication. Indeed, the agricultural crisis of 1965-66 in the Common Market owed at least partly to the attempt of the European Commission to acquire a range of autonomy in the performance of this function.

I suggest that the communication function is performed by two separate structures in the EEC, only one of which is specialized (the press) and neither of which is autonomous. As mentioned, the Council and the Commission each play a role, the Commission's role being considerably more important. The crucial role of the Commission in policy making is seen to rest partly on its ability to mobilize support among various groups, bureaucracies, interest groups, and the like. That this is important to their position as a vigorous proponent of integration is evidenced by the fact that at least three of the ten points demanded by the French as conditions for resolution of the agricultural crisis had to do directly with the communications and public relations activities of the Commission.[47]

The other structure concerned with the performance of the communication function is the European press and the Central Information Service of the Community. It is doubtful, though, how much impact the press has had in molding European public opinion. "The European press does not take the initiative in orienting the European mind to the Common Market. Common Market news is news, but it has to give up space on the front pages of the newspapers to local disasters, to news of national importance, to news of Southeast Asian, African, or other crises, and even to news of the United Nations, an institution generally more remote to the average European than the Common Market."[48]

In spite of this the apparatus of the European press is certainly impressive when judged by any supranational standards. By 1966 there were more than a hundred reporters accredited to the European Commission, and during 1966 the Press and Information Service spent $3.8 million, an amount that almost equaled that spent by the Department of Public Information of the United Nations.[49] These developments augur well for the emergence of a specialized and differentiated communications structure. The Community is organizing its resources in the most efficient and sophisticated way to harness support for its policies. Technical information is provided in abundance by the Statistical Office of the Community; documents are provided furnishing everyday proceedings and reports are given in the *Official Journal* of all decisions and regulations adopted; finally, popular information, speeches, and monthly reviews of Community affairs are given wide circulation. The Community even carried out an opinion survey to identify potential centers of resistance to European unity so that care could be taken to win them over.[50]

In the final analysis the central difficulty of the communication structures is not their lack of specialization but their lack of autonomy. The de Gaulle government was only the most careful among all the governments of the Six in keeping the information activities of the Community under close surveillance. As Hartley Clark put it:

> Commissioner Le Maignen suspected that the governments were fearful of Community autonomy in information, and the community is not entirely free to use media of its choice on the target of its choice. Not only did the Gaullist government frown on expansion of the staff of the Community's information service in Paris and threaten to remonstrate if the publications of that office were critical of official French action, it also restricted the Commission in Brussels. The Commission had been in the practice of publishing its proposals to the Council as supplements to the monthly *EEC Bulletin*, but the French demanded an end to the practice of publication prior to Council action as one of the conditions for their returning to Brussels after their boycott.[51]

The functions of rule making, rule implementation, and rule adjudication can be thought of in terms of the system's response to the demands made of it. Rule making has to do with forging common policies that are binding upon the member states. Most observers would concede that the nationally oriented Council of Ministers is the chief policy maker in the EEC. With very few exceptions the power to issue regulations (which are binding upon all member states) resides with the Council. The grant of power is not unlimited, however, since it is attenuated somewhat by provisions concerning other organs and how they impinge upon the Council. Spinelli, for example, argues that "the dynamism of the Common Market is entrusted essentially to the dialogue between the Commission and the Council of Ministers."[52] The Commission, first of all, is responsible for submitting proposals to the Council and in this way it helps to structure the way problems are approached. In addition, the Council may amend a proposal of the Commission only by unanimous decision, while the Commission is free to modify its proposals at any time.

The role played by the Commission in the formulation of Community policy has been the subject of much discussion and controversy. Much of the controversy has centered on the question of whether the Commission serves an essentially bureaucratic or political function.[53] It is often pointed out that the Commission is the only independent structure in the Community and that it alone is capable of representing the Community interest. The political role of the Commission has evolved over the years, however, and may have reached a high point around the middle of 1965. It was at the end of June 1965 that de Gaulle perpetrated the beginning of the Community crisis. Although the crisis began over some rather technical details concerning the financing of the common agricultural policy, the meaning of the crisis went beyond this. It was, as Louis Cartou said, "une crise des institutions."[54] Since the end of the crisis (January 1966) the Commission has become a more cautious body, inclined to sounding out national positions in great detail and not given to bold formulations of political programs. Cartou is right in arguing that legislation in the EEC has more and more taken on the character of bilateral negotiations.[55] The Commission also seems to have lost its initiative in representing the EEC to the rest of the world. In contrast with the important role played by the Commission in representing the EEC at the Kennedy Round of tariff negotiations, the preliminary negotiations in 1970 over British entry were almost completely bilateral in nature. In addition considerable doubt existed over whether the Commission, or some other less independent body, should represent the Community in the negotiations for the entry of Great Britain, Denmark, Norway, and Northern Ireland.

In the final analysis any success the Commission has in the rule-making process hinges on its appreciation of the limits within which it works, on its ability to sense in what directions the Council is willing to be budged. The Council simply would not succumb to a brazen Commission that formulated proposals without regard to national interests. Thus all signs point to the fact that the Community has not developed an autonomous set of rule-making structures. The dependence upon the Council members is evidence of this fact. Although we may agree that the Commission is influential we must also agree that Spinelli is correct when he argues that "influence is not government."

> The Commission has developed much influence and has produced important results because the governments have allowed it to do so. Everything remains precarious, however, precisely because that influence is not yet actually government. The Commission is really nothing more than a gigantic European pressure group which, aided by its official character, that is, by the blessing of the political authorities which gave it life, has brought most national administrations around to admitting the priority of European needs, if and when they can be demonstrated.[56]

Rule implementation is concerned with the enforcement or application of rules to concrete situations. The Commission is the institution most responsible for enforcement of Community policy. For example, the common agricultural policy, which has by this time become a very cumbersome bureaucratic problem, is administered by the Commission. In addition, the execution of Treaty provisions is left to the Commission as is supervision of all regulations adopted by the Council. The Commission has the power to issue recommendations and orders to states that violate the law of the Community.[57] If, for example, the Netherlands does not allow the proper quota of oranges to enter during a particular period, the Commission will notify her that she is in violation of a law of the Community. In most cases compliance is forthcoming.

It is clear that this function is performed neither by a specialized structure nor by an autonomous one. The Commission is clearly multifunctional, being preoccupied with articulation, aggregation, rule making, and rule application at various points. With respect to the problem of autonomy, the Commission's success has been linked to the relations it has cultivated with national administrations and the Commission bureaucracy. This has led one scholar to speak in terms of "bureaucratic interpenetration."[58] He has concluded that there is more intermingling of national and international bureaucracies as the "commitments undertaken by the states in the Rome treaty establishing the EEC become more vague. . . ."[59] Characteristically, the Rome treaty becomes vaguest in those areas which are more politically charged. The most autonomy is given to the supranational bureaucracy in those matters which are least controversial.

While the Commission's autonomy may be less than desired from the standpoint of committed Europeans it is nevertheless more than that enjoyed by probably any other international institution. The Commission has had a free hand in the formulation of proposals to the Council. It has also played an important part in the negotiating and bargaining process following submission of proposals. During this entire process the Commission remains independent of (though not insensitive to) the individual member states. Sidjanski points out that in the formulation of legislation the states respect the supranational character of the Commission and do not attempt to influence it.[60] Finally, the autonomy of that Commission is reinforced through structural factors, particularly through the fact that Commission members are not responsible to those who appointed them (the national governments) but only to the European Parliament, the legislature created by the Treaty of Rome.

The function of rule adjudication is concerned with the interpretation and resolution of conflicting claims. Rule-adjudicating structures serve as referees of sorts to interpret the rules to various players. The performance of this function is important not only for the obvious reason that it gives concrete expression to system rules but also because it serves as an indicator of whether or not compliance is forthcoming from discontented members.

The Court of Justice of the European Community, a highly specialized structure, is entrusted with the performance of the rule-adjudication function. The Court seems to surpass all other supranational courts both in terms of who can bring actions before the Court and in terms of the importance of its decisions. In the former regard it is significant that action can be brought before the Court not only by states but also by Community institutions or by private persons.[61] In the latter regard the Court has been appealed to freely by public and private institutions and its activities have increased at a pace equal to that of the Community in general. The number of cases on the Court's docket is increasing year by year. As with the Commission, however, whatever success the Court enjoys owes to its policy of going slowly. The Court has not yet experienced a real test case. Perhaps it will quietly nurse its strength until, when public support waxes strong, it will attempt to establish its powers more firmly.

Capabilities of the European Community

Having examined the conversion functions we now turn to a set of functions that describe the operation of the political system in its environment, the capabilities of political systems. These capabilities are extraction, regulation, distribution, symbolic capability, and responsiveness.

Almond and Powell define the extractive capability of a political system as "the range of system performance in drawing material and human resources from the domestic and international environments."[62] As such one can readily perceive the close association that this concept has to the definitions both of power as "the ability to mobilize resources in the pursuit of collective goals" and of politics, defined in terms of authoritative goal attainment.

There are three useful questions one can ask with respect to extractive capability. First, to what extent does the political system utilize human and nonhuman resources in the attainment of its goals? This includes the ability to utilize raw materials, technology, and leadership in the attainment of goals. Second, is the support among the population for system goals of a specific or diffuse nature? If support is unique to a given issue area then it will be difficult for the political system to harness that group's loyalties to system goals that go well beyond this. A system in which all support was issue-specific would approach the naked interest group model of politics, in which each group carries its demands into the political marketplace and bargains to see what it can get in return for concessions it is willing to make. It would be understating it to say that a political system operating under these conditions would find it difficult to get things done. Without a grant of credit, or a reservoir of political goodwill, every decision would have to be justified anew by policy makers. Third, is the extractive function backed up by force, other kinds of sanctions, or merely by goodwill?

The EEC appears to be extremely weak in terms of extractive capacity. In terms of its revenues, for example, there are no compulsory taxes. Most revenues are obtained either from voluntary contributions by member states or from levies on imports. Revenues in 1965 totaled only $160 million. The common agricultural policy alone was expected to cost about $1.3 billion by 1966-67.[63] Also, support for policies is tied to particular interests at different times and if there is not some concrete payoff in a particular policy interest groups cannot be expected to go along. Some observers look upon the Common Market as a rather large trade off between German industry and French agriculture. In some sense de Gaulle looked upon the common agricultural policy as a payment for French willingness to go ahead with integration in the industrial sector. Yet German agricultural interest groups, particularly the Deutscher Bauernverband (DBV), resisted the agricultural policy strenuously and exerted strong pressure on the Christian Democratic Union in this regard.

Indeed, a supranational agricultural policy was achieved only by very skill-ful maneuvering on the part of Erhard, the Chancellor of the Federal Republic of Germany, who succeeded in disarming the leader of the DBV, Edmund Rehwinkel, by agreeing to a substantial program of internal subsidies to affected farmers.[64]

That support tends to be tied to specific policies and has not yet become a generalized grant to conduct the business of government on a broad front is well illustrated by Gordon Weil:

> The German government was reluctant to agree to a common grain price which would mean that a large number of German farmers would be forced to leave the farms. Yet it finally accepted the price in return for promises that the Community would step up

its efforts to arrive at a relatively liberal negotiating position in the Kennedy Round of trade negotiations in Geneva. Italy was reluctant to accept common prices proposed for certain feed grains, but acquiesced after having been promised a new fruits and vegetables regulation.[65]

Finally, as already mentioned, extractions that do exist are completely voluntary and control resides almost completely in national hands. The one attempt to increase revenues and to transfer control of extractions from national to supranational control resulted in a grave crisis for the Community. The crisis, though complex, may be summarized as follows.

As part of the grain-price decisions in December 1964 the Commission was to prepare proposals on the financing of the common agricultural policy. Normally the Commission would have confined itself to the details of the technical implementation of agricultural finance. Such was not the case with this proposal. Two sections were especially controversial: the "own resources" section and the section pertaining to an increase of the powers of the European Parliament. With regard to the "own resources" part of the proposal, the Commission asked that revenues on imports from third countries be funneled into the Community treasury to be dispensed by a supranational authority. This would have meant the existence of a fairly substantial budget not subject to national control. This prompted the second proposal to increase the budgetary power of the European Parliament.

The second proposal would have simultaneously increased Community revenues, made them autonomous from national institutions, and transferred control to a parliament which it was hoped would eventually be popularly elected. It was estimated that by 1972 Community revenues would be of the order of $2.4 billion which would be more than adequate to finance the agricultural policy. It was also suggested that the Commission be given the right to propose other taxes.[66] Such proposals, if adopted, would seriously have enhanced the extractive capacity of the EEC if they had been adopted. The speed with which the de Gaulle government reacted and the gravity of the steps taken (French representatives were absent from June 30, 1965, to late January 1966) indicate that de Gaulle was very much aware of the far-reaching implications of the Commission proposals.

The regulative capability of a political system could be conceived in terms of a system's control over the behavior of individuals and groups.[67] Regulation then, is not directly concerned with the allocation of values but with compliance to decisions taken. In this sense the extent to which there has been compliance with the judgments of the Court and the regulations of the Council may be good indicators of regulative capacity. It is probably still too early to tell whether compliance is forthcoming since the seriousness of the laws is not sufficient to warrant deviance. The problems that emerge when common policies are effected, such as the common agricultural policy, are evident.

If a distinguishing characteristic of a political system is the employment of legitimate coercion the EEC must be judged very weak in this regard. Power to coerce lies completely with the national governments and not the wildest European dream would include a military or police capability in the near future. In large measure the strength of the Community lies in its peculiar ability to engage in an unobtrusive approach to integration, being careful to avoid confrontations that might result in a loss of power. The functionalist ideology holds sway. Federalism will be achieved "through installments," by the "slow, progressive coagulation of customs and interests around an integrated European bureaucracy...."[68] Functionalism stresses inconspicuousness, indirection, deferral of full-scale political union, and the immediacy of economic benefits.

If the Community is really one of administrators and businessmen, we should not be surprised to see the development of political institutions, especially those concerned with the control of human behavior, lag behind. If, as Etzioni suggests, "collectivities are not always coextensive in their action and their power dimensions" and communities may carry out more action than they control, the EEC certainly seems to be surging ahead in the former while leaving the question of control pretty much in national hands.[69]

Almond and Powell refer to the distributive capability in terms of the allocation of goods and services.[70] In large measure we ask who is receiving what share of the goods and services at the disposal of the political system. In this regard the small budget at the disposal of the European Community is an indication of its distributive strength. Yet the expenditure to finance policies has lagged far behind the Community's ability to make authoritative allocations so in this sense financial provisions may be misleading. The Council of Ministers is capable of considering some rather important issues and some of them are decided on the basis of qualified majority vote. Yet it is really only in the field of agriculture that the EEC has moved significantly beyond a customs union into a real common market organization.

Symbolic capacity, which can be viewed in terms of the society's symbolic identification with the polity, is usually treated as an unimportant matter. Little in the way of serious European political symbols exists yet, probably in large part because the functionalist conception of Europe is politically unglamorous. Whatever we may think of businessmen and civil servants it is difficult to think of them as political heroes.

Before one can go on to ask the question of whether a loyalty commitment on the part of Europeans exists, one must see whether the EEC is a "cognitive fact" for most Europeans. Some argue that it is not. As one author put it: "Much public relations work, whether by private associations, public agencies, or individual businessmen or educators, aims to impress upon the European public the simple fact that the Common Market exists."[71]

A great deal of attitude and opinion research has been carried out which challenges this view.[72] Jacques-René Rabier, director of the Press and Information Services of the European Communities, has carried out a series of studies on European attitudes which suggest that strong support for a politically federated Europe exists. On the basis of an analysis of a series of different samples, Rabier concluded that from six to nine adults out of every ten were in favor of a union of the peoples of Europe.[73] In a later study, undertaken at the suggestion of the General Directorate for Press and Information, but significantly, without intervention on its part, even more surprising results turned up. Table 1.1 presents some of the results.

TABLE 1.1

QUESTION: ARE YOU FOR OR AGAINST THE EVOLUTION OF THE COMMON MARKET TOWARD THE POLITICAL FORMATION OF A UNITED STATES OF EUROPE?
(PERCENTAGES)

	Germany	Belgium	Nether-lands	Luxem-bourg	France	Italy	European Community
For	69	60	64	75	67	60	65
Against	9	10	17	5	11	7	10
No response	22	30	19	20	22	33	25
Total	100	100	100	100	100	100	100

SOURCE: Adapted from "*Les Européens: 'Oui' à L'Europe.*" Public opinion poll taken in January-February, 1970, in the six countries of the European Community and Great Britain (Brussels: European Commission, May, 1970), p. 4.

Of those questioned, if the subjects who answered "no opinion" are eliminated, the percentages in favor of a United Europe were in the 80s and 90s. The Community average in favor of a United States of Europe was 87 percent.[74] If these results are taken at face value, one might infer that the attitudinal basis for a politically united Europe already exists. While not questioning the results of these studies on technical grounds it is well to keep in mind that the percentage figures arrived at are not self-explanatory. If we interpret these figures as evidence of a reservoir of well-developed loyalty for a politically unified Europe, we are probably making a mistake. The argument could be made that the concept of Europe is popular precisely because it is only dimly perceived and affects Europeans' everyday lives only peripherally. The idea of Europe is an exciting intrusion into their lives. The impact of a United Europe is probably unrecognized. This interpretation is given some weight by a public opinion poll carried out in 1970 by the Reader's Digest Association Ltd. of London. The results of this survey indicated that one out of five persons in sixteen European countries had not heard of the Common Market while only thirty-five out of a hundred could name all six members.[75]

The responsive capability of a political system can be viewed in terms of the extent to which claims made on the political system register as policies. A completely unresponsive political system would be one in which there is no relation between demands and policies. The EEC lags sadly behind in performance of this function. There is as yet no meaningful flow of demands into the political system. Structurally, most of the demands originate in the same place where issues are processed, within the conversion institutions. Thus the Common Market takes on an aura of unreality, of aloofness from the everyday problems of European life. Most Europeans simply are not a part of the input political process. Meaningful participation and responsible political behavior may have to wait until the distributive capacity of the EEC is greater.

Systems Maintenance and Adaptation

The final functions to be considered are those of political socialization and recruitment. Recruitment can be thought of in terms of the induction of new members to fill political roles so that the political system may be sustained with continuity. Socialization involves imparting knowledge, shaping attitudes, and helping to form role expectations for those occupying political roles.

Ronald Inglehart argues that in terms of socialization patterns, there are trends indicating deeper loyalty toward European symbols. In a comparative study of adult and child attitudes toward European symbols, he found consistently that children were more favorably inclined toward Europe than were adults.[76] This seems to contradict the point made previously that Europe was not even part of the average European's awareness. Perhaps there is a contradiction or perhaps affects are more fundamental than cognitions. It is possible that even a dimly perceived European political system may be regarded in positive or negative terms.

With respect to the recruitment of members into European political roles the picture is discouraging. Practically all the important positions in the Community are filled by quota, for example, the European Parliament has thirty-six members from France, Germany, and Italy, fourteen from Netherlands and Belgium, and six from Luxembourg.[77] The Council not only has its membership chosen through national procedures, its members are national officeholders who moonlight in the EEC. Commission members are chosen by convention so that France, Germany, and Italy have two members each and the other three have one each. In addition, as has been pointed out, Commission members remain to some extent dependent upon national officials if for no other reason than that they may want a job after they leave the Commission.

CONCLUSION

It was the chapter's purpose to shed some light on two primary considerations. First, an attempt was made to identify some conceptual similarities between theories of integration and development. Sometimes the boundaries of our fields are structured in such a way that fruitful insights and cross-fertilizations are impeded. In this case it was felt that a careful blending of integration and development theories clarified some relations and opened the way for fruitful insights in other areas. Second, it attempted to show how the contemporary process of integration in the EEC can usefully be conceived in functional terms. Both tasks are preliminary to a critical and meaningful hypothesis-testing stage and are intended only to serve as a backdrop for them. In subsequent chapters I hope to develop several of these functions in greater detail.

CHAPTER TWO

Interest Articulation:
Associational Interest Groups

INTRODUCTION

All political systems include some mechanisms for introducing issues into the political arena. This process, called interest articulation, is the initial phase of the conversion process, that is, the process by which demands made on the political system are translated into authoritative policies. The structures that perform the articulation function are important since they operate at the boundary between the social and political systems. They are in a position to affect and regulate the character of the flows between society and polity. For example, if interests are articulated by nonassociational groups, such as by a caste association in India, and if these interests are poorly differentiated from other caste characteristics (e.g., religious or language concerns), they will be difficult to aggregate into manageable sets of alternative policies. Socioeconomic demands will become infused with ideological concerns and the processes of bargaining, compromise, and accommodation will suffer. Legislative institutions will therefore be inundated with a welter of individual demands or a series of alternatives that would be unacceptable to some portions of the system. The result in either case will probably be inaction and no doubt will force the administration to assume a political role.[1]

One can view structures for interest articulation as gatekeepers of the political arena since they control in an important way the content of the issues allowed to enter. This view offers an intriguing opportunity for the study of power. Traditionally, power has been viewed as the capacity to enforce one's will in a particular issue area.[2] In addition to this approach we could also examine the success of various social groups in initiating issues, the probability that these issues will be dealt with by authoritative institutions, and finally, the capacity to suppress issues. Sociologists interested in the study of local community power structures have long recognized the importance of nondecisions.[3] Political scientists, on the other hand, have for the most part restricted themselves to instances involving the resolution of conflict, avoiding consideration of the sociological conception of power as part of an ongoing social pattern that has perhaps not yet become politicized.

23

In Western Europe and North America the vehicle through which demands are placed on the political system has tended to be associational interest groups, like trade unions, employers' associations, farmers' unions. Such specialized institutions reflect the development in the West of a specialized society with many problems requiring the expertise that only full-time, trained personnel can provide. It is to Durkheim's credit that he recognized the importance of those voluntary groups as more than a technical novelty of modern life and as a phenomenon with profound implications for contemporary society.[4] In traditional societies social life was organized around the family and ascriptive considerations weighed heavily in the political process. This type of social structure militated against both a specialized group life and a competitive political process. The family was the important group and social legitimation was effected through tradition rather than rationality. The rise of industrial society changed all this. Specialized groups and trades made it necessary to reach beyond the confines of the family and village and search for clientele in other places. Also, there was a need to bargain with these groups about the terms of interaction as well as the need to regulate their mutual behavior. These social changes provided the basis for the occupational group or what Almond calls the associational group.[5]

For Durkheim the essential component of modern life was its increasing structural specialization and the normlessness that followed in its wake. While Durkheim saw the emergence of voluntary groups as an antidote to the anomic consequences of differentiation, Tocqueville saw them as a counterforce to the atomizing effects of mass society. To put it differently, Tocqueville interpreted the importance of voluntary groups in terms of personal freedom whereas Durkheim viewed their importance primarily as a new social regulatory mechanism (i.e., from mechanical to organic solidarity). Weber carried this analysis one step further, interpreting the burst of activity by both voluntary groups and political parties as a consequence of the demise of traditional authority and the leveling effects of rational-legal legitimation.[6] Once the forces of tradition started to erode, the cultural and psychological supports of the established order weakened and in its place arose instrumental social and political structures.

INTEREST GROUPS AND THE EUROPEAN COMMUNITY

Although the creation and the operation of the EEC called a great many interest groups into existence[7] we should note that international interest groups existed before 1958. Sidjanski points out that the development of interest groups evolved in four successive waves, the first of which appeared with the launching of the Organization for European Economic Cooperation (OEEC) and the Marshall Plan.[8] In addition, the European Coal and Steel Community (ECSC), which came into existence in 1952, led to the emergence of a group of unions consisting of twenty-one members with headquarters at Luxembourg.[9] The third wave followed the establishment of the EEC. The implications of this wave were stronger, in terms of quantity and quality of group activity. Some groups formed immediately, anticipating the importance of the EEC experiment, whereas others waited until they were more directly affected. The final wave came with the arrival of the European Free Trade Association (EFTA) and brought fifteen new members to the international level.

The wave following on the creation of the EEC is the most important for several reasons. In EFTA, as well as in OEEC, interest groups did not fundamentally restructure their styles of activity but rather operated within the classic, intergovernmental framework. In these associations, the pressure brought to bear was exercised directly on governments who then participated in the making of common decisions. Since ultimate and effective power for such decisions resided with the member states and not with any super organization, interest groups felt little motivation to organize at the community level.[10] In addition, they represented only a very narrow range of economic life and did not nearly approach the spectrum of interests represented in the EEC. On the other hand, interest groups in the EEC displayed some novel forms of behavior.

The emergence and development on a large scale of interest groups at the Community level mirrors their development in Western, industrial society as a whole. Functional specialization and the growth of large-scale political and economic units have increased the physical and social space separating the elites from the masses. In a vertical sense, the development of interest groups can be seen as an attempt to close this gap both by the provision of expertise and the existence of full-time personnel whose task it is to provide vertical channels of communication and influence.

The pervasive development of interest groups organized at the EEC level is all the more important in that, for a variety of reasons, the gap between the European elites and the people is even more exaggerated than on the national plane.[11] Indeed, to the extent that institutional checks exist at the community level, they run horizontally, between equally elitist institutions. Vertical checks, such as between decision-making institutions and the electorate or between these institutions and some more popular institution, such as the European Parliament, are almost nonexistent. In addition, the Commission, which is the bureaucracy of the EEC, resembles a truncated administration in that it possesses no foundation.

> . . . the European Commission, unlike a national administration, does not have a complete administrative hierarchy at its disposal, it lacks the sub-structure and thus resembles a tree without roots, the consequences of this being that it has more difficulties in establishing the necessary contacts with the people concerned, may this be in order to get information and help from them, or inversely, to communicate its policies to them.[12]

Before examining the role interest groups play in the process of interest articulation two things should be mentioned. First, the number of interest groups associated at the level of the Common Market is not all the result of the birth and growth of the EEC. Part of this increase is a general phenomenon of the regionalization of organizations. This phenomenon includes a spreading-out effect on the part of national and subnational associations (e.g., a national trade union will establish a permanent organization in a regional organization) as well as a "splitting up" effect in which a universal or global organization sets up an office and establishes relations with a regional organization. The Confédération Internationale des Syndicats Libres (CISL) has since 1950 set up three regional secretariats, L'Organisation Régionale Européene with headquarters in Brussels, L'Organisation Régionale Inter-Américaine des Travailleurs with seat in Mexico, and La Confédération Régionale Asienne, New Delhi.[13]

.   A better grasp of this phenomenon is given in some figures that indicate that from 1954 to 1960 the percentage of regional organizations increased from 13.9 to 24.2.[14] This increase is considerable, given the rapid absolute increase of international organizations in general during this period.[15]

The second caveat to be made is that the Community interest groups must be seen in a much broader network of relationships in which national groups, international associations, and subnational groups also play a role. The presence of the United States is forcefully felt as the controversial Commission report on business interpenetration by the United States indicates.[16] It is important to note that this penetration is not limited to national actors. Many subnational actors are important. The state of Illinois exports more than any other in the U.S. and its largest customer is Europe. Thus it is not surprising that in 1968 Illinois established a permanent office in Brussels. New York, Ohio, and Virginia have also set up offices and emphasis is not only on exploiting outlets in Europe but in promoting business and trading opportunities for Europeans in Illinois.[17] This complex tangle of relationships should provide some warning against attaching too much weight to the isolated operation of European interest groups.

THE STRUCTURE OF INTEREST GROUP REPRESENTATION

What is the nature of the process through which issues emerge in the EEC? How are demands placed in the European political system? What are the structures in terms of which interest articulation takes place? Do such structures exist, are they differentiated from other societal institutions, do they possess autonomy from their national structural counterparts? These are some of the questions that need to be asked and they are all certainly not answered here. No assumption was made that associational interest groups perform this function, but an analysis of the decisional process in the EEC indicates that such groups do play a role, albeit far from one identical with national interest groups.

The three most pervasive structural characteristics of European interest groups are their number and sheer pervasiveness, their variety and their decentralization. Meynaud and Sidjanski note that as of 1966-67 there were more than 350 groups bearing expressly a European name in their titles.[18] These 350 groups are in turn part of a larger web of transnational relationships which involves many other nongovernmental groups and organizations. The same authors report that in the 1964-65 annual of the Union of International Associations there are some 1,720 nongovernmental organizations listed of which the authors estimate around 680 are European. The breakdown of these 680 organizations is enlightening:

These organizations break down approximately in the following manner: 350 belong to the European Community (340 adhering to the EEC and a dozen to the ECSC); about thirty stem from a concern with promoting the cause of European unity (so-called promotional groups); 190 correspond to the field of OEEC [Organization for European Economic Cooperation], OECD [Organization for Economic Cooperation and Development] and to organizations not belonging to the six; the remainder, that is to say about 110 organizations, constitutes a collection of diverse European groups as much in terms of the field covered as by the objective sought.[19]

Clearly this growth of interest groups at the Community level is one of the truly novel developments of international relations in the postwar era. Although it is a part of the general increase of international organizations, governmental and nongovernmental, it can be distinguished from this general growth both by its extent as well as by the peculiar functions performed.[20]

The important thing, as we shall see later, is the manner in which interest groups bring influence to bear on the making of policy. When we speak of integration, we require more than a simple intergovernmental kind of arrangement, in which groups exert influence on national ministers and organs who then go on to make policy. What we are dealing with in the European case, however, is the construction of an independent system in which groups directly coalesce at the European level and exert an influence directly on Community institutions.[21]

In addition to the above factors, the primary cause of the growth of these interest groups is the emergence of a new constellation of forces, a new decision-making center whose formal institutions are situated in Brussels, but loosely organized with several more or less distinct nodes of power and, above all, with supranational and national elements so intermingled as to render meaningless any talk about who is stronger and whether growth for one means decay for the other. It seems unlikely that so many groups would have sought formal association at this level if they could have operated just as effectively through national channels. This formation casts doubt on the often heard argument that power ultimately resides with the individual states represented in the Council of Ministers. This may indeed be the case whatever "ultimate power" may mean. The fact remains that there exists at the Community level a set of institutions whose vision is exciting enough, whose leadership is skillful, and whose capacity to produce policy options not generated through national apparatuses is so overwhelming that many hardheaded businessmen, farmers, union members, and others have found it to their advantage to set up direct relations with them. Although several shifting, loosely related power centers exist, the nodal point is the Commission-Council relationship. "To the extent that the Commission performs an autonomous function either in taking decisions itself or in elaborating proposals for the Council, it becomes a center of privileged interest in the eyes of the groups. It is this central wheel of the EEC, the Council-Commission tandem, which constitutes the decision center and consequently it is the object of solicitude on the part of groups."[22]

THE PATTERN OF GROWTH

By April 1961 many interest groups were organized with offices or official contacts in Brussels, or perhaps Paris, and met regularly with representatives of

Community institutions in a variety of capacities. As early as May 1961 forty agricultural interest groups had organized themselves at the EEC level and had taken up relations with the Commission. A year and a half later this number had increased to eighty-two.[23] An examination of the growth of formations for all interest groups is instructive. Figure 2.1 presents data on formation from 1957 to the end of 1969.

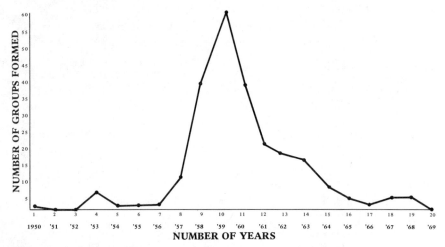

Fig. 2.1. Formation of interest groups at the European Community level. SOURCE: *Répertoire des Organismes Communs dans le Cadre des Communautés Européennes* (Services des Publications des Communautés Européennes, 1969).

We can see that 1959 was the peak year with heavy formations in 1958 and 1960 also. Then, overlooking some irregularity, there is a more or less gradual tapering off until by 1969 no new groups became associated. The fact that the growth pattern occurred in this way is probably partly a result of the slow reflexes on the part of national groups. A novel situation had presented itself which these groups could not fit into their stereotyped notions of national, intergovernmental organizations. Probably many groups remained quiet, hoping to act through national channels should the need arise. This hypothesis is borne out by Fischer, who, after viewing the pattern of growth, sent standard letters of inquiry to many interest groups. The results of his analysis led him to believe that many groups simply did not take the EEC seriously at the beginning.[24]

One final reason may be advanced for the rapid growth of interest groups. The Commission recognized from the start that it had a valuable potential ally in the interest groups. Vulnerable to the charge that they were an irresponsible, undemocratic body, the Commission was anxious to cultivate any contacts possible with the public and its organized groups. Thus from the start the Commission actively promoted the formation of interest groups. In its *First General Report on the Activities of the Community* the Commission frankly stated that the ultimate attainment of the goals of the Community may depend upon mobilizing public opinion, and always keeping in the foreground "representatives of those economic and social groups concerned, consulting them, advising them, even associating them with the work, where possible. . . ."[25] Their hopes about a possible ally were borne out during the agricultural crisis of 1965-66 when many groups took a firm stand for the Commission.[26]

VARIETY OF GROUPS

The range and diversity of groups is as striking as their pervasiveness. In addition to several general organizations, such as COPA (Comité des Organisations Professionnelles Agricoles) and UNICE (Union des Industries de la Communauté Européenne), there are a large number of highly specialized groups such as the Comité des Organisations Professionnelles Viticoles de la CEE, the Comité des Planteurs de Houblon de la CEE, and many others.[27] This diversity no doubt reflects the structural complexity and functional specificity of Western society. Groups no longer feel it advantageous to merge their identities with others. It is paradoxical that this fragmenting process, this structural or group fission, which entails the continuous breaking up of older units, is associated with integration. Yet it is this very process of fission that allows to these groups the necessary autonomy to probe for new contacts at the supranational level.

DECENTRALIZATION OF GROUPS

Even from the standpoint of their formal structure, European groups are very decentralized. There are practically no mechanisms (beyond gentle persuasion) to go beyond the wishes of the least cooperative member. COPA, for example, takes all positions by unanimity. The groups have proved to be tough negotiators for national positions and do not show much evidence of the Community spirit so often talked about. There are several institutional expressions of this high level of decentralization. In some groups, such as COPA, an important role is assigned to the organ directly representing the individual states, in this case the Presidium, which is composed of one member from each country, designated by their national organs.[28] Another sign of decentralization is witnessed in the adoption of common positions to be sent to the Commission. It is almost uniformly true that all positions are taken by unanimity. COPA allows for a minority position when it cannot muster agreement among individual members. Apparently, it is fairly common for groups to adopt, either in practice or formally in their statutes, this rule which allows for the expression of a minority opinion. This probably does little more than formalize the prevention of what would never occur anyway, viz., a coalition of national groups forcing upon another member an undesirable position. In addition, it has the advantage of allowing work to proceed, without degenerating into fruitless squabbling. The drawback, of course, is that what is passed on to the Commission may be a diluted, weakened version of the desired policy (in the case of excessive compromise) or a series of irreconcilable national positions which the Commission may find difficult to forge into an overall policy.[29] While no doubt such decentralization contributes to the safeguard of individual interests it can also prevent any policy from getting adopted. Protection may be secured at the price of deadlock. This general condition is reminiscent of the Fourth Republic in France where the ability to enact national interest legislation was also nonexistent.

UMBRELLA ORGANIZATIONS

While the proliferation, both in quantity and diversity, of European interest groups signified the development of a new decisional network, it also raised problems for policy making. How were the demands of several hundred groups, varying greatly in structure and technical concerns, to be met? How, especially in the absence of traditional aggregators of interest such as political parties, were a set of heterogeneous demands to be blended into a limited number of options to be presented to the Commission? Clearly, without some such mechanism to perform this function the Commission would be swamped with detail and rendered unable to pursue effectively its vital role of generating options attractive to Council members, while still upgrading the common interest.

The response was really more multitiered than this. One response to this problem was the emergence of a number of so-called umbrella organizations. These are peak organizations of an essentially confederal type, each of which includes or represents a number of similar national groupings. Among these are UNICE (Union des Industries de la Communauté Européenne) for industry, COCCEE (Comité des Organisations Commerciales des Pays de la CEE) for trade, COPA (Comité des Organisations Professionnelles Agricoles) for agriculture, and UACEE (Union de l'Artisanat de la CEE) for handicrafts. The statute of UNICE, which represents the employers of industry in the six countries, states that in matters of common concern, common interests as well as fundamental questions of common policy, it will be the spokesman for industrial groups in the six countries.[30]

This association, first as a specialized group and later as a member of an umbrella organization, gives rise to a form of "double representation."[31] The latter form seems to be the more important in terms of dealings with the Commission, which regards the general organizations as the official spokesmen of agricultural, industrial, and commercial interests. The actual relationships here are extremely subtle, though, and it would be a mistake to pass off the direct ties between the specialized groups and Community organs as completely unimportant. These specialized organs are called upon to meet with the Commission. In these cases, however, they serve as a provider of information and technical expertise concerning the questions of detail once general policy directions have been established. When the Commission is interested not in technical detail but in the political positions of national groups, in what the constituents are likely to accept, how much they are willing to compromise, they prefer to work directly with the umbrella groups.

The Commission's preference for relations with the umbrella organizations does not remove the problem of the variety of individual positions, it merely pushes the resolution of this problem down to another level. It allows the specialized claims of national groups to filter through the larger groupings first. The task of these groupings is to find, if not to create, common areas of concern as well as patterned axes of conflict. Metaphorically, these umbrella organizations can be looked upon as funnels through which a large, heterogeneous amount of information and demands pass. These demands and information are searched for common patterns and positions and in turn this reduced set of demands is passed on to Community institutions.

COPA, one of the most active of the umbrella organizations, represents fifteen basic national agricultural interest groups in addition to maintaining contacts with many specialized groups. Among others, it directly represents the Deutscher Bauernverband (West Germany); the Assemblée Permanente des Chambres d'Agriculture, and the Fédération Nationale des Syndicats d'Exploitants Agricoles from France; the Confederazione Generale dell'Agricoltura Italiana; the Katholieke Nederlandse Boeren-en Tuindersbond from Holland; the Alliance Agricole Belge from Belgium; and the Centrale Paysanne Luxembourgeoise from Luxembourg. Figure 2.2 gives a comprehensive idea of the groups involved. This chart gives an idea of the number of groups involved in agriculture. The question arises as to how common positions could ever come out of such a variegated assembly of interests. This problem would seem to be complicated by the absence of any compulsory mechanisms, such as majority voting. Article 15 of the statutes of UNICE requires that the Council of Presidents reach decisions unanimously.[32] It was already mentioned that COPA makes provisions for the expression of a minority opinion before passing on their positions to Community organs.

A brief examination of the structure of COPA may be illuminating. At the top of the organizational chart is the General Assembly, technically the supreme organ of decision, and composed of representatives of the member states. It is the Assembly's task to provide the broad policy options for agriculture and to set the guidelines for the more specialized work in COPA.[33] Since the Assembly meets roughly four times a year there is need for another institution to deal with the more continuous policy-making problems that are nonetheless nonadministrative in nature. Such a body is the Presidium which is composed of six members, one from each country, and designated by their national organs. The Presidium meets upon request of its president as often as needed but in any case not less than once a month: the Presidium occupies the central place in the nexus between the general policy-making activities of the Assembly and the more specialized concerns of the individual work groups (Sections Spécialisées: Groupes de Travail et Commissions). In this respect the Presidium is the conveyor belt communicating individual COPA interests to the Assembly and in turn carrying out and watching over the Assembly's decisions. Finally, at a lower rung of this political-administrative ladder there is a permanent secretariat headed by a secretary-general. This secretariat provides the administrative continuity needed for the day-to-day operations of COPA, proceeds with the administration of decisions already taken, and is responsible for maintaining permanent contacts between COPA and the relevant Community organs—in particular, the Commission and the General Directorate for Agriculture.[34]

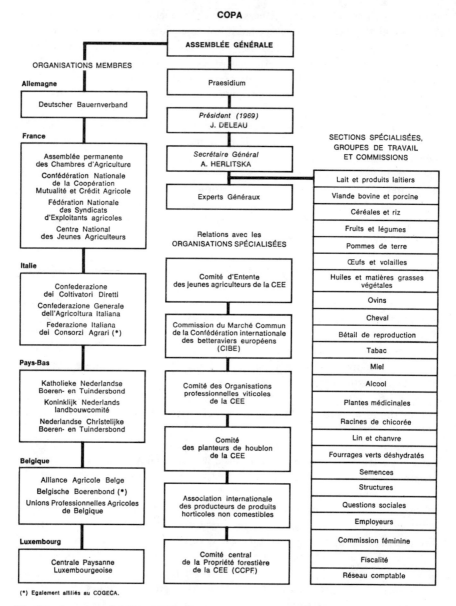

Fig. 2.2. Structure of COPA. SOURCE: *Documentation Européenne* (Brussels, 1969).

ROLE OF INTEREST GROUPS: ACTIVITIES AND ACCESS

How, if at all, do interest groups make themselves felt? In its attempt to avoid obsolescence the Commission promoted the idea that national interest groups should band together into peak organizations. Once this was accomplished it was left to these groups to decide on the particular mode of contact with influential Community organs. In any case, this depended to a great extent on the specific goal of the group in question. A great many groups are not set up to influence policy at all but only to keep au courant on developments in EEC and to report these developments to their constituents. Other groups are limited to making inquiries or to gathering information, whereas the more important ones are engaged in regular, institutionalized contact with Commission members and administrative personnel in the General Directorate of their interest. One could say that there are basically *four modes of activity in which Community groups engage:* (1) provision of information, expertise, and carrying out studies; (2) the coordination of national positions; (3) the pressuring of Community policy-making organs; and (4) the communication of mass demands to Community elites and inversely, the communication of Community positions and policies to the masses.

Information

The emerging Community system lacks structured, institutionalized, and differentiated organs for providing the detailed knowledge so crucially needed for policy making in an industrial society. One natural place to turn would have been the national administrations and, to some extent, the individual national bureaucracies are tapped for expertise. This gap in the Community system is being filled largely by representatives of interest groups. It is important to note that the views of these groups are sought not only for the working out of technical problems associated with the formulation of policy but also to sound out the limits national groups are likely to accept. The activities of COCCEE (Comité des Organisations Commerciales des Pays de la CEE) provide a good example of this form of activity. COCCEE continually engages in gathering information on the EEC and in passing on information concerning its positions to Community organs. The Commission consults it regularly and takes note of COCCEE's advice in an informal way. In addition, when the Commission notifies COCCEE that it is in need of expert advice, COCCEE designates the technical experts to go to the particular meetings organized by the Commission.[35]

Coordination of National Positions

One of the most important activities of the umbrella interest groups is that of coordinating the various national positions. It is not to be confused with the process of aggregation where individual positions are actually compromised and lose their separate identities. The role of European groups appears to be a more limited one involving merely a search for areas of agreement. Yet even this search performs a valuable service in narrowing the range of information that Community organs must confront.

The document describing the organization of COPA states that one of its goals is to "study and coordinate the suggestions of the constituent organizations with a view at common positions and present these to the institutions of the Community."[36]

It was recognized at an early stage of the Community's development that it was not to its advantage to offer views individually and that results were more likely to be achieved if actions were coordinated. COPA attempts to achieve coordination at its monthly Presidium meetings. UNICE, Fischer reports, did not provide for any legal link among its specialized groups and "had, therefore, no legal means later on to effectively regulate possible differences of opinions between itself and those groups."[37] What UNICE does to overcome this is to call meetings for all concerned parties in which information is exchanged, differing positions are aired, and a sense of one another's common and divergent points of view is acquired.

The umbrella organizations in general, and COPA in particular, suffer from a dilemma that is at once a strength and a weakness. These organizations attempt to cast their net as widely as possible, including a wide variety of opinions and positions, and in so doing they faithfully convey the views of national groups without seriously antagonizing anyone. The other horn of the dilemma is that, because of their reluctance and inability to forge effective compromises, these peak organizations find it difficult to be effective and dynamic spokesmen for their constituents at the policy-making level. Indeed, because of the loose, decentralized nature of the interest groups, a structure that offers maximum protection to national members, it becomes impossible to act when unanimous agreement does not exist. COPA, for example, could offer no leadership on the crucial question of farm prices because of lack of unanimity. Paralysis and protection appear to be opposite sides of the same coin.[38]

What do these organizations do then if they have no power of leadership in the face of disagreement and no power to effect compromises? They harmonize and coordinate, and by that we mean they search for preexisting areas of agreement, formalize them, and communicate the agreement to appropriate Community organs. Finally, they act to prevent, as the COPA document puts it, "toute dispersion des efforts et des moyens d'organisation. . . ."[39] In this sense they do cut down on administrative duplication and redundant statements of policy positions, a valuable service in itself as long as we remember that it is free from the compromises and aggregation efforts that must take place before issues reach the more crucial phases of the decision process.

Influencing Community Organs

The interest groups exert some influence every time they intervene in the policy-making process. National interest groups are not paying an international secretariat to altruistically supply information to Community organs to make policy that takes no account of their interests. Influence is an extremely subtle process, though. It should not be gauged in terms of the will of interest group over the will of a Community organ but rather in terms of winning over official representatives to their viewpoint. Thus, in one sense influence is not a separate activity but an aspect of all other activities. For example, information is not presented to Community organs in a neutral way but with a view toward influencing policy.

The stages where interest groups intervene most frequently, and where, therefore, they exert influence, are in the beginning when the basic policy is being formulated, and much later, when the details of the policy are being worked out. In the intial phase, the Commission calls upon interest groups for technical information and in turn distributes its documentation to the groups. It is doubtful if the information presented at this stage is as neutral as some observers have noted,[40] and it is probable that interest groups take this opportunity to assure themselves that the developing policy is proceeding within acceptable limits and slant their information to assure that it does. It also offers the Community organs an early check on what is acceptable to organized groups and provides them with guidelines for further elaboration of policy. (This initial phase serves as an early warning system.) At a later stage in this process of elaboration, when the atmosphere is more suggestive of bargaining than consultation and the provision of information, the interest groups still meet with Commission members, sometimes informally, sometimes in an institutionalized way. The more one passes from providing neutral expertise to bargaining over preferred policy positions, however, the more important becomes the role of national experts and correspondingly the less the importance of interest groups.[41]

There has recently been developing a new point of entry for exerting influence, viz., the actual initiation of a policy proposal. If such a development should become more widespread it would indeed be important for the emerging powers of European pressure groups. Initiation requires careful study, expert knowledge, and a sizable bureaucracy. Most of the pressure groups under discussion are strikingly lacking in this last requirement. It is undoubtedly one of the reasons why the actual initiation of proposals has occurred somewhere within the General Directorate responsible for the policy. It was only after this that pressure groups were then set into motion. As early as 1964, however, Professor Sidjanski noted a variation on this pattern:

> Group initiatives have lately become more frequent. To take only one example, the federation of bankers of EEC has formulated several proposals: the elimination of discrimination arising out of legislation or regulations, the suppression of all taxes or checques and commercial drafts with EEC. COMITEXTIL and many other groups continuously put forward their own proposals and suggestions to the Commission. In this way, they take an active part in the development of the Community, by urging and helping the Commission to undertake and to fulfill a multitude of tasks.[42]

In addition to the fact that influence is dependent upon the stage of the policy-making process in question we should also note that the structure of influence is multitiered, with umbrella organizations playing the role of coordinator and regulator of the more generalized aspects of policy and the specialized organs fulfilling the needs imposed by the more technical and specific demands of policy. Sidjanski correctly points out that UNICE does not try to speak on all questions concerning industrial activity but reserves its energies for common questions that raise general considerations of interest to all. In turn specialized groups speak on questions of detail and on problems that are peculiar to them.[43]

Finally, as to the direction of influence, we should remark that it is far from a unidirectional flow from the groups to Community organs. In many cases, a Community organ, usually the Commission, will attempt to influence the interest groups. The consultation phase involves more than the provision of information by interest groups; it also offers the Commission an opportunity to explain and to advocate. More importantly, the Commission is constantly attempting to win over group support as a source of reserve strength on which it can count. That this was a valuable strategy is seen by the important support given by key groups to the Commission during the 1965-66 crisis.[44]

Communication

A great many of the European groups do not attempt to influence the making of policy. They exist simply to communicate information concerning Community developments back to their membership.[45] Such groups play no outright role in the decision-making process but they are in a good structural position to become activated quickly should the need arise.

More important than the information function above is the development of a public relations activity on the part of some groups. They are the first examples of any Community organ attempting to mobilize and harness public opinion. This role is all the more important in light of the fact that the political and administrative apparatus of the Community is divorced from the masses and thus lacks popular roots. Some groups, like the Conseil National du Patronat Français, publish a periodical, Le Patronat Français, which attempts to reach a general readership. It is doubtful how successful these attempts are, given the relatively narrow interest span of the average citizen who is simply not likely to be interested in issues that do not bear directly upon him.

Limited evidence indicates that we should view this public relations activity in two lights: first, as an attempt to build up a reservoir of general support free from ties to a specific issue; and second, as a supplementary form of access when normal channels of influence are frustrated. The latter is the role that Meynaud and Sidjanski feel is important for public relations. They cite the example that the Counseil National du Patronat Français (CNPF) was oppossed to the date fixed for harmonizing the tariff union. After being frustrated in several attempts to deal with the French government it attempted to mobilize public opinion. By this circuitous route it hoped to influence the government.[46]

Another striking example of attempts to mobilize public opinion in the face of the closing off of other channels of access is provided by the agricultural crisis of 1965-66 in which French interest groups acted through both national and European channels. This crisis, though triggered by disagreement over some rather technical matters concerning the financing of the Common Agricultural Policy (CAP), in reality involved fundamental disagreements between the French and the remaining five countries about the strength of European political institutions. The French opposed the use of majority rule in arriving at Community decisions and they opposed the acquisition of an independent revenue base by the European Parliament. Since the Commission favored majority rule and independent resources for the European Parliament, the crisis involved a struggle between France and the Commission. In this case, it would have been inappropriate to apply pressure to the normal channel, the Commission, since it was the Commission's existence and vitality that were in question. It was clearly the

French government, as represented in the Council, that was the nub of the problem. Thus pressure had to be applied directly on the French government. This the French agricultural groups did, both by stimulating COPA to endorse its White Paper and by attempting to mobilize public opinion during the December 1965 elections.

The Introduction to the *Livre Blanc* included these words: "In the face of this disturbing situation [the crisis], the professional agricultural organizations have decided to undertake an information campaign destined to make known the grave consequences which would follow, for agriculture and for the whole French economy, from the halting of European construction."[47]

One can never tell for certain whether the role of interest groups, despite their strong stand, had any effect on the outcome of the French election of December 1965. Two of the candidates, Jean Lecanuet and François Mitterand, ran to a large extent on a European platform. De Gaulle won the election in a runoff but many observers feel that his weak showing led to his willingness to arrive at an agreement ending the crisis. In addition, the limited evidence offered by public opinion polls after the crisis confirms the view that, in the minds of the average voter, the European issue played an important role in the campaign. In a sample of towns chosen, the following results were reported in answer to the question: "le problème de l'Europe fut-il un problème dans la campagne électorale?" Seventy-nine percent answered yes, 15 percent no. The highest percentage was attained in Bordeaux with 84 percent responding in the affirmative whereas the weakest (European) results were in Lille with 68 percent. In all the other "villes" consulted, at least three-fourths of those interviewed testified to the importance of the European theme in the election.[48] Table 2.1 presents the results.[49]

TABLE 2.1

QUESTION: THE FIRST ROUND OF THE PRESIDENTIAL ELECTION IN FRANCE TOOK PLACE ON DECEMBER 5, 1965. IN YOUR OPINION WAS THE EUROPEAN PROBLEM AN IMPORTANT ISSUE IN THE ELECTION CAMPAIGN? (PERCENTAGES)

Answers	Total	Lille	Grenoble	Caen	Nice	Paris	Bordeaux	Lyon
Yes	79	68	76	82	80	79.5	84	83.5
No	15	23.5	19	11	13	15.5	9	12
No opinion	6	8.5	5	7	7	7	7	4.5
n	2116	290	332	254	122	592	276	260

SOURCE: Opinion poll conducted under the direction of D. Pepy, University of Rennes. Adapted from J. Pertejo, "Le thème européen dans les éléctions présidentielles françaises des 5 et 19 décembre 1965," paper presented to a seminar conducted by Professor D. Sidjanski (Geneva: Institut d'Études Européennes, May, 1967, p. 28, appendix.

MODES OF ACCESS

How does one characterize the modes of contact with Community organs? Are they sporadic or regular, institutionalized or noninstitutionalized, direct or indirect? Fritz Fischer identifies five types of access that can be detected: (1) information meetings; (2) consultation and expert meetings; (3) large-scale conferences; (4) working groups; and (5) institutionalized committees such as the Economic and Social Committee.[50]

Information meetings are general, fact-finding meetings at which interest group representatives get together and exchange views. The meetings may originally have been convened to make the groups aware of developments in new policies but inevitably the occasion is also used to advance the positions advocated by the groups. It is customary at the end of such meetings for the groups to draw together some statement of their position and submit these to the Commission.[51] It is an excellent example of the structurally double-edged nature of articulation. The Commission and the interest groups are both proposing almost simultaneously. It matters little that the Commission may have called for the meeting. Once in motion, the process can only be described in terms of a series of self-reinforcing activities.

In contrast with these information meetings, consultation and expert meetings do not come into play until the main outlines of a policy have been sketched. Then the experts are called in to fill in the detail and to enter into extensive consultations on the exact shape and form to give to the policy. Usually the Commission first sends the appropriate papers to the groups and requests their opinions. In addition to interest group experts, the process of give and take that ensues may include national experts, a group of which would be represented by each national administration. These experts, while not technically instructed by their national governments, are nevertheless sensitive to their views, and the technical advice given is no doubt sifted through national screens. An interesting by-product of this process is the dialogue engendered between national experts, drawn from the respective national administrations, and Community experts, drawn from the European interest groups.[52]

Conferences, such as the agricultural conference in Stresa, Italy, in 1958, provide a forum for discussion of general policy questions. Such meetings should be seen as efforts to achieve high-level policy agreement in a certain area, agreement that is necessary before any detailed work can take place.

Fischer notes that since the birth of the EEC, hundreds of working groups have been set up, again with membership mixed between the Commission and members of national administrations. Interest groups play an insignificant role at this point and are rarely asked to participate at all in these sessions.[53]

These modes of access are formal and institutionalized, that is, they are characterized by regularity of meeting time, specificity of place, proscribed membership, and the existence of a bureaucracy that records their activities and gives continuity to their aims between meetings. In addition to this there are thousands of telephone calls, personal conversations, private correspondences, and other contacts. These forms of access are characterized by their sporadic and noninstitutionalized nature. It is difficult to assess how important these relations are at this point, one reason being that many of these contacts are private and secret. Meynaud and Sidjanski feel that they can be very important and that the content of these relations can range from simple exchange of information and communication of dossiers and technical information to the transmission of opinions and orientations.[54] Finally there are relations between administration members of key interest groups that are regular and frequent but perhaps not official in the sense of being formally recognized in writing or in not having definite times and places of meeting. These relationships, for example, between high officials of UNICE and members of the Commission, may take place every day.

TARGETS OF INTEREST GROUP ACTIVITY

The targets of interest group activity are the focal points on which groups seek to exercise influence; they are potential leverage points for affecting policy. The identification of these points would in itself tell us a good deal about the European political system, possibly where its true decision-making centers are and where it is vulnerable to access. It may also be instructive to examine the targets of interest group activity for another reason. It sometimes happens that the pattern of group activity recaptures or retraces the more fundamental structure of the system. In this sense the established system will define the boundaries for the new structure (the interest groups). For example, interest groups in England focus on high level, peak organizations whereas in the United States, because of the decentralized nature of its federal system, one sees a multitiered system of group activity focusing on federal, state, and local levels. Thus, focusing on the constellation of group activity may be a backhanded way of learning about the European Community.

There is a wide variety of targets on which interest groups attempt to exert influence. In the perceptions of group leaders, at least, each of these targets can potentially influence policy. One could divide these targets along two dimensions, primary-secondary and national-supranational. Primary targets are those whose influence in the decision-making process is more or less certain as opposed to secondary targets, whose status in the decision-making process is more nearly consultative. National targets are those officially organized at the nation-state level such as the Ministry of Foreign Relations or the Ministry for Economic Affairs. Supranational targets are those uniquely organized at the Community level.

The two primary targets for interest group activity are the Commission and the Council of Ministers, both supranational groupings. Article 229 of the Treaty of Rome establishes the basis for the Commission's relationship with interest groups. The Commission is charged with assuring "les liaisons opportunes avec toutes organisations internationales."[55] This pressure has taken many forms, ranging from the institutionalized monthly meetings between the Presidium of COPA and Sicco Mansholt, General Director for Agriculture, to the more explosive outbursts typified by Edmund Rehwinkel's periodic attacks on the Commission.[56]

The Commission is by far the Community channel most often used by interest groups. In response to a set of interviews administered by a team of Dutch researchers, it was consistently argued by all groupings that the European

Commission was by far the most important target.[57] This is not surprising for several reasons. From the beginning there was an active attempt by the Commission to cultivate relationships with interest groups. In addition, the Commission has a permanent bureaucracy that gives it some stability and administrative roots. Third, the Commission has some influence on Community policy, a fact that could not have been unequivocally inferred from the formal structure of the EEC. Finally, although it is true that the Council ultimately decides, by the time a piece of legislation gets to the Council its general outlines have already been established. Thus the fact that the initial proposal for legislation comes from the Commission puts pressure on interest groups to lobby there. In view of the independence of the Commission from national authorities, interest groups clearly would be foolish to rely exclusively on national channels for representation of their interests.

A good idea of the frequency and scope of Commission contacts is provided by Lindberg and Scheingold. They present data to show that in the early 1960s the Commission met with interest group representatives, calling 733 such meetings in 1960; 856 in 1961; 1,344 in 1962; and 1,539 in 1963. These meetings took place over a large range of issue areas with, as one would expect, heavy concentration in agriculture.[58]

The Commission is the hub, the wheel around which organized interests consolidate in attempts to make themselves felt. It deals with making policy in its earlier stages of formulation and as such is an attractive target for many groups. It is this Commission role in the formulation and elaboration of policy that is important for the interest groups, for it is here that access is relatively easy and the policy situation still uncrystallized. The Commission's role in the later stages, for example, during the marathon sessions, the protracted negotiating sessions that precede the final stages of decision making, is almost completely insulated from the activity of interest groups.

The Council of Ministers, despite the fact that it is the ultimate decision-making organ in the Community, is not the object of influence of pressure groups. Undoubtedly, many pressure groups would like to bring influence on Council members but the Council is nearly impossible to penetrate and as the Dutch study put it, "le Conseil refuse catégoriquement d'être mêlé aux discussions entre la Commission Européenne et les groupes de pression."[59] Indeed, since the proceedings of the Council are shrouded in secrecy it is difficult for interest groups to know what is going on. Pressure group activity depends heavily upon the existence of institutionalized communication between pressure groups and their targets. Sometimes, during particularly important negotiations, such as the agricultural marathon sessions of January 1962, December 1963, and December 1964, an interest group, for example, COPA, will act on the basis of scanty information (derived, perhaps, from press releases, reading *Agence Europe,* an important European daily newsletter) and send a telegram to the ministers advocating a certain position.

There are many reasons why the Council is not frequently the object of group pressures. First of all, the Council presents a shifty and highly elusive target. It does not sit regularly; it meets sporadically and its membership may not even be the same from one session to the next. Second, the ministers who sit on the Council are full-time national politicians who cannot afford to be preoccupied with Community affairs. Third, the Treaty of Rome provides for the channeling of pressure group activity through the Economic and Social Committee which is in turn consulted by the Council. The Council has taken care to ensure that it could claim a variety of institutional buffers to absorb the dominant thrust of group activity. Finally, probably the greatest single reason for the unimportance of the Council is the fact that, since Council members are rather closely instructed representatives of their respective states, it would be redundant to try to influence them at the Community level. Why should groups change their geographical focus and attempt to deal with a shifting, uncrystallized institution when they have access to a more consolidated and permanent set of parallel institutions at the national level? Until the time when interest groups perceive that the Council of Ministers represents a distinct element in the policy-making process, that is, until they acquire some independence from their respective national ministries, they are unlikely to be a serious candidate for interest group activity.

The decentralized nature of interest group activity is thus reflective of the confederal character of Community politics in general. It is thus that the pattern of interest group activity helps us to trace out the more fundamental structures of the system within which it operates.

The secondary targets are distinguished by their essentially consultative nature and among these we include the Economic and Social Committee (ESC), the consultative committees, and the European Parliament. The Economic and Social Committee is composed of 101 members representing three groups: employers; employees; and a group including farmers, artisans, the liberal professions, and others. Thus the structure of this committee parallels closely the actual social cleavages in the component national societies. Despite the obvious aim of the drafters of the Treaty of Rome (the treaty establishing the EEC) that this Committee was to be an important channel for interest group activity, in practice it is not very important. One study notes that "La plupart des fonctionnaires ne tiennent pas compte des avis du Comité, très souvent ils ne les lisent même pas."[60] Many blame the Committee itself for its lack of influence, noting that it is given to slogans, it has no effective method of work, and its reports are of an inferior quality. It is interesting to note that in the initial years of the functioning of the EEC, agricultural groups took the Economic and Social Committee seriously and attempted to influence it. It soon became evident, however, that the effort was wasted, since the Council of Ministers did not heed the ESC's advice. This led to a reorientation of the activity of agricultural groups and a consolidation of contacts with the Commission.

It appears that the primary reason for the decline in importance of the ESC as a pressure group target is that it has been outbid and outmaneuvered by competing structures, particularly the Commission and possibly the consultative committees. While it is true that the Treaty provides that the Council of Ministers consult the ESC it must be admitted that the ESC does not occupy as strategic a spot as the Commission. The Commission is important in the position it occupies in the complex web of relations known as the Council-Commission dialogue. It is doubtful if the Commission would be as influential if it merely functioned as a conveyor of information and wishes. The Commission's influence is heightened when it can utilize a combination of information, persuasion, and harassment and when the Council is overwhelmed with detail and fatigue, in other words, during the marathon negotiations. The ESC is not equipped for such a role.

Another development may have affected the role of the ESC, viz., the emergence, as part of the agricultural regulations adopted on Jaunary 14, 1962, of a series of consultative committees composed of Community representatives, 50 percent from producer and agricultural cooperatives and 25 percent each from agricultural workers and consumers. They are convened either on the initiative of the Commission or professional groups and they discuss technical questions usually related to the application of decisions already taken.

These committees, being essentially involved in technical questions and blending further the activity of interest groups and the Commission, appear to result in the further consolidation of the Commission's position in the policy-making process and as such, siphon off interest group activity from other targets. This phenomenon results from the incredibly complicated system of market management set up by the adoption of the agricultural regulations of January 1962.

The European Parliament, like the ESC, is not very effective as a conveyor of group interests. Perhaps this is a sign of the general decline of parliamentary influence in the modern age where decision making under the welfare state demands new forms of political organization. The Parliament is accused of being "an institution of demagogues," of being aloof, and of not taking account of reality. A vicious circle argument is involved in that some argue the Parliament is weak because of its inferior personnel while others argue its personnel are inferior because the Parliament has no power. The fact that members of Parliament are not elected by popular vote and that the Community as yet has no independent resources over which they can exert control are two of the chief institutional weaknesses of the European Parliament.

LEVEL OF INTEREST GROUP ACTIVITY

Up to this point we have stressed the role of Community organs as targets of interest group activity. Yet attempts are often made to influence Community decisions through national channels. Indeed, since the final decision is taken in the Council of Ministers and since a substantial amount of the preparatory work takes place in the Committee of Permanent Representatives, it would seem natural, as Werner Feld has argued, for groups to attempt contacts with national governments and political parties.[61] The relative share of energy directed through national and Community channels varies with the member state as well as with the issue areas. For example, in France, especially under de Gaulle, there was a special disfavor for the intermediaries who stood between the state and the people,[62] whereas in Italy interest groups appeared to exert considerable influence, even in such areas as foreign economic policy. As a general rule, however, the more important the issue area, the greater the tendency for groups to operate through national channels.

The pattern of interest group activity as it develops in several of the member states is worthy of examination. It is generally agreed that in France the activity of interest groups has diminished under the Fifth Republic. French interest groups seldom channel their demands through either political parties or the Parliament. A substantial amount of contact transpires, however, through the so-called administration consultative, which brings together functionaries, professionals, and independent experts and facilitates an exchange of views between professional groups and the various administrations.[63] The objects of concern at these meetings are mostly of a technical and administrative nature whereas questions of genuine political scope are reserved for other arenas.

In Italy, interest groups have a considerable influence on the making of Community decisions. The structure of Italian interest group activity makes it necessary to distinguish between issues of a political-institutional nature and those that are primarily socioeconomic. What one author calls promotional groups tend to be very important in political-institutional questions (such as the fusion of the executives of the European Communities [EC]). On the other hand, interest groups, concerned with a specialized area of economy, are more important in questions relating to agriculture, industry, or labor.[64] The targets of these two types of interest groups are also different. For the most part, the socioeconomic interest groups direct their energy toward the Commission and the ESC whereas the promotional groups aim at the European Parliament. The former type of activity is intended to influence the outcome of a definite issue, the latter is meant to influence the political atmosphere or to rally public opinion. For example, there is the CISL, which has attempted—though not very successfully—to influence Community policy, with respect to the free movement of workers. Their weakness owes partly to the sometimes indifferent attitude of the CISL but in great measure it is a result of the fact that the Minister of Labor does not always maintain contacts with the CISL on Community matters. Other syndicates that represent only a minority of workers exert more influence and this owes partly to the fact that the parties to which they belong are dedicated to the solution of European problems.[65]

A number of groups are involved in attempting to influence Community decisions through national channels in Italy, perhaps reflecting the diversity of Italian society. Even the Confederazione Generale Italiana del Lavoro (CGIL), the Communist trade union, which is not represented at the Community level, attempts to influence Community policy through national channels. In this regard it takes a very active interest in European questions, publishing numerous documents and taking positions on important European questions. Also, the interest groups in agriculture, la Federazione Nationale dei Coltivatori deritti, la Confederazione Generale dell'Agricoltura Italiana and la Federazione dei Consorzi Agrari play an active role especially through le Comitati Italiano per le Relazioni Agricole Internazionali (CIRAI), a general agricultural committee which meets weekly to arrive at common positions in agriculture.[66]

THE PROCESS OF ARTICULATION

I have suggested already that the function of articulation is structurally diffuse, involving a variety of organs in the performance of this task. But how does this function transpire, how does it look in action? One simple formulation, certainly true, is that the Commission proposes and the Council disposes. This proposal may originate within one of the general directorates, for example, social policy, transport, or external affairs, or it may stem from a policy decision agreed to by the Commission members during one of their weekly Wednesday meetings. Such a view, while true, is nevertheless a blunt statement in that it ignores the multiplicity of mediating groups and structures that intervene between the time a proposal is put forward and its adoption. Indeed, it even obscures the manner by which an issue is put forward since it suggests that the Commission arrives at the proposal untarnished by the play of interest groups, national ministries, experts, and politicians.

It is likely that the formal stirrings of a proposal will take place within the lower levels of a particular general directorate, for example, agriculture, transport, external affairs. Many proposals emerge which never make it to the Council but are killed somewhere in the filtering process. But even before these formal proposals emerge a variety of groups are caught up in the process. Lambert gives us an idea of the comprehensiveness of this process.

> The Commission calls together, under the chairmanship of one of its own staff, the national civil servants working on a particular field. These are the men who commute regularly to Brussels from the Community capitals. Together, they go over the problems that have to be solved, and the various possible methods, as well as their own particular national difficulties. Then the trade unions and employers' organisations are consulted, at informal meetings and also the representatives of the industries directly affected. Everything that emerges is taken into account when the proposals to the Council are drafted and when they are examined and approved by the Commission itself.[67]

Thus associational interest groups are directly involved in the preproposal stage of interest articulation. They are also indirectly involved in that they engage in more or less daily contact and exchange of information with Commission members. Thus when a staff member draws up a proposal he is sensitive both to the needs and expectations of Community interest groups and he is usually advised, by virtue of contacts with members of the CPR of the positions of national leaders. Thus a proposal emerges out of a subtle interaction between the aims of Commission members, the options and constraints provided by the Treaty, the positions of national elites, and the influence of interest groups. A good example of this is provided by COPA's relation to the General Directorate for Agriculture. The General Directorate often submits drafts of proposals to COPA before finally presenting them to the Council and COPA members, for example, Secretary-General Herlitska may have sent letters and position statements to Commission members. The Commission's proposals on the fixing of prices for agricultural products are a good case in point.[68]

Immediately after the proposal emerges, and before it goes to the Council, the interest groups enter into another phase of collaboration. If they have not taken an active part up to this point, the Commission may communicate the content of the proposal to them or interest group members may hear about it reading *Agence Europe,* a detailed and highly accurate daily. The preproposal contacts described above usually make this form of information gathering unnecessary, however, which is fortunate since the definition of an issue is an important indicator of the limits within which it will be allowed to unfold. It would be clearly unsatisfactory for the interest groups to remain passive during this stage.

After this initial stage there are two stages during which the Commission may exert influence upon legislation, during the early stages when all groups take part in elaborating policy and a final state that involves close bargaining between the Council and Commission and upon which adoption or rejection finally hinges. In only the former of these stages do interest groups have any influence. Sometimes this influence is institutionalized in the establishment of a permanent committee with mixed composition (governmental experts and delegates of professional organizations) as, for example, the Committee for the Free Circulation of Workers. The latter phase of intensive Council-Community bargaining is simply too rapid and too secret for groups to play a role. In addition many of the technical considerations for which interest group representatives are so helpful have by this time been ironed out. The problems may now be of a more political nature. An exception to this occurred during the 1965-66 crisis when COPA and French interest groups reacted strongly to France's position. Although the controversy hinged on agriculture, reactions were forthcoming from both employers' associations and labor unions. For example, during the crisis, M. Buiter, secretary-general of the Secrétariat Syndicat Européen, met with Amintore Fanfani, acting president of the Council of Ministers, and expressed the anxiety of the free syndicates over the Community situation.[69]

COCCEE represents a kind of microcosm of the activities of interest groups, evidencing various forms of contact and influence, varying its pressure from information exchanges to stronger statements of political position, and cutting into the legislative process at various stages. It transmits information and opinions to members of the Commission's staff and it in turn is often consulted by the Commission. It designates experts for the "réunions d'information" organized by the general directorates and it may send an observer to the ESC when questions related to commercial policy are being discussed. It also designates three members to sit on FEOGA, the Fonds Européen d'Orientation et de Garantie Agricole. It is not an exaggeration to say that COCCEE is institutionally embedded in the Community legislative policy.[70]

Associational interest groups seem to play an important, albeit complementary, role in interest articulation, sharing the stage with the Commission itself, national bureaucracies, delegated national experts, and national politicians who make their day-to-day influence felt through the Committee of Permanent Representatives. It is difficult to detect a distinctly Community component in all this since the dominant pattern appears to be one of institutional blending of national and supranational elements which makes conceptual separation very difficult. Thus while the organizational component of associational interest groups is distinguishable (it has separate physical facilities, its own bureaucracy, distinct personnel), the functional component is not.

What we are witnessing is the struggle to settle what structure will become dominant in the performance of this function. The shifts back and forth between Commission bureaucracy, Community interest groups, and national ministries mirror a three-way tug-of-war in which there is a constant jockeying for positions. These three structures are not only bargaining about the outcomes of a particular policy. They are also bargaining about the very ways they will relate to one another in the future. In this competition, the demands of time, energy, expertise, and local knowledge press toward the elaboration of new structures whereas resources, entrenched bureaucracies, habits, and inertia help to propagate and give new life to old ones. The former set of considerations gives Community interest groups a one-upmanship while the latter tends to favor the nation-state. In this battle the nation-state keeps delegating and elaborating, entrusting its interests to proxies at the Community level. For example, one could view the CPR and the Special Agricultural Committee in this light, as two institutions that represent the national interests at the Community level and thus strengthen the probability that national channels can be used by interest groups. Whether this kind of elaboration will be effective in saving national channels from an evolutionary obsolescence or whether a clean structural break will be needed is now an unsettled question.

The one thing interest groups sorely lack in the exercise of influence is autonomy. The close relationship between the Council and the Commission reinforces this lack of autonomy and makes it difficult for interest groups to fundamentally reorient their expectations and activities. In this sense, poor boundary maintenance between Community and national components is reflective of the lack of autonomy at a higher phase of the decision-making process. Ultimately the tug-of-war will probably not be decided by interest groups but by the crystallization of more distinct and autonomous spheres for the Council and Commission.

INTEREST GROUPS AND THE INTEGRATIVE PROCESS

In what ways has the activity of the interest groups contributed to or detracted from the development of European political institutions? Interest groups have aided and could further aid the political development of European institutions in at least four ways: (1) by developing input structures; (2) by contributing to further differentiation of existing structures; (3) by contributing to the growth of a bargaining culture; and (4) by offering the possibility of closing the elite-mass gap.

INPUT STRUCTURES

Incipient interest group activity in the EEC marks the beginning of political participation at the European level. In a political system with neither effective political parties nor popular elections, the role of interest groups increases in importance. As modest as it may be at this time, the operation of interest groups provides one rationale for bringing checks to bear on those who wield policy. It also allows for some link between rulers and ruled and provides a transmission belt that channels individual wants and preferences to key policy-making institutions. Finally, there is some evidence to suggest that the development of political participation structures enhances the legitimacy of a political system.

> One of the advantages a democratic political system is supposed to have over other systems is that those who are able to participate in decisions will thereby be more satisfied with the decisions, and will be more attached to the system than are those who cannot participate. According to this hypothesis, a mutually beneficial exchange occurs between the individual and the political system. In response to his influential inputs, the system produces outputs that are in some way more beneficial for the individual than they would be without those inputs. The beneficial outputs, in turn, lead the individual, through his satisfaction with the system, to a higher level of attachment to that system.[71]

The intensive activity of interest groups has no doubt increased the amount of input load on decision-making structures. Today, labor, industry, agriculture, artisans, traders, and the consumer all make demands on European elites. This has led to a strengthening of input channels, indeed their institutionalization, in the sense of a regular, legitimate, bureaucratized set of structures exists to deal with these demands. For the most part these channels are utilized except in cases where groups feel that they do not offer a realistic hope for solving the problem. Such a case occurred in May 1968 when 4,000 Community dairy farmers demonstrated in Brussels against a Commission proposal. Lindberg notes that even these anomic outbursts in May, where cries of "Mansholt au poteau" ("Mansholt to the stake") and "Mansholt vendu aux margariniers" ("Mansholt sold out to margarine interests") were heard, are evidence of an emerging political process.[72]

FURTHER DIFFERENTIATION OF EXISTING STRUCTURES

It is also interesting to speculate as to whether the emergence of interest groups as an important political force will cause further differentiation in other Community institutions. For example, although both the Council of Ministers and the Commission play a role in the legislative process, the activity of interest groups has increased the strain toward a single structure taking over this function. The volume of information required to handle this new interest group activity necessitates a larger bureaucracy will full-time staffs dedicated to solving these problems. Thus despite the fact that the Council has avoided direct contact with interest groups, it has encouraged proxy groups (the CPR, national bureaucracies, and mixed working groups) to act in its stead. Still the Community system will be in an unstable equilibrium until these lines are more sharply drawn.

Interest group activity also points up the important absence of any structure performing the aggregation function. The lack of a party system to aggregate demands has led to heroic action on the part of the Commission, especially its role in the marathon sessions. At present this function is performed only in the most minimal sense by a host of different institutions. Some aggregation of interests occurs at the national level, where administrative gatekeepers winnow out demands on which it would probably be difficult to reach compromise. Additional aggregation occurs in the umbrella interest groups, in the Commission bureaucracy where proposals are being drafted, and in the CPR, when the agendas of the Council meetings are being prepared. The inadequacy of these structures in the performance of this function was aggravated by the flood of activity introduced by the interest groups. The already weak aggregation structures responded to these increased demands not through further differentiation but by straining the facilities of extant institutions. Thus the marathon session with its offspring, the package deal, arose to plug the gap caused by this structural deficiency. The marathon session is an extended meeting of the Council of Ministers, attended by Commission members and many others, which may last for several weeks, often involving several all-night sessions.[73] At these sessions agreements in the form of package deals (i.e., complex decisions reflecting trade-offs on many different but related issues) were reached which included important compromises that in other contexts seemed difficult to achieve. A good illustration is provided by the marathon session that ended on December 23, 1963, which culminated in an agreement on market organizations in the beef, rice, and dairy produce sectors. What is interesting is that, although as late as December 13, 1963, there was very little agreement on the basic issues, a perception of some package deal was present. On December 13, 1963, *Agence Europe* noted that: "One cannot help concluding that by and large the progress accomplished during this past session has been extremely modest. The Ministers clashed on all the important problems still unsettled in the draft regulations. As far as the 'rice' and 'beef' regulations are concerned, this failure may be explained by the common desire to reserve a good bargaining position for the 'package deal' next week."[74]

To put the functional significance of the marathon sessions and package deals in capsule form, I would say that: (1) both represent ad hoc responses to the growing demands on the Community's already inadequate aggregative structures; (2) both stress heroic leadership and strain existing institutions and personnel to the limit;[75] and (3) both plug the gap but do not solve the problem—indeed, by extending the life of present structures the evolution of distinct aggregative structures is impeded.

GROWTH OF A BARGAINING CULTURE

Interest group activity raises the possibility of a bargaining culture where demands in one sector are traded off for gains in another, where most issues are resolved by compromise and where logrolling and concessions are prevalent. The functional specificity of Community interest groups results in a set of pragmatic demands, divorced from the more turbulent and emotional layers of experience. These demands can be dealt with in a nonideological fashion and are in principle capable of being combined into general policy alternatives without difficulty. In short, the interest groups are responsible for setting into motion a set of demands that are capable of overriding ideological and political cleavages. These demands center on what Haas has called economic-social-welfare considerations and what Parsons has called the value complex of modernization.[76] The crucial question here is whether bargaining becomes truly intersectoral in nature, for example, among agriculture, transport, social affairs, labor, and so on, instead of predominantly intrasectoral, as has been the case to date.

INTEREST GROUPS AND ELITE-MASS GAP

The elitist and unpopular nature of the EEC is acknowledged by most observers. Council members are appointed national officials who sit ex officio. Commission members are appointed by member states and there is no direct election of members to the European Parliament. In fact, were it not for the interest groups, one would be hard put to name one way through which the average man can affect Community policy. The significance of interest group life is that it provides the organizational milieu so crucial in involving individuals in politics. Interest group activity could have far-reaching implications if it succeeds in anchoring the Community's top-heavy institutions in a popular base.

It must not be inferred from all this that interest groups constitute an unmitigated plus for European integration. Indeed there are some serious criticisms one could make against the political role of these groups. Perhaps most seriously the danger exists that Europe will become a giant welfare agency indulging the interests of all special groups and requiring sacrifices from no one. Adrien Zeller has noted that "It is no longer a secret, the mechanisms and policies followed to support agriculture profit essentially a minority of the large farmers."[77]

Zeller documents how Europe has become a haven for narrow pressure groups, sugar beet farmers, tomato growers, dairy farmers, and others. The sugar beet growers, for example, of whom there are two hundred thousand in the six countries, have benefited by the establishment of the EEC. For them a common price level meant an upward adjustment of prices. In this process the Confédération Internationale des Betteraviers Européens (CIBE) has played an important part. The agreements reached by the Community covering sugar illustrate some of the worst consequences of a political system whose center of gravity is found among pressure groups. An unsigned article in *Agenor*, a journal often critical of the EEC, describes it as follows:

> The common sugar policy gives the beet growers a double guarantee: a guaranteed price and a guaranteed market for reasons never explained, a "big" price of 223 dollars a ton is guaranteed for an output equal not just to 100% of normal consumption, but to 105%. And then, for the output between 105% and 135% of total needs a "half price" of 60% of the "big" price is also guaranteed! In short, the Ministers decided coolly and knowingly to subsidize the production of a surplus. Such a night-marish decision can only be explained as the result of late-night sessions, the steady pressure of the beet-

growers lobby, and the political need to placate the Belgians, the main party concerned, in order to get their agreement to the rest of the common farm policy.[78]

The establishment of the EEC seems to have served more as an excuse for pressure groups to wax fat than for economic rationalization to take place. The common agricultural policy has in fact resulted in greater inefficiency and higher prices to the consumer who pays roughly $3.5 billion a year to fund Community agriculture. The EC must be judged very inefficient in terms of its extractive capabilities. Also, as in most cases, unorganized groups will be the ones to suffer. This means that the consumer, laborer, and immigrant suffer disproportionately.

A second danger posed by interest groups, one in some ways already realized, is that the Community, penetrated by special interests, will be able to pass no Community-wide legislation. Zeller, examining price levels reached in wheat, sugar, and dairy products, concluded that the agreements were political compromises resulting from the doings of certain pressure groups.[79] There is of course nothing wrong with people pursuing their interests through organized pressure groups. The notion, however, that some general welfare function arises out of the play of discrete interests acting independently and with few restraints on their interest-oriented behavior is mythical. Groups have interests that are too narrow to engage the masses and as such are often unopposed. Their interests are also too focused to call into existence a countervailing organized group. In this regard, the advantage of group specificity is that few will perceive the group as a threat to their interests.

Still another danger posed by interest groups results from their operation in a truncated political and social environment. The institutional system of the EC is characterized by a legislature and an executive that are sensitive to the influence of interest groups. But interest groups have worked well in some domestic environments not only because they gave voice to specialized interests but also because they have been circumscribed by other political structures, for example, the political party, which serves as a mechanism for the expression of more general political sentiments. This does three things: one, it checks the unbridled expression of narrow interests by allowing for the expression of broader, evaluative dimensions; two, it restrains the operation of groups through periodic elections where unorganized groups can have a say; and three, it forces leaders to form coalitions out of different groups and thus to effect compromises and sacrifices.

A final danger posed by interest groups is that since they are functionally specific, representing highly differentiated areas of socioeconomic life, they present the possibility of not leading to political integration. This undermines the assumption of intersectoral dependence that was so central to early functionalist theory. It was this assumption that lay at the heart of the spillover process. The question now is whether economic life is so autonomous that integration in this sphere need bring about no politicization. The danger here is that the EC will become (or remain) an intergovernmental secretariat dedicated to working out the administrative details of nationally formulated policies. Also, what often is not recognized is that if articulation is too functionally specific, aggregation may be difficult. There will be limited opportunities for logrolling, trade offs, intersectoral and intrasectoral bargains.[80] Since issues revolve around a relatively narrow set of policy axes, the range of substantive material involved will simply not allow for the diversity and play of interests that could result in successful compromises.

Every political system must have minimal capabilities for extraction, regulation, and distribution as well as reserves of symbolic support on which to draw.[81] The EC is an active Community that extracts a substantial amount of resources from its environment. It sometimes does so inefficiently, though, indulging private interests rather than worrying about economic rationality. The surpluses created in butter and sugar are testimony to the pointless extraction taking place. Distribution is the single most important problem. The small farming population cannot continue to be served while the consumers pay. In terms of the development of regulatory structures the Community is still weak. It is true that a developing legal system does have power to sanction aberrant activities but what is most conspicuously lacking is the emergence of a common value system of procedural norms overriding partisan and group differences.

The strategy of Community leadership has been one of indulging private groups in the hopes that some reserve goodwill (symbolic capacity) can be built up. Up to now loyalties seem to be tied to specific issues and have been stubborn in their ability to generalize into more diffuse European attachments. Compromises have been tit for tat and have generally been solved by transferring expense to the more unorganized publics. More pessimistically, compromises more often take place within sectors than between sectors. Such a practice could well lead to the situation where a sector, by virtue of its own accomplishments, burns itself out, atrophies, and dies.

CONCLUSION

The most striking fact of the Community institutional system is the number and variety of interest groups that are involved. These groups represent, in varying degrees of strength, the entire spectrum of socioeconomic life. Organized groups tend to be strongest in industry and agriculture, weaker in labor, and weakest in consumer organizations. These groups conform to our notions of functionally specific groups, are dedicated to a particular task, and possess bureaucracy and personnel who labor to these purposes. This permits issues to be dealt with in a fairly calculating style with almost no ideological overtones. In all respects a bargaining style predominates. Involvement is nonsporadic, the concerns of interest groups being given smoothness and continuity by permanent secretariats whose business it is to maintain day-to-day contacts. The pervasiveness of pressure groups is all the more remarkable in that the Community system is only twelve years old. It appears that the general developmental trend of political systems is from the output to the input side, the exigencies of lawmaking and implementative machinery taking precedence over the luxuries of participation.

Another important point that emerges is that the Community system can be characterized by its "multiple crack" nature, a term used by Morton Grodzins to characterize the multiple-access nature of the American federal system. The EEC likewise offers many entry points for interest groups, both temporally, as the decision process unfolds, and in terms of targets. There are several places where a group may "grab on" and try to exert some leverage. This works against any one structure becoming too strong and thus makes it difficult for the member nation-states to manipulate and control at least one aspect of the influence process.

Perhaps the biggest lack in the interest groups is that of autonomy from the present systems, the member nation-states. Groups still operate through national channels and their influence is supervised on the supranational level by a variety of proxy groups. The dependent status of these groups also comes out in the way umbrella organizations arrive at common viewpoints. It often appears that these organizations serve as speakers for the national associations. If unanimous agreement does not exist at a COPA meeting, for example, vigorous action is not possible. This has affected COPA during the important negotiations on grain-price decisions.

There is more reason for optimism in the new institutional system that seems to be emerging and in which organized groups play an important part. Cross-system linkages between nation-states appear to be emerging and sometimes these seem to be at odds with a member state's own best interest. The outstanding example of this is provided by the agricultural crisis in which French farmer organizations vigorously opposed de Gaulle while German farmers, led by Rehwinkel's Deutscher Bauernverband (DBV), supported the French president. Such an alignment makes little sense if comprehended within a traditional nation-state context.

Notwithstanding this, the most important contribution of interest groups so far is that they have succeeded in effecting a partial reorganization of attitude and activities to a new focus. The way that interest groups rallied to the support of the Commission during the crisis is evidence of this as are the polls taken in France after the end of the crisis. Interest groups may provide the focus for engaging people in the participatory activity of the Community; they may be the transmission belt through which a European civic culture is built. The Community is desperately in need of something to undergird its economic structure, to prevent it from talking about nothing more than eggs in the shell, butter surpluses, and medium-term economic policy—in short, it is in need of a political structure that can engage the interests if not the imagination of Europeans.

Interest groups may prove to be crucial in one final respect. It is often noted that the Community is very open. This is because, structurally speaking, the Commission is an irresponsible body, appointed by the member states but accountable neither to them nor to some supranational element. This problem is aggravated by the gap caused by the gradual transfer of power from national authorities to European executives with the result that the domain under control of national parliaments is decreased while no corresponding structures have yet evolved at the Community level to take up this vacuum. In a situation so lacking of any popular restraints perhaps the emerging interest group web can play a role.

CHAPTER THREE

Interest Articulation:
Institutional Interest Groups

Not all articulation in the European Community is performed by functionally specific interest groups. In many cases claims are placed on the political system by groups or organizations not formally organized to pursue a specific economic or social goal. Indeed, in most polities a variety of input channels and structures exist for making claims on authoritative decision-making structures. In the developing societies, for example, the low level of structural differentiation, the weakly developed vertical links between the masses and elites, and the heterogeneous nature of existing groups all militate against a pattern of articulation dominated by specialized, single-purpose organizations. Weak vertical links would make it impossible to channel articulated demands upward to appropriate decision makers. The heterogeneous nature of existing groups would result in the expression of a set of demands that are so lacking in their ability to be compromised that decision makers would be faced with a myriad of conflicting claims, few of which could be collapsed into an overall program.

There are some restraints that are specific to associational interest articulation at the Community level. First, there is an access problem, which is both a logistical and a target problem. Some groups have not reorganized at the Community level either because they do not have the money to relocate or they do not feel such relocation will pay off. The problem of access to desirable targets is more serious. The Council of Ministers is a shifting body that has neither stable membership nor regularized dates of meeting. It generally convenes about twice a month and attempts to dispose of Community business in these meetings. In fact this arrangement is very inadequate and the Council, aware that it is not capable of responding to all Community issues, delegates its work to subsidiary institutions, in particular the Committee of Permanent Representatives. It also relies to a large extent on the activity and energy of the Commission to generate acceptable policies. In practice the Council is more or less limited to saying "yes," "no," or "try again" to the Commission.[1] These two factors, in addition to the fact that it is generally unsympathetic to cooperation with interest groups, make the Council an impossible target on which to focus for lobbying purposes. Yet the Council is the ultimate decision-making authority in the Community's institutional system. It is true that the Council works closely with the Commission and to the degree that this is so the problem is mitigated. One must not lose sight of the fact, though, that Commission contact with interest groups is for the most part limited to the earlier stages of the policy-formulation process. Once the broad lines of the policy have been fixed and the details filled in, the remaining bargaining, compromise, amendment, and policy changes are matters of Council and Commission concern. In any case, the Commission's role during these latter stages tends to shade off into aggregation, as illustrated by its role in formulating package deals during the marathon sessions.

A second restraint on associational interest articulation in the European Community stems from the fact that membership in functionally specific groups, because it is spread over six different sociocultural-political systems, tends not to be as overlapping as would be the case if all these groups were found in a single political unit. Local national differences, variations in the nature of economic systems—from the high degree of planning and state control in France and Italy to the freer, market-controlled economy in Germany— differences in the structure of agriculture and the like, all make it difficult to blend multinational differences. The upshot is the presence of a large number of groups, many of which present demands that can be aggregated only with difficulty. I argue in a later chapter that these demands are indeed aggregated but only through the emergence of a novel, bizarre, and heroic set of procedures which is coming to be known as the marathon session.

The third limitation on associational interest articulation is the absence of a formal structure to perform the function of aggregation, which is equivalent to saying that there exists no mechanism for coordinating the immense variety of highly disparate inputs. For an embryonic political system with as yet only loosely defined and underdeveloped political structures, this is a serious problem. The general response is that aggregation has been performed sporadically, in bits and pieces, by a number of different Community institutions.[2] Another response has been the necessity for the Commission to formulate proposals that encourage the consolidation of diverse demands. This stimulates single-purpose interest groups to think in more collective terms than would otherwise be the case and enables some modicum of compromise to take place right from the beginning. There is some evidence to indicate that this pattern is characteristic of developing societies. Rajni Kothari has observed that the nonaggregative character of interest groups in India has shifted the locus of articulation to institutional groups. This acts as a damper on the individualism of interest groups and fosters an ethic of coalition building among diverse interests.[3]

Performance of the articulation and aggregation functions has provided the setting for some of the most conflictive and harrowing Community experiences. This is reflected in the fact that most Community disagreements revolve around the questions of "what issues are permissible" and "who should sacrifice what and what should be received in return?" The Gaullist conception of the Common Market is one of an essentially delegate body empowered only to administer the details of programs decided on by the member states. From this stems the notion that permissible issues are technical in nature. The European Commission should therefore confine itself to making proposals along these lines. The problem of "who should sacrifice what" has received several formulations, ranging from Gerhard Schroeder's version of "synchronization" (basically a generalized version of tit for tat) to the Gaullist position that each state ought to be allowed to veto any proposal it does not favor. The absence of anything resembling a reservoir of diffuse loyalty has made states demand immediate repayment for any concessions and has contributed to the swell of a naked version of interest politics in which the public (i.e., those portions of the public which are relatively unorganized) is often the ultimate loser. As a counterpoise to this the Commission and the member nation-states themselves have acted as interest articulators.

THE NATION-STATE AS AN INTEREST ARTICULATOR

In many spheres of activity the nation-state has spilled out of its old shell and has yielded to a more diversified political life in which national and subnational groups may operate directly on foreign or supranational targets. At the same time the nation-state has lost some of its definition and has become penetrated by a variety of extraterritorial actors.[4] This has led some people to speak of an erosion of national loyalty or of the decline of the territorial state. Nevertheless the nation-state, despite the emerging Community system, is still the most meaningful focus of orientation both in terms of the loyalties it commands as well as its ability to move resources. For this reason the institutions of the emerging Community must be seen as representing a thin layer of carefully monitored activity and very limited autonomy. This becomes more and more the case the more salient and controversial the issue area becomes. It makes sense to focus on interest groups in their supranational context when the issue has to do with the level of insecticide in Italian tomatoes. It makes much less sense to do this when the question is one of foreign policy or defense. As Lambert puts it: "As the political implications of Commission proposals increase, so does its need to be aware of the political atmosphere. It may choose to make proposals not coinciding with the known wishes of a member country (its right to do this was at stake, and preserved, in the 1965 crisis) but then it must be able to assess the chances of support from the other countries toward achieving the solution it esteems best for the Community as a whole."[5]

The individual member states act as pressure groups in at least three ways: (1) as gatekeepers in deciding which issues are permissible for the Commission to raise; (2) as inside pressure groups influencing the content of proposals; and (3) as active participants in the conduct of Community negotiations which involve the important problems of foreign policy and defense. The difference between points 2 and 3 is that in 2 the nation-state makes itself felt through a proxy structure such as the Committee of Permanent Representatives whereas in 3 the nation-state is participating qua nation-state.

NATION-STATE AS GATEKEEPER

In the enthusiasm generated over what the Community is engaged in, it is some-times forgotten what activities are excluded from its purview. The Community has been primarily concerned with freeing restrictions to trade, establishing a common tariff wall, establishing market organizations in agriculture, and, in general, attempting to eliminate domestic barriers to the free flow of labor, resources, and capital. Thus, eliminating national transport discriminations, removing discriminations impeding the freedom of establishment of nationals in any Community country (e.g., a doctor should be able to establish a practice in any member country), and establishing a uniform patents convention are all staple activities of the Community. There is, however, a broad range of concerns that are excluded from the Community's jurisdiction. The individual member states act as gatekeepers of the political arena here, controlling the number and content of potential issues. Leon Lindberg has attempted to evaluate the Community's decision-making autonomy in a variety of issue areas.[6] Lindberg finds that in the areas of external affairs, public safety, civic rights, morality, patriotism, education, recreation, education, knowledge, and money and credit decisional power was almost completely in the hands of the member states. It is in this negative sense that the individual states are most important.

The concept of the nondecision has received important attention in the literature on Community power structures.[7] One of the criticisms to which political scientists have been vulnerable is that, since they operate within a decisional framework, they tend to view power in terms of the capacity of individuals to exert their will over others on a particular issue. Since it is not always the same individuals who have their way in each issue area, the conclu-sion is usually that local communities are characterized by a pluralistic political structure. Sociologists, however, by focusing on the recurrent social and economic patterns of a community rather than on specific issues, have come to radically different conclusions. Instead of limiting themselves to explicit deci-sions involving the resolution of conflict they have been more inclined to examine established institutions and have asked whom the functioning of these institutions benefits. Their substantive conclusions have tended to be that local communities are characterized by an elitist power structure. The important point for present purposes is that social institutions sometimes regulate the arena of contestable social problems. The individual national governments have played this role with respect to the Community political system.

In a more positive vein it should be noted that, since a majority of interest groups consider the flow of demands through national governments and minis-tries are more likely to be successful, the national governments have the oppor-tunity to influence policy here.[8] The primary targets are relevant governmental ministries and usually the Ministry of Foreign Affairs. Feld notes that in France, the premier and individual cabinet members are sought out on important questions. This gave de Gaulle a close watch on one of the most important aspects of Community development, viz., what issues are being debated.

For important decisions access to the premier and individual cabinet members is also sought. This seems to be the case especially in France, where de Gaulle and his cabinet play the decisive role in all economic matters and subordinate officials are reluctant in assuming responsibility for major decisions. The Conseil National du Patronat Français is said to have particularly good relations with Prime Minister Pompidou, and the representative of the FNSEA, France's largest agricultural organization, declared with pride that former agriculture minister Pisani always took the FNSEA viewpoint into careful consideration when making a decision in agricultural matters.[9]

THE NATION-STATE AS AN INTERNAL PRESSURE GROUP

There are a number of institutions in the European Community which represent the interests of the individual member states. The Council of Ministers is of course nothing more than a series of meetings between national ministers, for example, foreign ministers or ministers of agriculture. The Council, however, is not very important in the articulation of interests but its delegate body, the Committee of Permanent Representatives (CPR), is.

The CPR is a body of six members of ambassadorial rank, one from each of the member states.[10] The representatives serve a dual role. They are the ambassadors of their countries to the Community and they are the standing representatives of the Council of Ministers and engage in the preparation of the Council's work. Each representative is supported by a small secretariat composed of around twenty-five people. The work of the CPR is in turn closely coordinated with the respective national capitals through special coordination committees.[11] In this connection the permanent representatives usually travel to their respective capitals each week for consultation.

The official view is that the CPR is an ersatz negotiating body, setting the groundwork for the top level negotiations by the Council of Ministers. The process here is envisaged as one parallel to the detailed diplomatic footwork that transpires at lower diplomatic levels before summit conferences take place. "It is they (the CPR) who do the groundwork for the ministerial sessions, solving problems where they can, but above all sounding out the possibilities of compromise on the political issues."[12]

The task of the CPR is therefore seen as one of negotiation of proposals already on the table rather than the formulation of new proposals. The process of negotiation (including aggregation and rule making) is blurred by the interpenetration of Community institutions (e.g., the Commission is represented at the weekly meetings of the CPR) as well as by the Commission's desire to anticipate national feelings. The Commission utilizes the CPR to sound out its members on national feelings. The information gathered in this process no doubt affects the content of proposals even at this early stage. The reactions to proposals which do not conform to this collaborative process shed some light on its importance.

The Commission proposals in 1965 for independent Community revenue and increased powers of the European Parliament were not made in the traditional manner. The proposals were formulated by a small clique of Commission members who made little contact with either the CPR or national elites.[13] To make matters worse, Walter Hallstein, the president of the Commission, revealed these proposals to the European Parliament on March 24, 1965, a full eight days before they were submitted to the Council. This departure from established practice was seen (by de Gaulle) as an effort to mobilize opinion and give the proposals momentum before the individual nation-states could organize. This incident illustrates the importance which at least one nation-state (France) attaches to efforts to expand the Community decisional arena and the importance of channeling these efforts through the appropriate channels.

The swelling realization of the importance of the articulation process has led to an increased role of proxy groups at this stage. One indication of this is the invigorated role of the CPR after the 1965-66 agricultural crisis. Some observers feel that one of the important tasks of the CPR is to keep new proposals from sneaking in, and by doing so to serve as a watchdog for the nation-states. It raises the question of whether the integrity of the Commission's right to initiative could be undermined. Could the CPR define its agenda-setting prerogatives in such a way as to in effect offer new proposals? Or alternatively, could the necessity to include national views in the articulation phase ideologize the decision-making process from the beginning? Perhaps the difficult compromises worked out in the latter stages of the decision process would never have been possible if it had not been for the fact that everyone started from a set of givens generated by an independent actor. In fact the rationale on which the Commission's initiative is based is that discussion will be pitched first at a Community level and argued out in terms of Community solutions. Whatever the final compromise that emerges it will at least be assured that the "Community solution" is stated first. To argue the reverse, that is, that a common solution will emerge out of the bargaining of individual states, is wishful thinking. Dynamic leadership is crucial in emerging systems where consensus on a broad range of issues may be lacking.

The entire episode illustrates a move away from structural differentiation, involving as it does additional structures in the articulation process, structures that for the most part are more ideological than were previous groups. Finally, the sensitivity of the Commission toward national views, along with the extended process of sounding out individual national points of view, has the effect of diluting proposals even before they are submitted.

THE NATION-STATE IN EXTERNAL RELATIONS

In the domain of external relations, that is, in those areas in which the European Community confronts problems with respect to other countries, the individual member states play a strong role in the formation of issues. This is especially true when issues involve the grand questions of foreign policy and defense and less true when they involve commercial agreements. Negotiations in the former case have tended to fragment into patterns of bilateral contact involving heads of state or foreign secretaries while in the latter a much more complicated picture has emerged usually involving an initial phase where the individual nations set broad policy guidelines and a later phase where the details are worked out. Since the problem of external relations is dealt with in a separate chapter, I will only illustrate here.

The Kennedy Round of multilateral tariff negotiations (1963-1967) provides an excellent example of the Community in external relations.[14] The immediate initiative for these negotiations was provided by President Kennedy after de Gaulle's first "non" to British entry, in January 1963. Kennedy saw them partly as an effort to mitigate the impact of the EEC and to insure that Britain and the U.S. would still have access to a rapidly growing European market. Thus the origin of these negotiations was embedded in a very explosive set of political issues which included the role of Britain in the world as well as Kennedy's Grand Design for Atlantic partnership.

During the Kennedy Round negotiations the Six were represented by a single voice, the Commission, an indication to some of a qualitatively new dimension of integration, reflecting as it does the degree to which the Six became a unit with respect to external countries. This development is no doubt true to some extent, but its actual importance must be assessed in the context of the relations between the Commission and the member states (often acting through the Council of Ministers).

At first blush it appears that the Commission played a very strong role and possessed a wide measure of freedom to pursue the negotiations on its own. The Commission put forth some recommendations to the Council of Ministers in December 1963 for a mandate to open the negotiations. The mandate finally adopted by the Council was very similar to the Commission's draft proposal and indeed, as one observer points out, the Council's final negotiating position was very similar to the proposal.[15] If the mandate makes it appear that the Commission was a vigorous, independent supranational force during the negotiations, two qualifications should be noted: first, a substantial amount of attention was paid to national viewpoints in drawing up the suggestions; and second, the contacts between the Commission and the Council were very close during most of the negotiations. Sometimes the Council would determine in a very specific way the positions that the Commission should take. The Article 111 Committee, composed of national officials set up under Article 111 of the Rome treaty, met weekly with the Commission to give it advice. The same Committee also met in Geneva every week where observers from the member states sat in. This helped the Committee to fulfill its primary function of informing the Commission of individual national positions and also to assist in interpreting the Council's instructions to the Commission.

The Commission was limited in its ability to negotiate until toward the very end of the Kennedy Round. At that point the Council vested the Commission with the increasing margins of negotiating power that were so crucially needed in the day-to-day bargaining. Jean Rey, the Commission member who was leading the negotiations, was able to receive a permissive mandate from the Council and to reach an agreement with full Community backing.

The pattern of negotiations in the Kennedy Round involving the setting of broad guidelines by the Council and the close surveillance of the Commission's activities thereafter seems to be typical of the external relations of Community institutions. If anything, the member states seem to be acquiring more importance in articulating issues in this area. The negotiations concerning the entry applications of Britain, Norway, Denmark, and Ireland bogged down partly over the question of who would negotiate for the Community. "To a great extent, the nature of the negotiations will depend on who negotiates for the Community. It was evident at the March 6, 1970, Council meetings that none of the six member states was entirely happy about entrusting even a first phase of entry talks to the Commission, or even to the Council President, as was the case for the Yaoundé Convention negotiations last year."[16]

This negotiating pattern represents a setback from the previous negotiations where the Commission represented the Community position. The trend was buttressed by a growing bilateralization of talks before the actual negotiations got under way. Geoffrey Rippon, successor to Anthony Barber as British negotiator for entry into the EC, made the rounds of the EEC capitals to sound out the positions of various foreign ministers.[17]

INSTITUTIONAL INTEREST ARTICULATION: THE COMMISSION

The Commission of the European Community can be looked upon as an institutional interest group. An institutional group is a formally organized body which is set up to perform another function but which nevertheless expresses an interest of its own or acts as a vehicle for the expression of other interests.[18] The Commission was originally conceived primarily as a bureaucratic mechanism with power to "ensure the application of the provisions of this Treaty" and the capacity to "exercise the competence conferred on it by the Council for the implementation of the rules laid down by the latter."[19] In addition, the Commission was also empowered to make recommendations and to engage in the preparation of acts of the Council.[20] In practice the Commission is the primary body responsible for making proposals to the Council and in this process the Commission acts as a pressure group both for itself and for a variety of associational groups. The Commission's own interests are not of a concrete sort but rather are related to the growth of strong political institutions and democratic mechanisms. As a pressure group with its own interests the Commission has worked for eliminating the requirement of unanimity in the Council of Ministers, developing an independent resource base for the Community budget, increasing parliamentary control of the activities of Council and Commission, and democratizing (through popular elections) the European Parliament. As an institution furthering the interests of associational groups it drafts legislation and makes proposals to the Council of Ministers. This cuts down the variety of demands made even before the aggregation process has begun.

The Commission is the bureaucracy of the European Community although the functions it performs are not perfectly analogous to those performed by bureaucracies in the industrial societies of the West. It is charged with the tasks of being "guardian of the Treaties," executive arm of the Community, and initiator of Community policy.[21] We normally think of the second of these tasks as being central to the role of the bureaucracy.

The Commission is a collegial body of nine members[22] who are appointed by agreement of the member states but who, after appointment, are obliged to be independent of both the pressures and instructions of their governments. The idea behind this was that the Commission would be uniquely equipped to present a Community point of view and defend it during its negotiation with the Council of Ministers.

Each Commission member is responsible for a certain field of policy. Until the merger of the Commissions of EEC, ECSC, and European Atomic Energy Commission (EURATOM), each of the nine commissioners was in charge of one of the nine general directorates—External Affairs, Economic and Financial Affairs, Internal Market, Competition, Social Affairs, Agriculture, Transport, Overseas Development, and Administration. Each of these directorates was headed by a senior civil servant of a different nationality than the Commission member. Each general directorate in turn was subdivided into directorates and then into divisions. In essence, then, the structural setup is not much different from the national governments of Western Europe. The nine commissioners play the role of ministers and their staffs function as a civil service.[23] The total staff of the Commission is around 8,500 people and this includes "executive staff, translators, secretaries and technical personnel of all kinds."[24] The Commission is assisted by this bureaucracy in the preparation and execution of its work.

The Commission is a multifunctional body simultaneously carrying out legislative, implementative, and quasi-regulative tasks. The most important power, however, is the power of initiative and, with a few exceptions, the Commission has the exclusive prerogative in this field. Even this is not a departure from the role of bureaucracy in the West. The difficulty of separating political from administrative questions has long been recognized by students of bureaucracy. Coombes says, "there is a vast literature showing the tendency in practically all known types of political system for the 'Administrative State' to 'encroach' upon the 'territory' of other parts of the system, such as political executive, legislature, etc., and to acquire the latter's functions, such as political leadership, representation, etc."[25]

The Rome treaty explicitly takes this tendency into account by granting the Commission a role in the drafting and initiation of legislation. Whether consciously or not, the drafters of the Treaty provided for an institutional system in which the implementative component was not independent from political control. What is often called administrative may be nothing more than the working out of the more context-specific, local policies as opposed to the more general ones.[26]

Broadly speaking, there are three forms that initiation can take: studies reporting fact-finding efforts in an area; drafts of specific legislative proposals; and the preparation of broad memoranda designed to stimulate the consideration of certain issues. An example of the fact-finding role of the Commission occurred after the Agricultural Conference in Stresa in 1958 when the participants agreed that they could reach solutions only through a concerted effort. Yet they were unclear as to the specifics of what this joint action might be. It was left to the Commission to work out the common policy options, to make specific suggestions, and to assess the implications of a common agricultural policy for the rest of the economy and society.[27] On the other hand the Commission is often called on to submit proposals on concrete legislative items.

The agricultural packages adopted in January 1962, December 1963, and December 1964 were based on specific Commission proposals. Finally the Commission frequently carries out comprehensive studies to lay the basis for negotiation in a particular area. These may range from the problems associated with the applications for entry of Britain, Norway, Denmark, and Ireland, to problems of a common industrial policy and problems of structural reform of agriculture in the EEC. The memorandum of the Commission on industrial policy (*La Politique Industrielle de la Communauté*) illustrates this form of articulation. In a preface to the document the Commission outlines the purpose of the memorandum.

> The Commission considers this memorandum as serving as a basis for thorough discussion within the Community with the other Community institutions, Parliament, Council, also the Economic and Social Committee, the Consultative Committee of the European Coal and Steel Community and the European Investment Bank by and with the representative organs of the economic and social forces within the Community.[28]

Even more important have been other memoranda such as the "Memorandum on the General Lines of the Common Transport Policy" or the more recent and important "Memorandum on the Reform of Agriculture in the European Economic Community." In this memorandum, submitted to the Council on December 21, 1968, the Commission outlines the problems not only with respect to the operation of agricultural markets but also the more fundamental problems of agricultural structure. On the basis of this study the Commission set forth a series of economic and social measures which were intended "to bring about major structural changes in agricultural production and which involve heavy financial burdens."[29]

It seems clear that the purpose of these memoranda is to provide the stimulation so often needed to move ahead in an area. It also, by establishing guidelines, provides a focus for subsequent discussion and exchange of views by experts, national representatives, and interest groups. The declared aim of the "Memorandum on the General Lines of the Common Transport Policy" was to "stimulate an extensive exchange of views with all circles."[30] A similar case is provided by the famous *Action Programme of the Community for the Second Stage*[31] in which the Commission suggested possible directions in agriculture, transport, energy, social policy, monetary policy, external relations, and others. The result of this memorandum, as of the others mentioned above, is the politicization of an area of social behavior previously untouched. It is in this role, in broadening the arena of social conflict, that the Commission is able to provide grist for the Community's political mill. By providing stimulation to enter new areas, by coordinating the otherwise ad hoc nature of Community activity, and by providing a disciplined focus for discussion and collaboration, the Commission offers the hope that the EEC will push beyond a forum for the playing out of the sometimes incredibly narrow ambitions of its specialized groups. In the constant dialogue between the Commission, the interest groups, and the Council of Ministers, it is evident that the Commission is much more than a passive purveyor of interest group wishes. In fact it is the Commission that takes the initiative on almost all Community matters. A proposal for a regulation in agriculture, for example, may originate somewhere in the General Directorate for Agriculture. Members of an interest group, probably COPA, may become familiar with the proposal by reading about it in *Agence Europe,* or they may be informed by Commission members in the agricultural directorate. The Commission will then call together national experts and interest group representatives who at this point will take a very active part in a more detailed elaboration of the policy.

The direction of influence is not all one way, however. From their constant contact with interest groups, Commission members become sensitive to their demands. In addition the many "réunions d'information" between Commission members and interest groups provide an occasion for groups to state their positions on various proposals. In this sense, all articulation in the EEC is structurally double-edged. Although it is generally characteristic of social systems that the question of "who started X" is unanswerable, the Commission's one-upmanship is nevertheless important. The Commission is not put into a position of responding to a highly privatized set of demands which may be so lacking in their ability to be compromised that they offer little hope of being translated into policy.

The Executive Secretary of the Commission, Emile Noel, feels that the Commission's initiative is the most important part of the Community system. M. Cartou argues that this setup allows the Commission to bring to these decisions "a unity of view inspired by the Community interest."[32] Briefly, once the proposal has passed through an elaborate preliminary phase involving contact with national civil servants, interest groups, and the European Parliament, it then is presented to the Council of Ministers. The Council must either adopt or reject the proposal but can amend it only by a unanimous vote. This qualification gives the Commission an important advantage of flexibility in that coming up with an amended package at the right time may put even nationally minded institutions in a position where they have to choose between what the Commission offers and no policy. And in many cases no policy is not a feasible alternative owing to external pressures of one form or another. For example, the December 1964 negotiations on a common price level for cereal and the pressure on the Six to adopt a common negotiating position in the Kennedy Round negotiations each provided the key to breaking the Council's resistance. Cartou again has correctly pointed out that it is this procedure which has enabled the Community to overcome all crises, especially those in agriculture.[33]

The Commission can amend its original position and submit any number of revised proposals, right up to the time when the Council reaches its final decision. In effect, therefore, the Commission is articulating new proposals throughout the entire bargaining process. During some point in the negotiation process, however, interest articulation shades off into aggregation as amended proposals reflect the political compromises reached.

We have already mentioned that the formula "the Commission proposes, the Council disposes" is oversimplified. In practice the role of proposing is obscured by a variety of intermediary groups. Even before drafting a proposal the Commission consults the CPR to become sensitive to governmental views and it meets regularly with experts drawn from national administrations and Community interest groups. In the preparation of nearly all legislation Commission members make an effort to involve as many elements as possible. In the important field of agriculture, for example, Professors Lindberg and Scheingold note: "Mansholt (former commissioner in charge of agriculture) not only took 'constituency' interests into account, but he also co-opted those interests into the decision-making process so as to give them a maximum sense of participation in the great European enterprise. In so doing, he went beyond all the standard consultation procedures usually engaged in by the Commission."[34]

The extent to which this extensive consultation results in legislation which is merely sensitive to important national differences or whether the entire effect is to dilute the strength of the proposals is an open question.

Many observers feel that the Commission's initiative has been weakened since the agricultural crisis of 1965-66.[35] Indeed, the "Heptalogue," the document on which the Luxembourg Agreements that ended the agricultural crisis were based, established new guidelines for the relationships between the Council and the Commission. This was of course all part of de Gaulle's effort to limit the political role of the Commission. The "Heptalogue" admonished the Commission, before it initiated a proposal, to take up "the appropriate contacts with the governments of the member States, through the Permanent Representatives. . . ."[36]

In addition, the process by which the Commission engages national officials and other specialists in the decision-making process may retard the growth of a Community loyalty. If this penetration offers the opportunity to Europeanize national officials, it does so also to nationalize officials and policy. As Coombes points out, the extent of specialized decision making which this penetration involves poses a major threat to the institutional identity of the Commission.[37] The simple fact is that Commission members spend most of their working hours in contact with specialists and interest group representatives, rather than with their more politically minded colleagues in the other general directorates. The effect is that identities crystallize around administrative specialities rather than around general political problems. The inherent long-run danger is that the Commission could be reduced in status to that of an international secretariat.

The fear is reinforced by the fact that the Commission's more politically controversial proposals have been rejected by de Gaulle and were followed by a vigorous French effort to reduce the Commission to a delegate body functioning in a much more technical capacity. This was clearly reflected in the strong French reaction to the Commission's proposals for independent revenue and direct election of the European Parliament. The French correctly saw these initiatives as part of an institutional plan to give financial autonomy and some popular legitimacy to Community institutions. It confirms the view that the Commission's capacity to articulate issues is limited to acceptable issues more or less technical in nature.

Events since the 1965-66 crisis have not provided the basis for optimism. The most recent round of negotiations on agriculture have evidenced a disturbing tendency to bilateralize. At the Christmas marathon, from December 19 to December 22, 1969, decisions were reached on a financial regulation for agriculture, financial resources for the Community, and strengthened budgetary powers for the European Parliament. It is significant to note that the groundwork for these agreements was carefully laid at a summit conference at the Hague on December 1-2.[38] The upshot of the Hague meeting was that France agreed not to block the beginning of negotiations on British entry while Belgium, Germany, Italy, Luxembourg, and the Netherlands agreed to a financial regulation for agriculture. What is disturbing about this is not that agreement came out of hard political bargaining but rather that the Commission's position in stating the issues was circumscribed by an intergovernmental negotiation process. Fortunately the elements for a good horse trade were present. Even in systems more consensual than the EEC, however, it is sometimes the case that solutions involve sacrifices on the part of some members. One doubts whether the present institutional system is capable of even formulating such solutions.

There has been a great deal of discussion as to whether the Community's present decision-making process differs from that before the crisis. One view has it that the Community has weathered an important storm and goes about its business pretty much as before. One could point out that a huge amount of legislation has passed since January 1966. Some proposals have been accepted in the Council of Ministers by a majority vote, sometimes with France on the losing side of the coalition. This gives rise to a "business as usual" or "return to normalcy" interpretation of events in Brussels. That interpretation no doubt distorts the more subtle political changes that have taken place in Brussels, changes in the structure of influence relations among national governments, the supranational Commission, the Council, and the Committee of Permanent Representatives. It is true that France has not protested upon finding itself in a defeated minority but this in large part because, as has been pointed out, "when there are fears that France really would object, a great shuffling of stances takes place further back."[39]

Thus the changed nature of the Community decision-making process has neither been registered primarily through more defeated proposals nor through a reversion to a strict unit veto system. What has occurred is that the "rule of anticipated reactions" has induced the Commission to closely tailor its proposals to national expectations and wishes. It has also induced the Commission to more adequately sound out national viewpoints before submitting a formal proposal. It is in this political context that the increased importance of the CPR should be viewed, for in practice the CPR has become the vehicle through which national viewpoints have been represented. The relationship between the president of the Commission and chairman of the CPR has become very close. Weekly meetings are held between the chairman and the president at which time they decide what compromises will be acceptable to both sides. These compromises serve as the basis of proposals which eventually find their way to the Council of Ministers. That they are accepted at this stage owes not so much to the supranational tendencies of the member states as to the fact that care was taken to assure that proposals accorded with national specifications.

Yet, after all this is admitted, it must still be recognized that the hopes for a political Europe still center on the Commission. It is the Commission that functions to mobilize the biases of inarticulate groups. In this capacity the Commission offers the possibility of making the Community a reality to someone besides sugar beet growers and corporation executives. It is, in short, one of the few alternatives to a Europe of special interest groups. Despite the number of groups at the Community level the majority of people cannot enter the political process. As Schattschneider noted long ago: "Pressure politics is essentially the politics of small groups. . . . Probably about 90 per cent of the people cannot get into the pressure system. . . . Pressure politics is a selective process ill-designed to serve diffuse interests. The system is skewed, loaded and unbalanced in favor of a fraction of a minority."[40]

It still remains to the Commission to formulate general solutions which, in Schattschneider's phrase, "enlarge the scope of public conflict" by involving new groups and new issues in the political process.[41] One writer has referred to the process as the "governmentalization of social and economic structures."[42] The process, which involves the penetration of the associational interest group structure by institutional groups, seems appropriate to developing countries like India as well as to emerging systems like the EEC. The distressing fact is that in the seesaw battle over whether the Commission should be the articulator of a collective identity or the champion of special interests, the Commission has had more success when it has operated in the latter capacity.

CHAPTER FOUR

Interest Aggregation:
Bargaining and Coalition Processes
at the European Level

If pressure groups operate at the peripheries of the political system and if legislatures and executives comprise most of the activity at its core, it can perhaps be said that political parties form part of the important intermediary apparatus. This view is substantially accurate for most industrial democracies in the Western world. Interest groups have primary responsibility for mobilizing bias in the social system and for organizing discontent in such a way as to make it an active political ingredient. Political parties, on the other hand, concern themselves with the composition rules through which a set of more or less discrete interests will be balanced and aggregated. Parties are, in a sense, the fulcrum of the bargaining and coalition-building processes for numerous political systems. Since governments, even in demand systems with limited mobilization, cannot respond to the claims of organized interests on a one-for-one basis, it is generally recognized that some mechanisms for coalition building are essential. In this chapter I will address myself to the question of interest aggregation in the European Community.

In Chapter Two we examined the structure of interest group activity at the European level and found more than 300 specially organized interest groups. How do these interest groups get their demands translated into concrete decisions? How are conflicts between such groups resolved? Through what mechanisms? What impact do these groups have on the nonorganized public in the Community and what adjustments are made on this count?

There are two regions on the continuum of the Community policy-making process where the relevant structures are fairly clearly defined—in the region of interest articulation and later in the region where negotiations are in an advanced stage and where policy is often formally adopted. The interest-articulation structure is reasonably clear since there are several hundred organized, bureaucratized, specialized groups with offices, desks, secretaries, and filing cabinets. These groups, whatever their effectiveness in the political process, display a firsthand reality. They have none of that elusive quality associated with the more informal groupings incurred in many political systems.[1] The rule-making structure is clear since there are observable institutions responsible for allocating values. This holds true whatever the particular mix of powers and responsibilities

67

among the Council, Commission, and perhaps the Committee of Permanent Representatives. Where the Community insitutional structure becomes very fuzzy is in that region where the function of aggregation is generally performed. Indeed, it is questionable whether any structure (or structures) at all exists for this.

The Community political system has been described as both top-heavy— dominated by a curious admixture of elite technocrats and nationally self-conscious politicians—and bottom-heavy, influenced, penetrated, and captivated by the bustling, rapacious activity of several hundred hedonistic interest groups. In fact, the Community decision-making process can be viewed as simultaneously top- and bottom-heavy. The appropriate metaphor is not a pyramid dominated by its peak or base, but a dumbbell that sags in the middle. The absence of a well-organized system of transnational political parties is only a symptom, not a cause, of this. The causes lie at the level of the absence of popular elections for important offices, the lack of public interest (i.e., Community interest), legislation, and the crisis (or lack) of public authority in the Community. With respect to this latter consideration, it will be argued that Community institutions possess only ad hoc legitimacy; they do not possess general grants of power, that is, they cannot advocate legislation that is not directly tied to a specific group demand, even to the point of being incapable of formulating legislative packages that blend and compromise separate group demands. The upshot of this is the emergence of a petty bargaining mentality, an avoidance of genuine public interest legislation, and, worst of all, the encouragement and cultivation of an interest group individualism in which organized group demands are dealt with in a fragmented and isolative way, discouraging the processes of competition, bargaining, and coalition building.

The most striking feature of the confusing mass of Community activity is the almost total absence of democratic institutions at that level. There are first of all no general, popular elections for any important institutions. Thus there is no way that the masses of people, part of whose loyalty and activity belongs to the European political system, can choose between alternative conceptions of Community policy. In addition, the absence of elections deprives the Community political system of attention and legitimacy that may arise as a result of mobilizing aspects of electoral activity. For the most part, European political parties are nonexistent and there has been an absence of serious movement toward integration on their part.[2] It is true that they operate to some extent within the European Parliament, and much is sometimes made of the role of the party groups and the seating arrangement by parties.[3] Nevertheless, it must be recognized that the role of parties is quite negligible on important issues and that the Parliament itself is an impotent institution.

The chief tasks of Parliament are to dissolve the Commission should it choose to do so and to be consulted by the Council with regard to various legislative proposals it may be considering. The former power is practically worthless for two reasons. First, the Parliament's primary ally is the Commission. It is, after all, the Commission that has been most strenuous in its advocacy of increased budgetary powers for the Parliament as well as direct elections of its members. Second, should the Commission be dissolved, the Parliament has no power over its manner or content of reconstitution. It is thus a hollow power. Concerning the second task of the Parliament, its right to be consulted by the Council of Ministers on proposed legislation, two things should be kept in mind. The opinions that the Parliament renders are purely advisory. They are in no way binding on the Council. Since the Commission has access to a continuous flow of national bureaucrats and interest group experts, and since there exists a multitude of working committees and delegate bodies charged with the preparation of legislation, Parliament is deprived of its traditional source of strength as a reservoir of manpower and expertise crucial to the formulation of policy. A final reason for the lack of parliamentary control stems from the fact that it is consulted only late in the decision-making process. Often the time for response is not adequate and the opinions may reach the Council too late to be taken into account.[4]

One final observation should be made, since it is relevant for the proper understanding of the process of interest aggregation in the Community. This is what could be called a functional derangement between the Community institutions and the people for whom it presumably acts. The Commission is held responsible to the Parliament but the Commission is more an initiating and implementive than a policy-making body. The Council, which is the ultimate decision maker, is held responsible to no one at the European level. But neither can the national parliaments be said to control the Council. Parliamentary control is eroding internally so that national parliaments have a difficult enough time controlling national policy. The Parliament, which is perhaps the most representative institution (in spite of the fact that its members are not directly elected), is deprived of political power generally. This problem becomes more and more acute as an increasing range of functions are transferred to the Community level. It is in this uncertain political environment that the subsequent discussion must be understood.

STRUCTURES ASSOCIATED WITH PERFORMANCE OF AGGREGATION

There seems to be no specific structure in the European Community which is concerned with the aggregation of the multiplicity of demands made by interest groups. At least there is no crystallized structure whose primary intent (or function) is to create coalitions of interests. It is admittedly a difficult task to assess this in a political system characterized by the structural-functional fluidity of the EC. Yet, several contenders like political parties and the Parliament can be eliminated easily since, in the former case, they are barely existent and, in the latter, its powers are negligible. The Council of Ministers also presents itself as an unlikely candidate. Although it is among the most powerful of Community bodies, this power rests more on some ultimate ability to veto proposals of the Commission. In terms of its capacity to create options, formulate detailed proposals, and build coalitions the Council is a weak body. It is composed of representatives of the individual member states who at the same time are officeholders in the separate national ministries. They are thus simultaneously full-time employees of a domestic political system and representatives of a supranational system. Since the primary responsibility of the Council is to the nation-states its members must continually rely on proposals formulated by the more supranationally oriented Commission. Thus the Council's role is not in creating viable decision-making packages but in accepting or rejecting them.

Other structures are not so easily disqualified. It is not completely clear how much bargaining and compromise goes on in the umbrella interest groups. Indeed, the structure and behavior of these groups varies so much that it may be difficult to generalize. As Nielsen notes: "Some groups are well-organized institutions with an administrative apparatus, such as COPA and UNICE (the federation of employers' organizations) that perform a significant interest aggregation and provide an accommodation of different positions and demands; others are just weak bodies the activities of which rarely extend beyond acting as a post box between the commission and the national member organizations."[5]

As indicated, COPA, one of the better-organized peak organizations, does attempt to aggregate interests of groups under it. Indeed, one of the professed goals of COPA as expressed in one of its internal documents is "to study and to coordinate the suggestions of the constituent organizations with a view to arriving at the taking of common positions and to present these to the Community institutions."[6] In practice, however, at least until recently, there was very little yielding of nationally held positions at this level of the bargaining process. The decision-making procedure in COPA indicates this. When the Commission is formulating a piece of agricultural legislation it will often consult COPA to sound it out on its position. The request is referred to the relevant specialized section (e.g., if it concerns the market organization in rice it will be referred to the specialized section on rice) where the members attempt to come to a common position. These positions are then transmitted to the general experts (Experts Généraux, see fig. 2.2) who examine them and often note their reactions to them. Before these positions are sent back to the Commission as a formal "prise de position" they must go to the Presidium where they are approved. If the position is not found satisfactory to all interest groups concerned a minority opinion is simply filed. This would seem to indicate that rather than compromise at this stage, a dissatisfied interest group simply transmits this dissatisfaction in the form of a minority report.

There is, however, some evidence to suggest that at least some aggregation does occur through these umbrella groups. First of all, where several national interest groups from the same country are involved, there is often coordination among these groups before the national view is channeled to COPA. This is not important in Germany where the Deutscher Bauernverband is the only agricultural organization to speak of, or in Luxembourg, where the Centrale Paysanne Luxembourgeoise is the only agricultural group. Italy, Belgium, and the Netherlands, however, have three agricultural groups associated with COPA while France has four. The coordination among interest groups within each country varies, being low in Italy and fairly well developed in the Netherlands. In fact the three Dutch agricultural organizations that are affiliated with COPA have established a joint international secretariat to harmonize their actions and to try to coordinate their positions.

Feld has noted that national interest groups felt that their demands were somewhat weakened when they were channeled through the European umbrella groups.[7] This may in effect be a backhand way of saying that national viewpoints are somewhat compromised in the process of working through these groups. Nielsen argues that this way of making decisions in COPA is increasing. In 1964 COPA suffered from a lack of influence in the agricultural negotiations to set a common price level for cereals. The strong differences among national groups prevented COPA from taking a positive stand. Presumably COPA has learned its lesson and now makes more of an effort to come to an agreement before the final stages of the bargaining process. Differences still exist but the decision-making process is increasingly characterized by compromise, give and take, and logrolling.[8]

The Commission, as the most active, and possibly the most complex Community institution, deserves a careful examination in the context of interest aggregation, especially so since it is to the Commission that the elusive Community interest concept is entrusted. Thus, even though Commission members are appointed by the respective national authorities, they are to act in the general interest of the Community and in complete independence from national authorities (Article 157 of Rome treaty).

In light of the fact that the Commission is charged with the promotion and protection of the Community interest and is often referred to as the conscience of the Community, it is surprising that more of the various attempts to categorize the functions that the Commission performs do not include any notion of the Commission's role in promoting the collective good, however vague this term may be. The Commission is said to be in charge of initiating legislation, implementing laws, and acting as guardian of the Treaty[9] while others say it has responsibility for initiation, negotiation, and administration of policy.[10] Dahlberg's category of "negotiation" may point to the role of the Commission in coalition building. In fact this process of negotiating national positions is not only involved in the confrontations between Council and Commission which characterize the late stages of the process. The elaborate soundings that the Commission takes of the individual interest groups before policies are even formulated anticipate the more explicit negotiations that follow. The Commission, confronted with a deadline and a mandate to get things done (set either by the Treaty of Rome or by the Council of Ministers), is encouraged to find the broadest possible coalition of interests. To do this it must "create a 'social' basis for its package deal by creating cross-cutting coalitions of interests. This is most likely to come about through bringing as many groups as possible into the political process."[11]

Despite the fact that the Commission has the legal grant (from the Treaty) to perform a coalition-building function, many factors would seem to work against this. The mere fact that the Commission is responsible for the formulation, drafting, initiation, and implementation of Community policy is enough to suggest that it is already too overburdened to devote its energies to anything else. For the time being we will defer this question and turn instead to some consequences of the absence of specialized aggregation structures.

ABSENCE OF SPECIALIZED AGGREGATION STRUCTURE AND ITS CONSEQUENCES

The absence of a specialized interest-aggregation structure has created a strain on existing Community institutions. At the boundaries of the political system there is a huge interest group network which is continually pressing to have its demands translated into policy. At the center of the political system there is a Council of Ministers which functions in an ad hoc, intermittent way and whose primary preoccupation is with national concerns. There is also the Commission, which is, of course, a full-fledged European institution but it is already saddled with several other important Community functions so that it cannot dedicate its full energies to the building of coalitions.

The fact that the existing structural framework is inadequate to handle the demands placed on it has had several consequences. First, it has encouraged the search for high-consensus areas and has led to extensive probings of individual national attitudes even before the negotiation phase. Second, it has fostered the evolution of processes that function as filter systems and time-savers. The purpose of these new processes is to separate technical from political questions and to free the Council and Commission to devote more of their attention to the latter. Third, the overburdening of Community institutions has led to the decentralization of decision making. And finally, it has encouraged heroic action as a means for stretching out extant structural resources to their fullest.

High Consensus Issues

Since the Luxembourg Agreements in January 1966 (marking the termination of the agricultural crisis) there has been a tendency to seek areas where agreement is easy to come by. The more controversial questions having to do with political union, social policy, and the powers of the European Parliament have not been as vigorously pursued as might be expected, at least up until the Hague Conference in 1969. Whether this conference signifies a relaunching of ambitions to politicize Europe or whether it is merely a carefully circumscribed mandate by the individual states to proceed in certain areas still remains to be seen. There has been a parallel movement to closely identify Community initiatives with the interests of powerful interest groups and the desires of the member states. Thus the Commission has played down any conception of a Community interest that is not at the same time the interest of each member state. This action has led to (or hardened) some fundamental defects in the operation of the Community. Since most interests are fragmentary and since a majority of them conflict with other interests, it follows that any attempt to use these interests as a basis for policy making involves compromise. This is true at least if one makes the additional reasonable assumption that one interest is not to dominate all others with which it comes into conflict. But compromises involve sacrifices and sacrifices are hard to justify in hedonistic settings. Since compromise involves sacrifice and since rewards and burdens are never equally distributed, least of all for a single policy, there is a low probability that the incentives to agree to a policy in any given case will be forthcoming. The careful cost-benefit scrutiny given to Commission proposals denies this.

The Community has always argued that integration was based on some variant of enlightened self-interest whose central institutional mechanism was the exchange system. That system was to lead to a net increase in rewards for all and an even distribution of burdens to all members. The formula points to a fundamental defect in the operation of Community institutions. The Community bargaining system is one of naked utilitarianism where gains and losses are carefully calculated for each issue and occasionally over several issues. It is my argument that such bargaining systems cannot possibly work in practice for two reasons. First, the exchange systems in large societies are extremely complex and extend over multiple issues for multiple countries. It is nearly impossible to perform the bookkeeping job in just one of these complicated transactions. Talcott Parsons treats the problem extensively in *The Structure of Social Action*. In his critique of classical utilitarian theory Parsons presents Durkheim's position on the contract relationship. "Durkheim notes that the possible consequences of the relations entered into by agreement, both to the parties themselves and to others, are so complex and remote that, if they all had to be thought out *ad hoc* and agreed to anew each time, the vast body of transactions which go on would be utterly impossible."[12]

But if each transaction, agreement, or policy is not justified in terms of self-interest, then how is it possible to get things done? Durkheim provided his famous answer to this in his statement "tout n'est pas contractuel dans le contrat," loosely translated as "there are noncontractual elements in the contract." These noncontractual elements are embodied in the cultural norms, sentiments, and values surrounding the contractual setting as well as in the law. Much of this is simply accepted (unconsciously) and there are rules that do not have to be renegotiated from issue to issue. The problem with Europe is that there is not much in the contract which is noncontractual.

The inability of the bargaining system to effect real compromises has forced the Commission to occupy itself with the limited concerns of organized interest groups. If these concerns are narrow enough they will not engender countervailing pressures and unwanted controversy can be avoided. Much as in the United States, the tendency to cultivate the support of these organized groups is a response to a crisis in public authority.[13] By directly basing action on the desires of specific organized groups, the Community creates the impression, to use a phrase of Theodore Lowi's used elsewhere—"that power need not be power at all, nor control control."[14] Lowi's analysis can be carried further. To closely tie Community policy to organized groups and to national desires is to destroy political responsiblity. And given the fact that not much political responsibility exists anyway, it frustrates any hope for it developing.

The Commission, sandwiched from above and below, is caught in a cruel dilemma. By appealing to a burgeoning interest group base it runs the risk of parceling out political authority to the several hundred groups who have neither the ability nor the desire to engage in serious political compromises. Nor are they suited to winning the support of broad sectors of the public. Their interests are admittedly narrow claims which would seem ludicrous to present as general interest legislation. Yet parceling out authority would eventuate in the destruction of political responsiblity. There is no way to call 350 groups to account for their behavior. They are too numerous, their work too invisible and admittedly self-interested to make them account for their actions.[15] The other part of the dilemma arises from the danger that, by catering too closely to national demands, the Community runs the risk of making it appear as if no Community at all existed, or that its primary function was increasingly one of facilitating "concertation" among the members and institutions of the EEC.[16]

Filter Systems and Time-Savers

One of the responses to the overload of Community institutions has been the evolution of processes responsible for pruning the number of issues that reach the Council and Commission in the later stages of the decisional process. The function of these new processes is not to aggregate the multiplicity of demands made on the political system but rather to edit them so that only the most politically controversial become objects of the attention of Commission and Council members. In an organizational setting characterized by the absence of public authority there is a dual decision-making tendency. On the one hand decision making is highly fragmented and decentralized with power distributed over many groups. At the same time there is a parallel tendency for controversial issues to get pushed up to the highest rungs in the hierarchy. This is true even when the decisions to be made are relatively trivial. The emergence of these filter systems should be seen as an effort to regulate the volume of the upward flow of issues. Two of the most important of these procedures are the Points A and the written procedure.

In 1962, the Council of Ministers, with the agreement of the Commission, instituted the Points A procedure which works essentially as follows: The CPR meets in full session several times a week. On many matters that they discuss the CPR is able to come to full agreement. These matters become A points and are generally adopted by the Council without debate at the beginning of its sessions. Although the decisions taken by the CPR are occasionally important, their character, as Noel and Etienne put it, is "more technical than political."[17] This same procedure is applied in basically the same way by the Special Committee of Agriculture, to which the Council refers Commission proposals concerning agricultural matters.

The Treaty of Rome charges the Council not only to take all major decisions of political importance but also matters considerably less important. All decisions made with respect to the harmonization of technical standards, even points as technical as the size of driving mirrors and the characteristics of cut glass, are to be taken by the Council acting unanimously.[18] As the volume of work of the Community increased, both in its technical and political aspects, the Council became quickly burdened and sought outlets to aid them. The Commission's full-time delegate body, the CPR, seemed the appropriate institution to handle this increased work load. Because of the heavy volume of work associated with agriculture alone, the Special Committee of Agriculture was created.

Since the Points A procedure is basically a response to the structural inadequacy of the Community, especially in terms of the absence of an effective, specialized aggregation system between the interest groups and the legislative institutions, it is not surprising that this procedure has become more important as the volume of Community activity has grown. The procedure emerged in 1962, when the Community political system achieved takeoff stage. In 1964, during which the Council held fifty-six sessions, there were 138 matters that were treated as Points A.[19] By 1970, by contrast, the number had grown to 599. Probably more important than the gross increase in volume is the possibility that the procedure may show signs of being used even when substantive disagreement exists.[20] Unfortunately no solid evidence exists on this matter.

The written procedure performs much the same function for the Commission. Even more than the Council, the Commission is overburdened by demands on its time and resources. As the common agricultural policy developed, a huge amount of technical legislation emerged along with it. This technical legislation threatened to saddle the Commission and to make it the Commission's full-time preoccupation. One means of freeing itself from spending too much time on these technical proposals is the written procedure by which copies of proposals that require little discussion are circulated by Commission members throughout the week. If no one objects to the proposal within a specified time period (usually one week), the proposal is deemed accepted by the Commission as a whole.[21] This serves to free Commission members to deal with more important issues at their weekly meetings.

Both the Points A and written procedures are important developments. Although neither involves the elaboration of a new structure and neither introduces any interest aggregation, the effect of the procedures is to mitigate the lack of such structures. Most political systems effect a decrease of demands on decision-making institutions by collapsing demands made through articulation structures into general legislative packages which involve a variety of subcoalitions. The Community procedures bring about this reduction through a self-conscious sifting or winnowing process. Although this does not solve the problem of the necessity of building coalitions, it does free the Council and Commission from the distraction that would result if it had to deal with the full range of problems at top-level policy-making sessions.

Decentralization of Decision Making

A further response to the increase in the volume of demands made of European institutions is the decentralization of decision making. This performs the same function as the procedures discussed in the preceding section, namely it frees policy makers to focus on the more important matters. The manner of achieving it is slightly different. Whereas the Points A and written procedures work on the principle of regulating the flow of demands to the Council and Commission, the decentralization of decision making attempts to make routine the handling of the more technical dimensions of decision making in delegate bodies. The out-standing example of this administrative decision making takes place in the management committees (Comités de Gestion). It works roughly as follows: there is a distinct management committee for each class of agricultural product. When the Commission is interested in passing implementive legislation in a particular field it sends its draft proposal to the appropriate management com-mittee which then decides, by a weighted majority (twelve out of seventeen), to give an opinion. Although the Commission is not bound to accept the opinion of the management committee the consequences of a Commission and management committee disagreement are interesting. If the Commission and the management committee agree, the implementing decision is final and there can be no appeal by the Council. If the Commission renders a different opinion, the matter then goes before the Council of Ministers which has the power to reverse the Commis-sion's decision within one month if it so chooses.[22]

The institution of the management committees is very active and impor-tant. It is not a mere institutional embellishment. Noel reports that during the fourteen months from March 1967 to April 1968 there were more than 200 meetings of the various management committees, after which nearly 600 Commission regulations and decisions were adopted. None of these occasioned a conflicting decision by the Commission.[23]

The management committee system delegates downward a huge amount of the more technical legislation that has evolved with the progressive establishment of the common agricultural policy. This system emancipates the Commission from a large amount of detail but it probably does little to enhance the auton-omy of the Commission even in this rather administrative area. The Council wanted to assure that these issues would be dealt with in consultation with member governments. Thus the composition of these committees includes repre-sentatives from each of the member states. By doing this the Council is freed from the necessity of having to keep a close watch over this area of policy in which technical questions seem to have a propensity of becoming controversial. The management committees are vicars for the interests of member states and are expected to act as a kind of early warning system. A disagreement between the Commission and one of the management committees is taken as a sign of a possibly controversial issue.

Heroic Behavior and the Marathon Session

Weber tied the emergence of charismatic leadership to periods of deep social transformation, periods during which there occurred fundamental realignments of social roles and normative orientations. It was during these periods that individual leadership became important. In one important sense the European Community is undergoing fundamental changes: it is a system that is just emerg-ing, struggling to come into existence. Whether it does come into existence and what form its political institutions assume will have serious implications for national political systems. In addition, although much of the activity in the Community is extremely routinized (especially the administrative decision making) there is a basic structural uncertainty among the various roles in the system. This condition permits flexibility on the part of individual leaders in their attempts to establish clearly the identity of one structure. This leadership flexibility is most clearly reflected in the Commission, where, despite the fact that it wears many different hats, it has attempted to establish the priority of its political role.

I define heroic action as action, either individual or structural, in which resources are pushed far beyond their normal limits in order to achieve desired goals. Heroic leadership involves more than long hours and hard work. It involves some conception of extraordinary effort and mobilization in the pursuit of political goals. In the European Community heroic action becomes manifest in two ways and these correspond to two levels of abstraction: on the individual level, particularly in the importance of two figures, Sicco Mansholt, former head of the General Directorate for Agriculture, and Walter Hallstein, the former president of the Commission; and on the structural level, particularly as manifested in the decision-making style embodied in the marathon negotiations.

In response to an extensive survey conducted by the Europa Institut in Amsterdam the authors of the report show that what struck the interviewers most in response to the question about where the interest groups had contacts in Brussels was how often Mansholt was mentioned.[24] The importance of Mansholt in cultivating contacts with interest groups before the important agricultural proposals were put forward is documented by Lindberg and Scheingold:

> Mansholt not only took the "constituency" interests into account, but he also co-opted those interests into the decision-making process so as to give them a maximum sense of participation in the great European enterprise. In so doing, he went beyond all standard consultation procedures usually engaged in by the Commission. He actively stimulated the creation of Community level farmers' organizations (over 100 now exist). He consulted them at every stage of the process of preparing for changes in policy, thus forcing them to try to reach common viewpoints, rather than expressing six national ones. . . . It is no accident that Mansholt is so well-known among European farmers, or that he has usually been able to count on their support when his proposals have gone to the Council of Ministers.[25]

The activity of Mansholt is extremely productive in terms of defining issues and raising them to a level of consciousness so that they become part of the agenda of the Community's decision system. But it does not solve the problem of how the different components of the agricultural picture are to be put together in any package. Nor does it say anything about how policy in agriculture is to relate to policy in other sectors. Finally, of course, it has little direct bearing on getting the policy adopted although it is surely formulated with this in mind. The primary mechanism through which adoption is accomplished is the so-called marathon session.

The marathon session refers to the extended negotiation among the Council, Commission, Committee of Permanent Representatives, and national experts which occurs during the final stages of the decision-making process. It is during these sessions that most of the political compromises among the member states occur.

The marathon session, as a technique for the negotiation and aggregation of Community interests, has been in existence since 1961. It was during late 1961 and January 1962 that the first agricultural marathon session was held. Subsequently, during the period from December 1961 to May-July 1966 there were five marathon sessions.[26] These sessions can basically be seen as a response to two things. One, they represent an attempt to compensate for the absence of any serious process of interest aggregation before the later stages of the decision process. The compensation occurs not through the utilization of a specialized structure, but through an excessive taxing of the resources of those already in existence. Second, it reflects the fact that the Rome treaty is in part an implementive treaty, and it sets deadlines for the completion of certain goals. This acts to produce a deadline mentality in which everyone is called upon to devote all his energies to meeting the deadline. For example, the 1961-62 marathon was concerned in part with the transition to the second stage of the elimination of tariffs, the 1964 marathon occurred over the deadline for a common grain price, and the 1965 marathon was deadlocked over the issue of a financial regulation for agriculture. The upshot of these deadlines is predictable. Serious political differences are allowed to cumulate until the deadline approaches. Then the appropriate ministers convene and may sit for several weeks in a row, enduring all-night sessions, if necessary, in an attempt to come up with a solution. Von Geusau has rightly characterized the marathon session as "le processus de décision typique d'un système en crise permanente."[27]

During these sessions the advantages of the Commission are highlighted. Its right to make proposals and its in-depth knowledge of national positions make it a natural vehicle for the rapid generation of package deals. Such packages represent in reality attempts to put together coalitions even at that advanced stage. The role of the Commission is particularly important since it is in at least an organizational sense outside the conflict. That is, the Commission is not officially tied to any national delegation and therefore does not have to plead a special case. It thus appears as a legitimate mediator which can provide impartial initiatives to at least set the context for the bargaining discussions. A mediator is especially required because of the structure of the latter stages of the decision-making process. Von Geusau describes this situation accurately:

> In the first phase, the national delegations have a tendency to harden their positions right up to the moment where progress no longer appears possible through debate. At this time the session is interrupted in order to permit the Commission to elaborate a new compromise and to the ministers to consult their governments. After the Commission has had time to formulate its package deal, the ministers resume the negotiations. Compromise is finally reached at a nocturnal hour when the most obstinate delegation yields to the majority, or the most fatigued delegation yields to the strongest delegation.[28]

The marathon sessions and package deals, albeit ad hoc and intermittent, seem to be an important part of the bargaining process. In the next section the conduct of negotiations in the agricultural sessions of 1961-62, 1963, and 1964 is examined in more detail.

DECISION MAKING IN THE AGRICULTURAL SECTOR

The making of policy in the agricultural sector has occupied more time and energy of Community politicians than any other issue. Many aspects of this policy are extremely complicated, especially those concerning pricing and support systems. What follows is an attempt to trace some of the highlights in the development of this policy from 1958 to 1965. Hopefully some idea of how the Community coalition-building mechanism works (and does not work) will emerge.

After the Stresa Conference in 1958 in which the member states put forth their proposals on agricultural policy, a lull followed during which the Commission studied the agricultural situation in consultation with national administrations, expert groups, and agricultural organizations. The Commission then drew up a set of general proposals that were thoroughly examined by EEC organs and national representatives. The agricultural section of the Economic and Social Committee (ESC) as well as the Agricultural Committee of the European Parliament closely appraised the proposals.[29] Progress after this was extremely slow, so slow that Shanks and Lambert were led to remark: "As the end of the first four-year stage of the Common Market transition period drew near, not a single decision had been taken; it had become clear that the foundations of the common policy had to be treated as a single whole, and that the twelve separate pieces of legislation which the Commission had prepared must be approved in one vast package deal.[30]

Then on January 14, 1962, after more than several hundred hours of intense negotiations, the Council of Ministers adopted a series of proposals by the Commission through which agricultural policy ceased to be a purely national concern. One aspect of these decisions was simply an agreement in principle to arrive at a common price for cereals. At this time, however, neither the content of the price nor the timetable for aligning national prices was decided upon. The agreement to agree was one aspect of the decisions. The other part concerned the regulations designed to bring about common organization of the agricultural markets. The actual system is extremely complicated and we need not be concerned with it in full here. The most common form of organization was based on the system of variable levies, which worked roughly as follows: Over the course of the transition period obstacles to trade in agricultural products were to be reduced to zero (i.e., tariffs and quotas were to be eliminated). This would open up the markets of countries where agriculture was high-priced to the cheaper products of other countries. Since the price of agricultural products reflected a variety of conditions (efficiency of productivity being only one), this was not altogether desirable. Thus, until the unified price stage was reached, there would be a transitional period during which the variable levy scheme would operate. This is in effect a multiple-tiered levy that protects member states from one another as well as from outside countries. The levy is basically an import duty equal to the differential between the price of the product in the importing country and its price on the world market. The same general procedure holds for the calculation of the levy whether the imported product is from a member or from a nonmember country. The only difference is that in the case of imports from member countries the levy is reduced by a standardized amount in order to place member states in a favorable competitive position in relation to non-member suppliers.[31]

In contrast with the progress made in the removal of restrictions to trade in agricultural products, only very modest headway was made concerning the question of common price. The big stumbling block here was the well-organized agricultural interests of West Germany, who opposed any suggestion of a decrease in their high prices. This posed the problem that if prices were to be aligned through gradual narrowing of the forks, the final alignment was likely to be much closer to the higher German prices than to the lower French prices. The problem was solved later (December 1964) through adoption of the Mansholt Plan, which aligned cereal prices in one step.

Several things should be noted about the role of the Commission during the period leading up to the adoption of these decisions. First, the Commission played an important role in the process of putting definite content into Community initiatives. The structural position of the Commission, the fact that it was not an ad hoc Community structure (as was the case with the Council of Ministers), that it had a number of dedicated loyalists and a full-time bureaucracy to study the problems in agriculture, all worked to shift the initiative to them. The ministers of the six member states were able to agree on the broad outlines of the common agricultural policy. Thus at the Stresa Conference in 1958 they were able to set out some broad goals with respect to agricultural cooperation. The means of working out the attainment of these goals was left to the Commission. The Commission began by carrying out studies of the agricultural situations in the member countries and by taking extensive soundings of the individual national positions. In this regard the Commission's formulation and initiation function runs into its coalition-building function.

Lindberg describes the role of the Commission during this period in terms of stimulating contacts with agricultural interest groups as well as maintaining fairly constant working relationships with the individual national ministries. Throughout the first four years (1958-1961) the Commission, under the energetic leadership of Sicco Mansholt, held numerous meetings with agricultural producers and agricultural workers. It kept close ties with COPA (the umbrella interest group in agriculture) and periodically submitted working papers to it as one way of achieving feedback on the agricultural situation in the individual countries.[32] It surely appears that this process of sounding out, of probing national experts and interest groups on their positions, of suggesting tentative proposals, and then of retracting and modifying them to suit member state needs, comes close to interest aggregation. Were this initial groundwork of compromise not laid, the negotiating process at later stages of the decision-making process would be much more difficult.

It also seems clear that the Commission was not a simple servant of the demands of individual member states along with the respective interest groups. From the very beginning the Commission stressed that the solutions to the problems in agriculture could not be dealt with effectively on a classic interstate level. True community solutions were needed which might have to go

beyond the minimal demands of any individual member state. The Commission
was faithful to this credo, and consistently advocated policy lines that were at
odds with one or another member. Lindberg comments on some of the specific
positions of the Commission: "The Commission espoused a distinct set of values
in making its proposals: that liberalization in other spheres must go hand in hand
with liberalization in agriculture; that structural reforms should take precedence
over price supports; and that a lower price price level ought to be achieved in the
interests of consumers and to keep the Community competitive on the external
market.[33]

The point illustrated here is that the Commission had its own conception
of some notion of public interest and they pursued this conception while at the
same time attempting to cultivate the support base among key groups. It is true
that the Commission's proposals, as adopted in 1962, were different from the
proposals originally made. Lindberg concedes that some of this change can be
attributed to the pressures exerted by interest groups and national ministries.[34]
But the direction of these changes was by no means entirely from Community-
centered to state-centered legislation. Thus the Commission was able to maintain
a sense of Community purpose throughout the negotiation process.

This coalition-building process set the stage for the success of the marathon negotiations in November-December 1961 and January 1962. By October
of 1961 basic positions had been thrashed out, areas of disagreement had been
pinpointed, and coalitions in the more noncontroversial areas had taken place.
As the end of the year approached a flurry of negotiations broke out. Yet, in
spite of four extensive Council of Ministers meetings in late November and
December, no agreement was reached. The end of the year passed without a
satisfactory agreement. Then the intensive phase of the marathon negotiations
began. The Council agreed to stop the clock and to extend the session until some
agreement was reached. After forty-five separate meetings, seven all-night
sessions, hundreds of hours of negotiations, and three heart attacks, an agreement was finally reached.[35] There could hardly be a better example of the
heroic dimensions of the marathon process. The structural inadequacy of the
Community to handle the problems of aggregation, the absence of a specialized
structure to cope with this, resulted in a marked overtaxing of the resources of
structures designed to perform different functions. Thus the Commission, which
is formally the initiator and implementer of Community legislation, took on the
role of coalition builder and aggregator.

The regulations adopted by the Council in January 1962 did not set up
market organizations for all agricultural products. Thus after the January session
the Commission set out to draw up proposals for organization in the beef, veal,
rice, and fruit and vegetable sectors. The Commission also had its work cut out
in terms of the large number of implementing decisions that were required to
bring into force the market organizations already decided upon. In addition,
there was the explosive question of the common grain price still to be decided.

At its session of December 23, 1963, the Council, again after much difficult bargaining and fear of failure, arrived at a set of decisions setting up
market organizations in the beef, rice, and dairy produce sectors. Decisions were

also taken on financing the common agricultural policy and the Kennedy Round. No final action was taken on the Mansholt Plan (for unification of grain prices) and it was simply tabled until spring.[36]

Although negotiations were long and difficult, by December 1963, Community negotiators had acquired a sense of the saving grace of the package deal.[37] In this decision, even more than reflected in the January 1962 decision, the maneuverings of the Commission seemed to play a decisive role. In view of the fact that the Council could get nowhere considering agricultural items one by one, the Commission drew up proposals in which special interests were carefully locked into a broader system of rewards and sacrifices. And again, as in the other decisions, a grueling marathon session characterized the end of the negotiating period.

The dominant pattern of integration in the agricultural sector was a non-incremental one. Initial disagreements over the specifics of working out the policy resulted in paralysis. But a general commitment to move ahead in agriculture, manifested not only in the Rome treaty but also in the personal guarantee to de Gaulle, as well as the self-imposed deadlines generated by the crisis atmosphere, tipped the initiative to the Commission. The Commission was the only institution with a full-time bureaucracy and energetic political leadership. This permitted the human resources necessary to generate quickly the successful options. Indeed, the primary power of the Commission probably lay in its ability to generate options under stressful conditions.

The preceding discussion suggests that interest aggregation is performed in the European Community, at least minimally, and that the European Commission is the most important structure in its performance. I say minimally, since the process of coalition building seems to fall far short of what usually characterizes domestic political systems. The two principal limitations are in terms of the scope of aggregation and the timing. Aggregation generally takes place within sectors, not across sectors, although there are some exceptions to this (e.g., positions on trading in the Kennedy Round were part of a package along with grain prices). In areas where there is not sufficient intrasector variability, coalition building and package deals are impossible and stagnation is the result. The timing limitation concerns the fact that most of the aggregation is telescoped in the latter stages of the decisional process where the Council of Ministers and national politicians are intimately involved. The culmination of this inadequate aggregation along with the desire for some policy and approaching deadlines to complete such policy provided the context for the marathon sessions. These sessions are to be seen essentially as institutional compensatory mechanisms for other structural inadequacies. Whether these marathon sessions and the frantic negotiations they entail are likely to be the long-term answer to the Community's problem of building political coalitions is a question to which we now turn.

DIFFICULTIES OF THE COMMISSION AS INTEREST AGGREGATOR

In political systems there is not the close connection between form and function which one finds in biology. Still the characteristics of a structure do have implications for its ability to perform a function. There are at least three structural characteristics of the Commission which work against its ability to perform the aggregation function in the long run.

The first structural characteristic of the Commission is that it is subjected to an institutional overload. In simpler terms, it has too much work to do, both in terms of the sheer volume of work demanded from it as well as the scope of the tasks. The Commission's roles are variously characterized as that of initiator of legislation, implementer of Community policy, broker among differing national viewpoints, guardian of the Treaty, conscience of the Community, and chief institution responsible for administrative decision making. Each one of these tasks requires much time and energy, and the fact that the Commission has had a supply of dedicated politicians and civil servants has not been enough. Just to formulate the details of proposals in agriculture, for example, has demanded a huge amount of time. Not much help was received in the drafting of major pieces of legislation from any of the other Community institutions. The same may be said for the implementation of Community policy—also a full-time job. The gradual establishment of the Common agricultural policy has brought with it the necessity to enact a large volume of implementing legislation. The Treaty of Rome, in Article 155, states that the Commission "shall exercise the powers conferred on it by the Council for the implementation of the rules laid down by the latter." As Noel and Etienne point out, the Council has made extensive use of this legal basis for delegating powers to the Commission: "The Council has made wide use of possibilities, with the result that the Commission now enjoys extensive powers over the daily running of the agricultural policy, customs union, commercial policy, animal and plant health matters, etc. In general all current implementing measures are adopted by the Commission after consultation with various committees."[38]

If one adds to formulation, initiation, and implementation the monitoring of many day-to-day activities of the Community, one begins to acquire a feeling of the extent to which the Commission is burdened. To some extent the Commission avoids the distractions of the morass of detail by itself delegating to administrative decision-making bodies, as is the case with respect to the management committees where the Commission sets broad limits for making decisions. The specific content of the decisions is left to the individual management committees.

The second structural defect of the Commission is that it has no direct links with the people of the Community and this has serious drawbacks in terms of the ability of the Commission to widen the scope of political conflict. Since the Commission is structurally set up to deprive it of legitimacy (i.e., it is a technocratic body appointed by the individual governments), it is in an awkward position whenever it casts itself as the defender of the public interest. If we take the public to mean all those people who are affected by Community policy but are deprived of access (in the making of that policy), it becomes a serious matter.

The Commission seems to be caught in a vise. To the extent that the Commission is the driving force behind significant Community legislation it will enhance the emergence of groups whose demands will have to be listened to. This would seem to lead to the institutionalization of some form of popular checks, such as elections of members of the European Parliament or making the Commission a representative rather than technical body. To the extent that the Commission cannot produce legislation with impact of this proportion it will not have to worry about legitimacy. Thus the Commission seems bound to live either in a world in which it has significant impact but is involved in constant crises over legitimacy or one in which its impact is essentially bureaucratic but where crises over legitimacy do not emerge. It appears to me that the Commission itself originally opted for the former strategy, attempting to develop legislation with a true Community flavor. But this line of action came to an uncertain halt in June 1965 when the French walked out of the Common Market negotiations. The immediate cause of the walkout was the attempt by the Commission to link some technical provisions for financing the common agricultural policy with increased powers for the European Parliament. The turn of events after the resolution of this crisis in January 1966 was in the direction of more cautious proposals, more detailed soundings of national positions, and a de-emphasis on developing any legitimacy basis for the Commission. In the place of the Community interest the Commission substituted the interests of specific pressure groups. Thus, for example, the formulation of policy in the agricultural sector was developed in consultation with agricultural interest groups. This is fine as far as it goes but one should carefully note that the common agricultural policy (CAP) is affecting many people besides the Community farmers. Community taxpayers are paying nearly $4 billion a year for the CAP with the net result of higher consumer prices. In addition, the developing countries are being hurt by having markets closed off, markets for which they often can produce commodities—of cheaper price and better quality. The problem is, therefore, not only one of responding to organized group demands. It is also one of enlarging the scope of conflict by drawing these potential groups into the political process. A narrow cultivation of ties with organized interest groups will simply not do. This should not be taken as a criticism of the Commission, which has clearly attempted to speak to as large a political constituency as possible. Indeed, the Commission until 1965 never attempted to play down its political role. Clearly, political leadership has gone about as far as it can in attempting to construct its own basis of legitimacy.

The third, and last, structural defect of the Commission is the conflict among the alternative roles it must perform. The Rome treaty foresaw no inconsistency in the alternative tasks it imposed on the Commission. The Commission was to be the initiator of Community legislation as well as the implementer of that legislation. It was to be the politically creative component of the system (initiating legislation and building coalitions) as well as the bureaucratic component (administering legislation).

As Coombes has brilliantly argued in his *Politics and Bureaucracy in the European Community* these two roles are at odds with each other and are constantly struggling for supremacy.[39] In its bureaucratic role, the Commission is asked to be neutral, to do the legwork of the Council in politically noncontroversial ways, and to carry out detailed studies within carefully circumscribed limits set by the mandates of the Council of Ministers. It is also expected to objectively implement Community policy and to keep member states in line according to such policy. In this role, the Commission is not expected to foster bold political initiatives, unrequested by national authorities. Nor is the Commission expected to appeal to the people, to cultivate support for itself, or to seek to strengthen the Community institutions. It was largely because the Commission departed from this essentially bureaucratic conception that the French pulled out of the Common Market in 1965.

On the other hand the Commission is really expected also to play a political role. The presentation of initiatives is the best example of this role—initiatives are inherently political. As we move further and further away from the period in which the content of the Commission's proposals are determined by deadlines in the Treaty, we can expect this political role more and more to be highlighted. Also, the Commission's role as mediator and broker among national interest groups as well as its importance in later stages of the decision process are crucial to the Community political process.

In any case, the Commission cannot avoid either of these roles, at least given the present structuring of political institutions in the EC. The Commission is condemned to an institutional schizophrenia. The absence of other structures to create and initiate legislation and form coalitions necessitates this condition. There is a structural-functional vacuum in the EC and the Commission, as the structure with the most resources and flexibility, is most capable of filling it. These conditions lead, of course, to a fundamental dilemma for the Commission. If the Commission wants to become a political body it must emphasize values, such as representativeness, legitimacy, and the influx of new values. It must depart from the organizational values of efficiency, consistency, uniformity, and professionalism. Recruitment should then emphasize political savvy at the expense of technical expertise. On the other hand, part of the success of the Commission is that it is a streamlined bureaucracy with high internal cohesion and expertise. As such, by underplaying its political role, the Commission took advantage of one of the characteristics of the military in developing countries— its efficiency. The efficiency of the Commission, its ability to act as a strong force in generating legislation, and its cohesiveness, all can be threatened by the assumption of a more openly political role. As Coombes perceptively points out:

> . . . it is bound to threaten institutional identity and purpose by multiplying values and loyalties within the organization. At least it might bog the organization down in interminable internal frontier disputes and "party" squabbles. Indeed, there is evidence that this has increasingly come to be the case, with more and more issues needed to be voted on by the Commissioner and an increasingly dominant role being played by·the cabinets. Above all, it conflicts with the Commission's administrative function in that the implementation and defense of Community policies calls for organizational characteristics such as consistency and uniformity.[40]

I have argued that there is an absence of interest-aggregation structures at the Community level which has harmful implications for the later stages of the decision-making process. It is also partly responsible for a crisis in political responsibility and authority. It is not likely, given current circumstances, that political parties will emerge to fill this vacuum. The primary reason (i.e., manifest reason) for the existence of parties, viz., to elect leaders for public office, does not exist.

There are possible solutions within the existing structural context. The Commission could continue to act out its heroic pattern and perpetuate the decision-making style embodied in the marathon session. As the Community moves away from the period of euphoria surrounding the first decade after its formation this is likely to be a more difficult course of action. A second possibility is that the Commission could effect a structural differentiation through a substantial delegation of its powers to administrative decision-making organs. The Commission has already begun to explore this option with the management committees. What the Commission does with these committees is to lay down broad mandates and then loosely monitor their activities. Should the Commission succeed in shifting the more technical aspects of its work to other organs it may in effect free itself to operate at a more political level. This is how structural differentiation often occurs—not by the overnight creation of a new structure but by the slow, progressive coalescence of old activities around new organs.

CHAPTER FIVE

Policy Making in the European Community

Policy making, involving the allocation of public values, reinforced through recourse to legitimate sanctions, lies at the heart of the political process. Policies are those binding rules by which the political system responds to the conflicting demands made of it. A highly developed political system could be viewed as one that acts together on a broad range of issues (scope) or one that acts together on many problems within one issue area (intensity). Integration can also be viewed in these terms. Philip Jacob and Henry Teune conceive the "essence of the integrative relationship . . . as collective action to promote mutual interests."[1] But cooperative activity is not all there is to politics. We must also be concerned with the modes through which policies jointly arrived at are enforced or else we run the risk of confusing politics with other modes of corporate problem-solving activity. Almond has suggested that political policies are distinguished by virtue of the fact that they may be enforced by resort to legitimate force.[2] One way of viewing political integration then, would be in terms of a vector variable, the resultant of two lines, one of which represents scope and intensity of coopera- tion, the other standing for the extent of coercive and persuasive compliance.

Most accounts of integration in the EEC stress the gap between economic and political integration. For example, the Dutch monthly, *The Common Market,* catches the spirit of this view: "Anyone reviewing the development of EEC since its beginning must be struck by the contradiction between the Community's unparalleled success in the economic sphere and the growing political discord between its members. While the treaty was carried out at great and even accelerated speed, the lack of agreement on the ultimate aims and methods of European unification has grown ever more obvious. How can we explain this paradox?"[3]

The view is widespread that no political integration has occurred. This is explainable partly on the grounds that some scholars see politics primarily in terms of grand issues, power diplomacy, nuclear policy, and large defense ques- tions.[4] To them Europe is no political system at all but rather a collection of specialized technocrats scampering around in white coats, standardizing road signs, and fixing the level of insecticide permitted on oranges. The success of the

87

technocrats, according to this view, is attributed precisely to the fact that they concern themselves with uncontroversial, nonpolitical questions. It is certainly the case that functionalist ideology, which permeates so much of EEC thought, studiously avoids open political confrontations in favor of a quiet, unobtrusive discharge of technical functions which stresses incrementalism, unintended consequences, and spillover.[5] The functional path to political community is, to quote Max Beloff, "federalism without tears."

The view here is that it is meaningful to speak of a European political community. Instead of asking whether the Common Market countries have a common defense ministry and whether they have relinquished their sovereignty on questions of national defense, I ask if any common authoritative allocations of values are taking place. The political process in the EEC hinges on such allocations of values, their implementation, enforcement, and adjudication. The task here is to identify the structures responsible for making and implementing rules as well as to examine the processes and interactions of these various structures. Most of these structures are of course embryonic, not highly institutionalized, and often inchoate. In addition, the distribution of power among the several community institutions is by no means a settled matter and in large part the drama of community activity highlights internal power struggles where different structures jockey for superior positions. In short, the Community is in the throes of deciding the question "what structures will perform what functions?" This fluidity of structural functional connections compounds the difficulty of a functional analysis since now not only is the operation of a structure and its place in the larger system problematic but also the identification problem is troublesome, that is, what structures in fact are performing what functions? Finally, it must be emphasized that EEC political structures are multifunctional; it is rare for one structure to perform a single specialized function. By the same token it is rare for a particular function to be performed by a single structure.

PRINCIPAL STRUCTURES THAT ACCOUNT FOR POLICY MAKING

Although decision making in the EEC is an enormously complicated process, three institutions are of primary importance in forging common policies. These are the Council of Ministers, the Committee of Permanent Representatives, and the Commission. Before examining the complex ways in which these institutions intermingle, a brief review is taken of each separately.

The Council of Ministers has been invested by the Treaty of Rome with the chief lawmaking power of the Community. It alone may decide on policy binding on all member states. The Council was originally composed of six members, one from each of the six signatories.[6] At present there are nine members. Members are not full-time Community officials. Usually they are the foreign ministers, agricultural ministers, or other appropriate representatives at the national ministerial level. The composition shifts with a shift in the content of proposals before the Commission. Thus if the issue being discussed is important enough, or if the content is so diffuse as to affect several departments, member governments may send several ministers.

Voting procedures in the Council are complicated and vary with the content of the issue being discussed. Many decisions, however, are reached by a qualified majority on proposals initiated by the Commission. Before January 1, 1973, a qualified majority usually meant obtaining twelve out of seventeen votes. According to the voting formula provided by the Treaty of Rome, Italy, France, and Germany had four votes each, Belgium and Netherlands two each, and Luxembourg one. In the event that the Council amended a Commission proposal, it had to be adopted by unanimous vote.

Because the Council is composed of part-time ministers it must delegate much of its work to continuous groups. It places its trust in the ability of these groups to effectively screen out detail and separate rubber-stamp issues from controversial, politically loaded ones. Thus when the ministers arrive in Brussels for Council sessions there is no need to go through proposals in full detail. Neither is it necessary to engage in extended "cloakroom politics" or "cocktail-lounge diplomacy" as one author put it.[7] Preliminary questions have already been decided by a group of advance teams, the chief of which is the Committee of Permanent Representatives. Emile Noel, executive secretary of the Common Market Commission, describes this process of delegation:

> When the Council has before it a Commission memorandum of general scope or a proposal on a well-defined subject, it entrusts the preparation of its discussion either to an ad hoc committee of senior officials (for example, the Special Committee on Agriculture) or to one of its permanent committees (groupes de travail), of which there is one for each branch of the Community's activities. The work of these bodies is coordinated by the Committee of Permanent Representatives . . . which prepares the work of the Council by functioning as a committee of ministerial deputies.[8]

The Commission is generally thought of as the executive body of the Community although this is not a simple matter. Leon Lindberg, in his pioneering work, notes that the Commission has the responsibility for representing the Community as a whole.[9] There are parallels here to the presidency in the United States, the constituency of which is national, and the Senate, the constituencies of which are more local. There are thirteen Commission members (before January 1, 1973, there were nine) who are appointed through national processes but once in office, they may not receive instructions from their governments. Their technical backgrounds and aloofness from national political processes, in addition to their full-time status as European civil servants, tends to induce in them a Community viewpoint. Thus the Commission is often the Community organ most closely associated with Community success. Erstwhile president, Walter Hallstein, referred to the Commission as "the engine of European integration."

Out of the welter of activity in which the Commission is engaged it is possible to abstract at least three roles for which the activity of the Community is fundamentally important. The Commission functions as an initiator of Community policy, as a pressure group in the adoption of Community legislation, and as a guardian of the Treaty and regulations of the EEC.

The most important power of the Commission is the power to initiate legislation which the Council may consider. Several advantages flow from this.

First, the limits of the legislative battlefield are, in a sense, marked off and the general content of the issue is placed within certain limits. These features may be altered only by an amendment by the Council which requires a unanimous vote. Second, the element of timing is important.[10] The success of the Commission is in good part attributable to its sensitivity in selecting the proper occasion for battle. When the proper constellations of events emerge the Commission has enough foresight, skill, and political acumen to seize upon them. The ability of the Commission to operate most effectively in an environment in which multiple conflicting forces are present is evidenced by the negotiations to achieve an agreement in grain prices in December 1964. Throughout these negotiations the position of the Commission was enhanced by the necessity of the Six to adopt a common position on the Kennedy Round of tariff cuts. The Commission exploited this desire to go forward in tariff cuts to overcome the resistance of the Council in the agricultural agreements.[11]

The second hat the Commission wears is that of a pressure group influencing EEC policy. The Commission neatly combines its role as initiator with that of pressure group. It is the ability of the Commission to do the advance work in formulating proposals that enables it to acquire an expertise and intimacy with proposals which makes their advice invaluable. Two other factors add to the Commission's role as pressure group: first, the Commission has a great deal of influence in the direction of public opinion. The extent to which members may freely engage in activities of this sort is severely circumscribed by the desire not to run afoul of the graces of the Council. Also the Commission has a wide range of contacts with the member governments and with the national bureaucracies.[12] All these factors make the advice and activity of the Commission particularly salient to Council members.

The third function performed by the Commission is that it acts as guardian of the Treaty and executor of Community policy. "The Commission sees to it that the Treaty's provisions and the decisions taken by the Institutions are correctly applied. It is responsible for maintaining an atmosphere of mutual confidence."[13]

The Commission thus acts as a kind of watchdog, assuring that the minimal conditions of security and stability exist within which economic integration can take place. It contributes to an atmosphere of trust and reciprocity and it acts as a lubricant to ease potential friction. The Commission is clearly an implementer of Community policy here, translating general policies into specific applications with contextual meaning.

The implementive powers of the Commission have grown as the common agricultural policy took one frantic bound after another and created the need for a corresponding bureaucratic structure. Thus it is not surprising to find that the activity of the Commission follows closely behind that of the Council. Noel summarizes the activities of the Commission:

> ... between 1958 and July 1, 1962 (when the first agricultural market organizations began to function) a total of 55 Regulations came into force, of which only nine were executive Regulations issued by the Commission. In the three months between July 1 and

October 1, 1962 the establishment of the first agricultural market organizations (grains, livestock products, fruits and vegetables) led the Commission alone to adopt 70 implementing Regulations. To give another example, in 1964 the Commission adopted a total of 124 Regulations, almost all of which were connected with the administration of the market organizations set up in 1962 and with the establishment of three further organizations (milk and milk products, beef and veal, and rice).[14]

Before moving to an examination of how policy is hammered out in practice, which involves an examination of the interaction of a variety of institutional components, we must recall the Committee of Permanent Representatives. The CPR is composed of one representative of ambassadorial rank from each of the member states. The Committee performs important functions in working along with the Commission on a day-to-day basis in preparing Community policies. It also acts to sift out controversial policies at an early stage of the decision-making process so that members will have adequate time to act.

Although the CPR is only elliptically referred to in the Rome treaty, it has, according to Spinelli, "become one of the most important cogs in the Community machinery."[15] The CPR started out as a preparatory committee for the Council but gradually its powers have grown, so that it now represents a rival power center to the Commission. Lindberg is no doubt correct in arguing that sooner or later the Council would have to establish some structure for preparing its decisions ahead of time.[16] The Council is institutionally unsuited to meet the burdensome demands made of it. It is, after all, the chief lawmaking structure and as such should have an ongoing organization, stability, continuity, and adequate time. Of course, it has none of these. Spinelli puts the problem this way: "The Council faces a very serious contradiction between its duties and the nature of its composition. Actually, the deliberative body in a very active, living community should have functional and structural continuity analogous to the legislative chambers in the individual states. Instead, since the Council consists of national ministers who are involved above all in the direction of their national departments, it can actually have only an intermittent existence."[17] The emergence and growth of the CPR can be seen as an adaptation to this institutional defect.

THE POLICY-MAKING PROCESS

To describe the process by which authoritative policies are decided upon and implemented by reference to the formal procedures outlined in the Treaty of Rome does violence to the complex, operational manner through which rules are hammered out. As Emile Noel explains: "The Treaty provides the foundations, but the house itself has still to be built. Once the structure is there, the Institutions will also have to frame Community policy and apply it from day to day. To guide the whole of this process the Treaty makes the Commission today the architect of the new building and tomorrow the initiator of the common policy."[18]

Whether this description is true in any extended metaphorical sense, we can certainly agree that it catches the spirit of the relationship between the

Treaty and the institutions it creates. Lindberg has discussed how the Rome treaty is basically a "traité cadre," a framework treaty that "contains more or less precise statements of goals and sets up an institutional system to achieve them."[19] In this sense the Treaty sets the institutional boundaries and the limits of the possible. Within these boundaries, which are not only fuzzy but also elastic, there is ample room for innovation and manipulation in arriving at common negotiating positions.

The function of rule making essentially resides in an institutionalized dialogue between the Council and the Commission. Also entering into the process are numerous expert groups, the CPR, the Economic and Social Committee, the European Parliament, and a variety of pressure groups. Thus the performance of the rule-making function involves simultaneously many different structures. The pattern of relationships has by no means crystallized into its final form but rather represents a shifting set of interactions in which national and supranational elements are very much in the process of jockeying for one-upmanship. In many ways, recurrent strains and crises in the EEC are symptomatic of attempts to change these patterns of relationships.

The mix of national and supranational elements in this dialogue seems ingeniously calculated to propel the Community toward common policies in many fields while at the same time insuring the preservation of national interests. Structurally, the task of safeguarding national interests has been deposited with the Council, on which one minister from each of the states resides. Similarly, the Commission is invested with the European point of view. This institutionalized competition is evident in the actual policy-making process. "The submission of a proposal by the Commission initiates the dialogue between the national governments represented in the Council (the members of which express their national points of view) and the Commission—a 'European' body called upon to express the interests of the Community as a whole and to seek 'European' solutions to common problems."[20]

We have mentioned that the Commission, on almost all matters, has the right to propose legislation while the Council disposes. The Treaty also states, in the very important Article 149, that "When, pursuant to the Treaty, the Council acts on a proposal of the Commission, it shall, where the amendment of such a proposal is involved, act only by means of unanimous vote."[21] The Council-Commission dialogue, however, goes well beyond this. In practice the respective prerogatives of initiation and adoption are circumscribed by both structural and attitudinal factors. The structural factors must include mention of the proliferation of specialized groups, ad hoc committees, and recognized institutions such as the CPR and the Economic and Social Committee. Attitudinal factors include a sensitivity on the part of the Commission as to the limits of what the Council will accept and a willingness, on the part of Council members, to concede that many problems do not lend themselves to national settlement, and are more rationally handled on a transnational basis. The Commission will have to take into account the different conditions obtaining in each of the member states in order for a proposal to have a serious chance of being adopted. The wide differences in agricultural prices among the six member states provide an example of the national diversity that the Commission must take into consideration. Table 5.1 gives one an idea of this diversity.

TABLE 5.1

DIFFERENCES IN PRICE SHOWN BY THE CHIEF AGRICULTURAL PRODUCTS IN THE MEMBER STATES OF THE EEC 1958-59 (ARITHMETIC AVERAGE = 100)

Product	Germany	France	Italy	Belgium	Luxem-bourg	Nether-lands
Wheat	109.4	74.9	109.1	100.4	123.3	83.0
Rye	116.7	71.0	101.7	87.1	138.9	84.7
Barley	134.6	76.6	93.4	105.1	98.9	91.4
Oats	121.2	83.6	84.3	100.3	110.5	100.1
Sugar beets	122.3	81.5	103.9	92.8	--	99.1
Milk	101.6	92.1	98.7	94.3	116.1	97.8
Cattle	101.3	87.8	113.7	89.5	105.9	101.8
Pigs	110.0	93.7	105.7	84.9	115.3	90.4
Eggs	109.4	89.8	113.1	94.5	119.9	73.2

SOURCE: EEC Commission, Proposals, Part I, 21. Reprinted from Leon N. Lindberg, *The Political Dynamics of European Economic Integration* (Stanford, Calif.: Stanford University Press, 1963), p. 225.

The genius of the Commission is its ability to comprehend national differences while still preparing and formulating proposals that attempt to go beyond the "minimum common denominator."[22] To this end it is incalculably aided by the complicated, ambiguous process by which other Community organs as well as national and ad hoc groups penetrate and influence the decisional process. While this ambiguity, or decisional fuzziness, does not magically churn out Community solutions where no agreement exists, it nevertheless does obscure exactly what has been sacrificed by dovetailing specific positions into general decision packages. If it appears that a little ambiguity in the policy-making process is functional, it is equally plausible that an institutional setup that pits the Commission against the Council would not be best suited to effect this ambiguity. In this sense, the evolution of a complicated process involving the mediation of a variety of structures between the Commission and the Council acts as a political lubricant and precludes confrontation politics.

The path that a proposal may take is by no means fixed from issue to issue. But since the Community's most successful rule-making apparatus is in agriculture, this issue is used as an illustration. Figure 5.1 illustrates the typical flow of policy in the field of agriculture.

The shaping of a proposal is likely to originate in the appropriate general directorate of the Commission, in this case agriculture. It may originate at the behest of a Commission member, a Council member, or a bureaucrat. Sometimes an agricultural pressure group may be responsible for articulating the interest. At

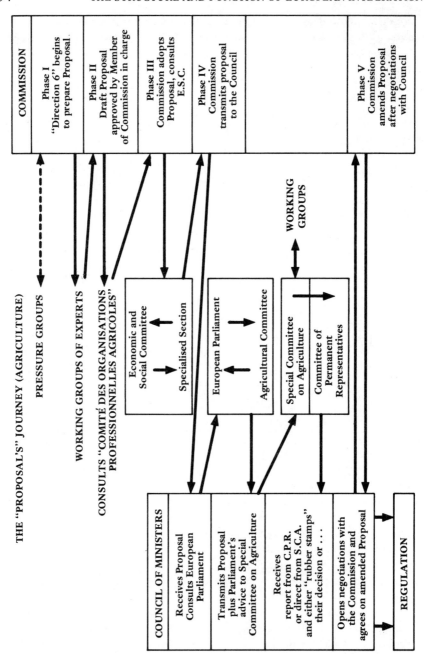

Fig. 5.1. Typical flow of policy in the field of agriculture. SOURCE: From Stephen Holt, *The Common Market: The Conflict Between Theory and Practice.* Copyright © 1967 by Stephen Holt (London: Hamish Hamilton, 1967), p. 58. Reprinted here with the permission of the publisher.

this stage, however, it appears that articulation by associational interest groups must take a back seat to articulation by institutional groups. The Commission and its General Directorate are two such groups. This stage is perhaps one of the weakest links in the entire policy-making process, reflecting the tendency for issues to be conceived apart from the interest group context operative domestically in each of the member states. This defect itself is becoming somewhat less forceful by virtue of the growth of interest group associations at the Community level.

After the issue has arisen, the Commission is likely to set up a series of working groups. Some of the membership is drawn from interest group representation at the Community level and some from the national level.[23]

The next stages are somewhat less definite. It is helpful to quote extensively from Stephen Holt here:

> When the working groups have completed their task, the draft proposal is approved by the Member of the Commission in charge, and in the case of agriculture, Mansholt now consults with the Comité des Organisations Professionnelles Agricoles. After these discussions have been completed, the draft proposal is now ready to go to the full Commission for approval.[24]
>
> We now proceed to the next stage of the proposal's journey, when the Commission sends it to the Council of Ministers. If the European Parliament and the Economic and Social Committee have not been previously consulted by the Commission, the Council will probably consult these organs at this stage. The Council sometimes does this voluntarily and sometimes because it is required to by the Treaty, depending on the subject. But to settle its own view on the proposal, the Council hands it to the Special Committee on Agriculture (if the proposal is not on an agricultural subject, it goes straight to the Committee of Permanent Representatives who take charge of all preparatory work on the Council's behalf).[25]

The CPR helps to fill the institutional lacuna caused by the intermittent qualities of the Council's existence. It gives continuity, structure, and specialized knowledge to the policy-making process. It acts as a surrogate Council in matters not pressing enough to warrant the Council's attention and, in addition, it performs an invaluable winnowing function in isolating the crucial political questions for Council consideration. Finally, the Commission has learned to use the CPR as an experimental laboratory, testing out ideas and attempting to discover, as Lindberg puts it, the "limits of the possible."[26] The value of such a procedure is that it provides a loose advisory opinion of what policy-initiating groups are likely to expect. It is significant that the agricultural crisis of 1965-66 was in part set off by the failure of the Commission to clear its proposals through the CPR.[27]

The final stage of the rule-making process involves the Council and the Commission most directly. By this time much of the detailed and less controversial portions of the proposals have been eliminated. What is left may or may not provide the materials for a joint solution. The difficulty of negotiations at this stage is well known. "This is the final stage of the dialogue between the

Commisson and the Council, a dialogue which as often as not is long and stubborn. It should be remembered that the Commission is free to amend its proposal right up to the moment a decision is taken and as the struggle enters the last round, the Commission has most of the strong cards in its hands."[28]

This flexibility cannot be exaggerated. During the lengthy marathon sessions that characterized agricultural negotiations the Commission was free to offer last-minute compromises. That this is a real power is evidenced by the creative role of the Commission during the December 1963 agricultural marathon:

> In two hours, between 0100 and 0300 on Sunday, December 22, the Commission drew up and presented to the Ministers an overall package deal, thanks to its perfect knowledge of the dossiers and the positions and legitimate interests of the member states. When it took its decisive initiative, the Commission had to be certain that none of the elements in its proposal were unacceptable, at first sight, to one of the member states: there thus had to be an intelligent balance of reciprocal concessions, and allowance had to be made for all the essential interests at stake. The final result has shown that the Commission had perfectly calculated the moment for intervention and the balance of concessions.[29]

The Council and Commission can engage in meaningful dialogue at this stage because the detailed groundwork has been laid. And if there has been an effective performance of the aggregation function, it facilitates the task of top policy makers who are offered several well-defined alternative policies.

This process of selection, compromise, screening, and forging alternative policy proposals out of a variety of separate national demands highlights the importance of the aggregation function for effective policy making. The entire process is subjected to a complex editing procedure in which parts unacceptable to individual governments are taken out and other, merely objectionable parts are blended into larger, more acceptable proposals. The process is more than one of give and take; it is also partly a process of obscuring the components in terms of which a meaningful give-and-take calculation can take place. The institutional diversity provided by the Community method is peculiarly fitted to this end.

It is doubtful if the Council could become the nucleus for a true supranational form of decision making given the sporadic nature of its activities as well as the domestic constraints and pressures under which it operates. Yet it seems improbable that the present machinery will persist in all its complexity. Commission members are already overburdened with the executive weight of the common agricultural policy. Council members already complain of their lack of time and expertise to deal with Community affairs. In the presence of this kind of strain, the pressure seems to be in the direction of a further elaboration of structures. In the absence of a strong European will for common policies the present institutional diversity is tolerated and justified in terms of its tempering and refining effects. Should a clear European purpose develop this same machinery is likely to be viewed as obstructive.

To a certain degree, recurrent crises in the EEC can be interpreted as growing pains along the road toward increasing structural differentiation. Here I do not mean to imply that movement in this direction is inevitable, only that certain pressures exist for it. Crisis in the EEC seems to occur when a threat to the ongoing institutional pattern is posed and efforts are made by one structure to siphon off functions performed by others. For example, the "own resources" controversy that partly instigated the French boycott of the Council meetings concerned an attempt by the Commission to alter the balance of financial control in the Community's favor.

The dilemma of the Community is this: the supranational force is the Commission and its autonomy and independence from member governments allows it a high degree of decisional latitude. It is this same autonomy that makes the Commission an unpopular body. An effective supranational organ will have to retain some of the autonomy that the Commission now possesses while acquiring some popular or responsible base. It is likely that any attempt to do this will be met by vigorous national opposition.

INDICATORS OF POLICY FORMATION IN THE EEC

There are several advantages to general comparative schemes as outlined by Gabriel Almond or David Easton. First, such conceptual schemes provide us with a common language in terms of which we represent the observational world. Second, a set of categories (in this case functional categories) is suggested with which we can evaluate experience. Third, the categories suggest interconnections and therefore imply theory. To some extent the question whether a conceptual scheme is a good or bad one hinges on whether its categories can be formulated as theoretical statements.

If Almond has contributed much in the way of an abstract, conceptual schemata, Leon Lindberg and Joe Nye have performed valuable translations. Lindberg has performed the valuable service of applying Eastonian systems analysis to the EEC.[30] There is much that is helpful in applying Almond's framework to the EEC experience. Nye has made important contributions in exploring the dimensional nature of integration.[31] Instead of viewing integration as all of one cloth he has made an attempt to isolate its significantly different components. These are necessary pretheoretical tasks. Before we can make general statements expressing relations among variables, we must identify the components of these variables.

After conceptual schemes are provided the task of the social scientist becomes one of anchoring abstract concepts in an empirical base and ultimately, relating these categories to one another in terms of general theoretical statements. The former task requires that we operationalize our concepts and find indicators for them in the empirical world. Yet the literature of political integration demonstrates a remarkable reluctance to make concrete our notions of political integration by specifying indicators.[32] When talking about political integration most scholars seem to have a merger of distinct sovereignties in mind, or at least a common defense ministry. This is a relatively insensitive indicator of political integration, insensitive in the sense that it remains indifferent to a substantial range of political cooperation below that threshold. In addition, it is no wonder, given this hard test, that it is commonly asserted that political

integration lags behind economic integration. In the absence of separate measures of economic, social, and political integration, the interrelations among them
are undemonstrable.

I propose that the indicators of policy making in the EEC be based on the
performance of political functions in general where the performance of functions is shifting to a new, more comprehensive unit. The indicators center on
political structures and the weightings are determined by the activity of these
structures.

It was decided to try to find suitable indicators for all three of the output
functions: rule making, rule implementation, and rule adjudication. There are
certain advantages in dealing simultaneously with all the indicators of the output
functions since by doing so the question of whether the adjudication function is
empirically distinct from those of rule making and rule implementation becomes
answerable. The indicators chosen are listed in table 5.2. These indicators should
provide us with an operational way of asking whether or not Europe constitutes
a political system. Can Europe be characterized as possessing a set of structures
whose activity significantly affects the distribution of values? Do these indicators describe coherent patterns of activity or are they unstable from time
point to time point? Finally, do these indicators cluster together in coherent
patterns, that is, how many components of integration are described by our
indicators?

TABLE 5.2

INDICATORS OF POLITICAL INTEGRATION

1. Communications of the European Court of Justice
2. Judgments of the Court
3. Court rulings
4. Court decisions
5. New cases brought before the Court
6. Parliamentary questions and answers
7. Regulations of Council of Ministers: the true laws of the Community, binding and
   directly applicable in all member states
8. Council information: communications requesting information on the part of the
   Council
9. Commission regulations: regulations adopted by the Commission to put into effect
   regulations adopted by the Council
10. Directives and decisions of the Commission: directives bind any member state to which
    they are addressed on the result to be achieved, while the means is left open to national
    discretion. Decisions are binding on those to whom they are addressed
11. Recommendations and opinions: these have no binding force whatsoever

RELIABILITY OF INDICATORS

Ideally, each of the eleven indicators specified in table 5.2 will not be tapping a
separate dimension. Hopefully several of them will cluster into a reduced set of
political integration factors with which one can deal more parsimoniously. The
task ahead is therefore one of dimensional analysis. I proceed in two ways. First,
I adopt a correlational approach to the formation of indexes. The basic measure-

ment model adopted here is the multiple indicator model. The primary assumption of this model is that if two or more indicators are part of the same concept, they will intercorrelate. The second approach is to subject the indicators to a factor analysis. This technique is particularly appropriate for our purposes since one of its functions is to uncover the underlying components or factors in a larger set of data.[33]

One way to approach this problem would be to correlate our indicators for specific issue areas. Table 5.2 lists the eleven indicators on which analysis was carried out and table 5.3 presents the correlations for the activities of the European Parliament, the Council, and the Commission in the field of agriculture.

All indicators in table 5.3 except indicator 6, Commission recommendations, intercorrelate significantly. This leads me to believe that we are dealing with a concept possessing functional unity and stability, in short, a reliable concept. Still, we do not have any clue as to how many dimensions are included here. In answering this question factor analysis will be of some help.

In addition to looking at political integration in agriculture, one could also apply the same logic to the activity of the Parliament, Council, and Commission in all issue areas. When we examine the pattern for total political integration (see table 5.4) we find the pattern much the same as in agriculture. The one difference is that indicator 6 seems to be more sensitive to the other indicators now. As a matter of fact, the entire correlation matrix has only two entries that are not significant at the .05 level. This buttresses my conviction that we are dealing with a stable concept.

Although the evidence for reliability is now fairly strong we still cannot proceed to form composite indexes of political integration until we resolve the dimensional problem, to which we now turn.

Most of the literature concerning international integration assumes that political integration is a unidimensional concept. This is a strong assumption and one that can have a serious effect on the outcome of a study. The view here is that before making an analysis concerning relationships among variables, the major working concepts must be dimensionalized and their internal theoretical

TABLE 5.3

CORRELATION AMONG INDICATORS OF
POLITICAL INTEGRATION IN AGRICULTURE
$n = 39$

Indicator	1	2	3	4	5	6
1. Parliamentary questions	1.00					
2. Council regulations	.408[a]	1.00				
3. Council information	.447[a]	.353[a]	1.00			
4. Commission regulations	.507[a]	.876[a]	.497[a]	1.00		
5. Commission directives	.451[a]	.472[a]	.699[a]	.615[a]	1.00	
6. Commission recommendations	-.026	.035	.186	-.037	.195	1.00

[a]Pearson's *r* significant at .05 level.

TABLE 5.4

CORRELATION AMONG INDICATORS OF
TOTAL POLITICAL INTEGRATION
$n = 40$

Indicator	1	2	3	4	5	6
1. Parliamentary questions	1.00					
2. Council regulations	.679[a]	1.00				
3. Council information	.509[a]	.466[a]	1.00			
4. Commission regulations	.332[a]	.710[a]	.221	1.00		
5. Commission directives	.528[a]	.553[a]	.723[a]	.369[a]	1.00	
6. Commission recommendations	.408[a]	.420[a]	.548[a]	.173	.690[a]	1.00

[a]Pearson's r significant at .05 level.

and empirical boundaries probed and sharpened. In a sense this is a logical extension of the search for functional unities, since dimensionalization focuses on the problem of discerning whether a particular phenomenon has one, two, or n sets of organized properties. It is true that through correlational analysis the homogeneity of a set of indicators was considered, but this was done only in a gross sense. All indicators were considered together and no attempt was made to differentiate subgroups or independent clusters within the data. What should we do, for example, if two independent clusters of correlations exist in the data? If we add together indicators from these clusters, we may in effect wipe out any relationships that existed between each of these variables and some dependent variable.

A bivariate correlation matrix is not very helpful in ascertaining dimensionality. This is because only dyadic correlations are given. Nothing is said about the general position of each variable with respect to a general construct. For example, two bivariate correlations (A and B, B and C) may be high internally and yet not show significant correlation between them (i.e., AC will be low). Conversely, bivariate correlations may be low and still possess part of some construct by virtue of shared variation with a third variable.[34] A correlation matrix simply will not answer these questions for us.

Factor analysis, which can be loosely considered as a multidimensional generalization of Guttman scale analysis, seems to be the appropriate statistical technique here.[35] As one observer put it, factor analysis starts with the assumption that a matrix of correlation coefficients is not so complicated as it appears to be. In this sense, the primary function of factor analysis is to reduce a larger set of correlations into a smaller set of factors or dimensions. Generally this is done by searching the correlation matrix for clusters of variables that share common sources of variance. The proof of whether or not two or more variables have common sources of variance is determined by whether they load (i.e., correlate) on the same dimension.

The following are the basic questions the factor analysis addresses itself to:

1. What is the basic pattern or structure of the data?
2. What reduced set of dimensions can account for the entries in the correlation matrix?
3. What variables load highly on what factors?
4. Is there a unidimensional pattern or is what we refer to as the richness of political events manifested in several distinct underlying dimensions of integration?
5. Finally if the patterns presented are multidimensional, how can these dimensions be meaningfully interpreted in theoretical and/or common sense terms?

The procedure is to specify a set of indicators for a concept, present the factor structure that these indicators form, and proceed to analyze this factor structure.[36] On the basis of these interpretations will be decided which indicators to discard, which to retain, and out of those retained, which to put into clusters for index formation.

We can begin much as we did with the correlation analyses, by factor analyzing the eleven indicators of agricultural political activity in the EEC. The factor structure in table 5.5 is for the third rotation. After much deliberation it was decided to treat agricultural political integration as two-dimensional. Thus I labeled Factor I as general political integration factor and excluded only variables 3, 4 and 11 (Court rulings, Court decisions, recommendations and opinions). I also decided to construct an index on the basis of Factor III. The deviant behavior of variables 7 and 9 are the convincing facts here. Why do these two indicators (Council regulations and Commission regulations) which behave almost identically with the other indicators on Factor I) suddenly break ranks and load highly on Factor III when the others do not? The theoretical interpretation here is that both of these indicators are lawmaking measures, one of the Almondian functions I spoke of earlier. One would expect each function to have a certain amount of behavioral autonomy. Granted that this interpretation rests on shaky methodological grounds, I still formulate it as a separate measure of political integration in agriculture. I do this partly because the factor structure for the indicators of total political integration supports and brings out more clearly the factorial distinctness of the rule-making dimension.

Total political integration represents the gross amount of political activity underway in the Common Market, irrespective of issue area or country (see table 5.6). The indicators are the same as for political integration in agriculture with the exception that there are two additional ones: indicator 12 is a measure of the number of delegations and foreign missions accepted by the EEC during a given time period; indicator 13 is a measure of the amount of activity that transpired through the European Development Fund in a given period. This is also reflective of the international activity of the EEC.

The factor structure in table 5.6 is for the third rotation. The interpretation of these factors is much less strained than for political integration in agricultural factors. It seems clear that Factor I represents the rule-adjudication

TABLE 5.5

FACTOR ANALYSIS OF INDICATORS OF
POLITICAL INTEGRATION IN AGRICULTURE

Indicator	Factor I	Factor II	Factor III
1. Communications of the Court	0.749	-0.366	0.143
2. Judgments of the Court	0.693	0.176	-0.298
3. Court rulings	0.127	-0.126	-0.610
4. Court decisions	0.122	-0.769	0.095
5. New cases brought before the court	0.902	-0.245	-0.101
6. Parliamentary questions and answers	0.668	0.223	0.125
7. Regulations (Council of Ministers)	0.659	0.009	0.587
8. Council information	0.797	-0.162	-0.288
9. Regulations (Commission)	0.811	0.059	0.466
10. Directives and decisions (Commission)	0.817	-0.356	0.026
11. Recommendations and opinions	0.062	-0.807	-0.078
Percentage of variance	38.959	12.347	8.804

NOTE: The underlined numbers were considered to be significant and are used to form composite indexes of integration based on the addition of several indicators.

function factor. But, it is contaminated with one housekeeping indicator (8) and one implementation indicator (10). Indicator 8, a measure of Council information or communications, seems to represent a normal maintenance function, activities performed by every formal organization just to serve itself rather than being a goal it accomplishes in relation to its environment. Indicator 10 is a measure of the directives and decisions of the Commission of the EEC. As such it is not surprising to find it in the same cluster with adjudication indicators. In the growth and development of political functions one expects rule making to precede adjudication and implementation: one cannot enforce and litigate until one has at least an embryonic system of rules. In addition, one would not expect legal activity to develop only with the formulation of laws. If laws were hammered out in a vacuum and never became a part of the social fabric, we would not expect much litigation. A case in point is the amount of litigation in the courts since the federal government of the United States involved itself in enforcing and implementing civil rights legislation.

Factor II in table 5.6 appears to be a rule-making one. Indicator 6 has to do with legislative activity, whereas indicators 7 and 9 are directly related to the number of regulations produced by the Council and the Commission. It is important to note that indicators 7 and 9, especially, are characterized by their binding equality. Regulations have the force of real Community law and are directly enforceable in all member states. The fact that these three indicators, 6, 7, and 9, load so low on the other two factors reinforces the clarity of this interpretation. Factor III is an external relations factor. We shall, however, only

TABLE 5.6

FACTOR ANALYSIS OF INDICATORS OF
ALL POLITICAL INTEGRATION IN THE EEC

Indicator	Factor I	Factor II	Factor III
1. Communications of the Court	0.572	0.552	-0.241
2. Judgments of the Court	0.822	-0.018	0.043
3. Court rulings	0.064	-0.204	-0.508
4. Court decisions	0.351	0.025	-0.102
5. New cases brought before the court	0.832	0.340	-0.225
6. Parliamentary questions and answers	0.202	0.689	-0.418
7. Regulations (Council of Ministers)	0.163	0.908	-0.129
8. Council information	0.765	0.294	-0.337
9. Regulations (Commission)	0.112	0.819	0.205
10. Directives and decisions (Commission)	0.684	0.467	-0.309
11. Recommendations and opinions	0.226	0.349	-0.701
12. Foreign delegations and missions accepted by EEC	0.201	0.029	-0.801
13. Activity transpiring through EDF	0.182	0.350	-0.745
Percentage of variance	27.709	21.410	18.175

NOTE: The underlined numbers were considered to be significant and are used to form composite indexes of integration based on the addition of several indicators.

retain indicators 12 and 13. Indicator 11 will be dropped in spite of its high loading since it makes no sense theoretically.

In summary, then, factor analysis was utilized to aid in the dimensionalization process and three distinct dimensions emerged: a rule-making dimension, a combined rule-adjudication and implementive one, and an external affairs dimension. This lends some empirical support to the threefold output scheme with, however, the qualification that court activity and implementive activity come out on the same factor. There are several interpretations for this. First of all, there is as yet only a minimal level of structural differentiation in the performance of these functions. The complexity and ambiguity of the entire policy-making process offers striking evidence of poor boundary maintenance. Second, it appears that the implementation and enforcement of Community law is the weakest link in the political system. Performance has certainly outrun control in the EEC. Third, the enforcement and adjudication functions have been closely associated in the EEC. W. Hartley Clark gives an idea of just how undifferentiated these two functions are:

> Up to mid-1962 the Commission had received sixty-eight complaints against the way national administrations had applied regulations. So new was the problem of enforcement to the Common

Market that at the same time thirty of these had not yet been examined in any way, and sixteen of them were just being studied. That left twenty-two cases in which the Commission had actually acted as policeman. In twelve of them the offending administration made the necessary adjustment after the matter was called to its attention by the Commission. It was necessary to go a step farther and render an opinion in ten cases, but in only five of these did the offending administration then comply. The five most difficult cases had to be taken to court. Going to court was threat enough to make a national administration back down in one case, and the case was withdrawn. In two others, the European Court upheld the Commission and the last two were still pending.[37]

Now that composite indexes have been formed on the basis of factor analysis we are in a position to assess two important matters.[38] First, we can ask whether significant growth in the activity of political structures has occurred since the inception of the EEC in 1958. My notion of growth is similar to Kenneth Boulding's "simple growth," that is, "the growth or decline of a single variable or quantity by accretion or depletion."[39] It does not include changes in structure, level of organization, and the like, an example of which would be increasing structural differentiation. Second, we can ask, in an empirical way, whether the EEC is a political system. It has certainly been a working hypothesis that the EEC is not made up of random structural components but that the components form some interlocking system. The operational test of "system" is whether elements (structures and functions) we have specified are related to each other so that variation in some elements is related to variation in others.

One way to get an idea of the progress of political development in the EEC is simply to plot the activity of its institutions in terms of a composite index or of their political integration.[40] Figure 5.2 gives us an idea of political activity from 1958 to 1967 in the fields of agriculture and transport. We can see from the plot that political integration remains at a very low level until the beginning of 1962, then rises gradually, peaking several times probably representing the agricultural marathon sessions of January 1962, December 1963, and December 1964.

It is instructive to examine these patterns of political integration for all issue areas. Figure 5.3 (p. 108) presents the plot for these data. A gradual but clearly discernible rise in political integration over the ten-year period is evident. Both of these plots lend some evidence to the growth of political structures in the EEC. It should be added that owing to the standardized nature of the data (all scores are expressed as T-values, where $T = 10(x) + 50$), the increases appear much less dramatic.

The second consideration is that of empirically assessing whether components of the EEC are interdependent. One way to do so would be to correlate activities among different components of the system. For example, one could see if activity in one issue area affected or was associated with activity in other issue areas. Another tactic would be to see whether the development of political structures bears any relationship to the development of structures in other parts of the system, for example, the economic.

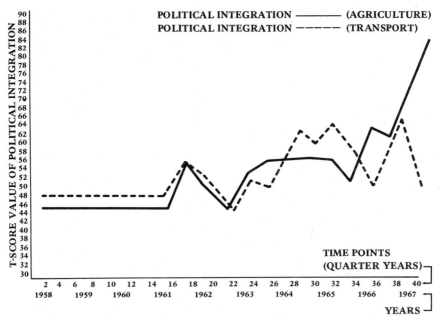

Fig. 5.2. Political integration in agriculture and transport for the EEC (1958-1967). SOURCE: Reprinted with permission of publishers from James A. Caporaso, *Functionalism and Regional Integration: A Logical and Empirical Assessment.* Sage Professional Papers in International Studies (Beverly Hills, Calif.: Sage Publications, 1972), Vol. 1, No. 02-004, p. 52.

The most basic requirement of a system is that its components be related to one another. If a set of components were completely indifferent to one another we would speak of a random aggregate and not of a system. Table 5.7 presents the correlations for political and functional integration in both agriculture and transport. Functional integration is measured by trade data in the case of agriculture and railroad activity, by inland water activity and tourist flows in the case of transport. We can see that all the coefficients are fairly high, indicating a good deal of systemic interdependence. It is noteworthy that the correlation between political and functional integration in agriculture (.863) is higher than the correlation of political integration in agriculture with political integration in transport. This suggests that the links within issue areas but across analytic systems (i.e., from political to economic) are more well developed than those between issue areas within the political system.

Testing hypotheses concerning relations between integrative patterns in several sectors probably comes very close to testing the spillover proposition. While the factors on which spillover depends are somewhat ambiguous, one usually thinks of spillover in terms of integration in one sector forcing or causing or being associated with integration in related sectors.[41] The functional approach offers some fresh ways in which to handle the spillover problem. Questions concerning the relationships between two sectors can now be looked at in terms of boundary maintenance. The argument that functionally diffuse

TABLE 5.7

ZERO-ORDER CORRELATIONS FOR AGRICULTURE AND TRANSPORT

Variable	1. Agricultural (political)	2. Transport (political)	3. Agriculture (functional)	4. Transport (functional)
1. Agriculture (political)	—			
2. Transport (political)	.604	—		
3. Agriculture (functional)	.863	.422	—	
4. Transport (functional)	.392	.234	.514	—

SOURCE: This table is reprinted with permission of the Publishers, from James A. Caporaso, *Functionalism and Regional Integration: A Logical and Empirical Assessment*, Sage Professional Papers in International Studies (Beverly Hills, Calif.: Sage Publications, 1972), Vol. 1, No. 02-004, p. 53.

TABLE 5.8

CROSS-SECTORAL SPILLOVER

	Agriculture (P)[a]	Transport (F)[b]	Agriculture (P)[a]	Transport (F)[b]
Political integration 1	.478	.281	.546	.159
Political integration 2	.406	.434	.582	.416
Political integration 3	.713	.253		

[a] P = political.

[b] F = functional.

SOURCE: Reprinted with permission of the Publishers, from James A. Caporaso, *Functionalism and Regional Integration: A Logical and Empirical Assessment*, Sage Professional Papers in International Studies (Beverly Hills, Calif.: Sage Publications, 1972), Vol. 1, No, 02-004, p. 56.

NOTE: Political integration 1, 2, and 3, refer to dimensions 1, 2, and 3 of all political integration data less the data for agriculture and transport. These data had to be removed in order to prevent a redundant correlation. Thus the factor analysis for this set of data was not identical with the factor analysis for the total political integration set. Political integration 1 represents a general political integration factor; Political integration 2 represents a rule-making or legislative factor; and Political integration 3 represents the adjudication component.

sectors exhibit weak boundary maintenance can be translated into a suggestion that integration in diffuse sectors will generate more spillover than integration in functionally specific sectors.[42] The logic of such a hypothesis could be cast in terms of the poor boundary maintenance or of high permeability of diffuse structures. The high autonomy or separability of functionally specific structures could lead one to believe that integration in these sectors would be more autonomous.

If certain assumptions are made, the data lend themselves to an approximate test of this hypothesis. The primary assumption is that agriculture represents a diffuse sector while transport represents a functionally specific sector. This assumption would seem to have high face validity in that we usually associate agriculture with the less modern, more diffuse kinds of societies while recognizing that transport is part and parcel of a differentiated society. The need for a specialized transport system does not even arise until a society becomes specialized enough to call into existence structures to coordinate activity and to carry out the interchanges among various, spatially remote societal components.

Examined are the intersector relationships among three dimensions of political integration (1, overall integration; 2, rule making; and 3, rule adjudication) and political and functional integration in agriculture and transport. Table 5.8 presents these correlations.

TABLE 5.9

SIGNIFICANCE TESTS FOR SECTORAL SPILLOVER

Dimension	Agriculture (F)[b]	Transport (F)	Difference	t- or z- value	Significance at .05 level
Political integration (1)	.478	.281	+.197	1.23	no
Political integration (2)	.406	.434	-.028	0.17	no
Adjudication (3)	.713	.253	+.460	3.21	yes

Dimension	Agriculture (P)[c]	Transport (P)	Difference	t- or z- value	Significance at .05 level
Political integration (1)	.546	.159	+.387	4.9	yes
Political integration (2)	.582	.416	+.166	1.4	no
Adjudication (3)	.802	.514	+.288	2.3	yes

[a]Significance is based on a one-tailed test.

[b]F = functional.

[c]P = political.

SOURCE: Reprinted with permission of the Publishers from James A. Caporaso, *Functionalism and Regional Integration: A Logical and Empirical Assessment*, Sage Professional Papers in International Studies (Beverly Hills, Calif.: Sage Publications, 1972), Vol. 1, No. 02-004, p. 56.

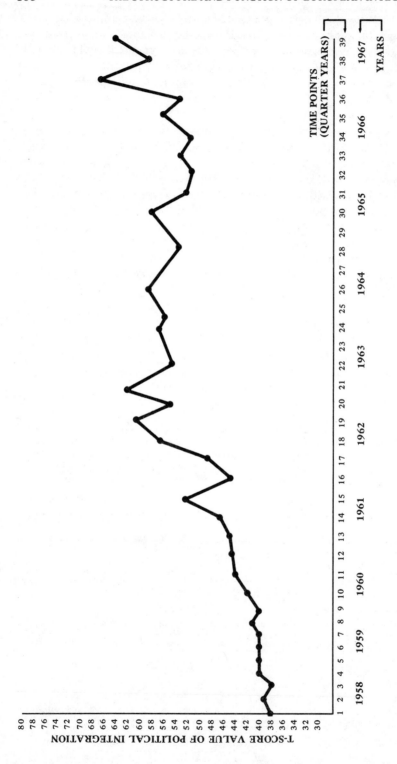

Fig. 5.3. Total political integration.

According to my hypothesis correlations between agricultural integration (functional and political) and political integration in other sectors should be higher than corresponding measures of association for transport. I employed three such measures of political integration in table 5.8. In only one case did the theory fail to predict the correct direction of differences between these co-efficients. This was for the second dimension of political integration (rule making) with functional integration in transport, the correlation for transport being .028 higher than that for agriculture. The fact that the predictions were in the correct direction, however, does not make the differences between the coefficients significant.

To assess whether these correlations differ significantly, we must utilize the formula for computing the difference between nonindependent correlations.[43] The evidence presented in table 5.9 (p. 107) is somewhat ambiguous. In three out of six cases the differences turned out to be significant. The direction of all except one of the paired correlations, however, was predicted correctly and two out of three of the nonsignificant differences ($t = 1.23$ and 1.4) came very close to being accepted. $t = 1.4$ is significant at the .10 level and $t = 1.23$ is significant at the .15 level.

To summarize the meaning of table 5.9, we note that the t's in the lower half of the table are generally higher than those in the upper half. This suggests that there is more dependence or permeability from the political to the political rather than from the functional to the political. In any case, the hypothesis appears to be confirmed that diffuse sectors are more likely to be associated with high spillover.

CONCLUSION

The evidence presented here indicates that Europe is characterized by a steady development of its political structures. In addition it seems reasonable to refer to the EEC as an emerging system if for no other reason than the fact that it possesses a set of structures whose activity is interdependent. In the next chapter I pursue the assessment of linkages within the EEC but from a slightly different perspective.

The primary purposes of this chapter were to translate integrative events in the EEC into the grammar of functional analysis in order to acquire access to its theoretical resources and to supply dimensions for the integrative process. The latter exercise was carried out with the intention of assessing to what extent empirical patterns of behavior conformed to the conceptual categories outlined by Almond and Powell in their discussion of conversion functions. An interesting question for the future hinges on whether distinct functions of adjudication and implementation will emerge. At this point they appear to be inseparably intermingled.

CHAPTER SIX

The Development of System Linkages in the European Community: A Quasi-Experimental Analysis

In previous chapters the patterns of political behavior in several functional areas within the European Community were explored. The purpose was not simply to describe but more specifically to sort observations into empirical categories that would hopefully be useful for theoretical analysis. The guiding metaphor I adopted was provided by structural-functional analysis. The operation of various structures in the EC, such as interest groups, the Council of Ministers, the Commission, and expert groups, were examined with an eye on the role they played in the operation of the larger system. This step was seen as necessary to any future comparative analysis as well as to any analysis of relationships within the Community itself.

To be tested now is the extent to which some of the linkages within the EC have developed. Despite the fact that we have observed an impressive growth on the part of many of the Community's structures, it is entirely possible that linkages among these structures are very weak. Some scholars have said exactly this. Altiero Spinelli has argued that despite its impressive growth in some respects, the European Community is in fact a loose conglomerate of many different power centers that hang together in a decentralized and poorly coordinated existence.[1] If this is true it may not be appropriate to speak of the Community as a system at all but rather as a set of separate systems that are bonded only by having been called into existence by the Treaty of Rome. In this chapter I test the question of the development of linkages among the component parts of the Community. Since a specified set of linkages are examined, this chapter should not be taken as a definitive statement on the existence of linkages in general.

Before testing the extent of these linkages I want to clarify the two dominant ways in which scholars have approached the concept of integration: as growth and as social coordination. On the one hand, integration has been used to refer to the process whereby structures and functions emerge and develop at a new level that is more comprehensive than the previous levels. Here the dominant focus seems to be that of growth without much attention to the ways in which these growing parts interrelate. This conceptual orientation is illustrated

111

by Deutsch's definition of integration,[2] Inglehart's focus on the growth of favorable attitudes toward European institutions,[3] by Bliss's focus on the political development of European institutions,[4] and by Lindberg's and Scheingold's emphasis on the growth of a decision-making capacity for European institutions.[5] In addition, Hughes and Schwarz, in clarifying their concept of political amalgamation, explicitly point out the similarities between this concept and notions of growth in performance capabilities of political systems appearing in the development literature.[6] There is some evidence to suggest that in both biological and social systems, performance capabilities tend to emerge first and are later followed by coordination facilities.[7] Although these two dimensions are by no means independent (e.g., a total lack of coordination may not allow the system to exist at all), it is my working hypothesis that emerging systems dedicate more of their energies to development in their early phases and worry about coordination problems later. In another chapter I argue that this is indeed a good strategy and that an emphasis on developing the Community's coordination and cohesion at an early date will probably foreclose the possibility to grow and branch out later.

The second use of the concept of integration has been to refer to the processes of social coordination. As Brickman has pointed out, theorists who have tended to work within the systems tradition have tended to view problems of coordination as important. He notes that since "the system perspective places stress on the internal relationships of the system, the problem of coordination of subsystems is patently a critical one."[8] Talcott Parsons adopts this perspective when he is led to ask how complex social systems whose component parts are highly specialized can avoid operating in ways that do not involve conflict among the parts of the systems. Parsons sees part of the problem's solution in the development of a specialized integrative subsystem, responsible for the scheduling and coordination of the component parts. The attention that Haas and others (e.g., Schmitter and Puchala)[9] have directed toward the concept of spillover also reflects an interest in particular kinds of intrasystem linkages as does Morton Kaplan's interest in integrative processes as "regulatory processes which join systems or organizations with separate institutions and goals within a common framework providing for the common pursuit of at least some goals and the common implementation of at least some policies."[10] Of course the specific mechanisms through which coordination is brought about are varied. Socialization processes are responsible for altering the attitudes and loyalties of members of the system in such a way as to bring them in line with values and norms of the collectivity and hopefully to dovetail individual motivations with the goals of the political system. Allocative processes attempt to distribute rewards in such a manner as to satisfy significant portions of the public and to command the legitimacy of as much of the public as possible. The distinctive aspect of these allocative processes is that they are backed up by a legitimate system of coercive sanctions. Exchange processes attempt to bind together diverse interests by establishing some exchange of valued things between them. Both allocative and exchange processes are distributive. They are distinct in that the former is supported by a system of sanctions. As a result, allocative processes tend to deal with public goods (i.e., those that are in varying degrees indivisible for a given population) while exchange processes deal with private goods.

SYSTEMS AND LINKAGES

In previous chapters I have outlined the notion of system and have given it an interpretation in structural-functional terms. For the purposes of this chapter it is sufficient to view a system as a set of elements (components) that to some extent interact with one another.

Interaction is only one of the ways in which a system may be bonded. Others include homogeneity of parts (e.g., morphological similarity), common loyalties of component parts to a third unit, the envelopment of several components by an additional structure, and the sharing of subparts by several units. In this chapter attention is confined to only one type of bond, namely interaction. Whatever we may say about the importance of the other linkages, it seems clear that interactions are crucial. Campbell sees the common fate of the system's parts as a crucial element in any empirical assessment of systemness.[11] If parts of a system are capable of thriving or dying without affecting other parts, we would not be inclined to treat these parts as being very cohesively related to one another. Similarly, Singer defines a system in terms of interdependence, as does James G. Miller:

> By a social system, then, I mean nothing more than an aggregation of human beings (plus their physical milieu) who are sufficiently interdependent to share a common fate (Campbell) or to have actions of some of them usually affecting the lives of many of them.[12]

The meanings of "system" are often confused. The most general, however, is: A system is a set of interacting units with relationships among them.[13] Other views of system retain the focus on interdependence but shift attention to a more cybernetic perspective, as in Buckley's definition of a system as a collection of "elements in mutual interrelations, which may be in a state of 'equilibrium', such that any moderate changes in the elements or their interrelations away from the equilibrium position are counter-balanced by changes tending to restore it."[14] The crucial point here is that the interactions that characterize the system are not strictly determined. There is some "system slack"[15] or in Miller's terms, a "zone of stability." Miller defines this zone as the "range within which the rate of corrections of deviations is minimal or zero, and beyond which correction occurs."[16] Up to a point, changes in the behavior of one part of the system may not call forth responses from other parts of the system. Once a certain threshold is passed, though, the operation of another variable is begun. If the operation of this variable works to restore the values of the other variables to their original position, the system is characterized by negative feedback mechanisms and static equilibrium. If a new equilibrium is established we say that the system is characterized by negative feedback and dynamic equilibrium. On the other hand, if the variables called into play operate to throw the other variables still further away from their goal state, we say the system is characterized by positive feedback and disequilibrium.

THE LOGIC OF EXPERIMENTATION

In this chapter an attempt is made to test the simplest of a class of linkages, those based on linear, single-bonded effects, the products of visible, short-range impacts. There is no focus on curvilinear effects, more complicated delayed effects, compensatory changes, and multiple-bonded relationships.[17] Since the causes and effects examined here are generally of short duration and since their interpretation is surrounded by many equivocalities, it is necessary that some ground rules be adopted. The ideal design for strong inference would be a true laboratory design where one has access to precise laboratory equipment and can randomly assign subjects to treatment and control groups. But, we are interested in real social situations where self-selection into groups occurs and where confident controls over potentially confounding variables are usually not possible. Similarly, when one is interested in social processes in which he has little or no control over either the independent variable or the context in which it occurs, there is little hope that unequivocal effects can be demonstrated through invoking verbal arguments. In a richly textured world where all variables are allowed to fluctuate simultaneously, there is little constraint on the conclusions that one can draw. In short, there is little place in research concerning ongoing social and political processes for the equipment and technology of the laboratory, its neat separation of subjects into experimental and control groups, its abrupt, incisive administration of the stimulus (independently of other similar administrations), and its precise recording of the response. We cannot voluntarily manipulate the independent variable and there is usually a substantial lapse of time between the occurrence of the event in which we are interested and its presumed effect. Finally, since we cannot achieve the closure (isolation) surrounding experimental tests, we are denied the experimenter's luxury of adopting strong assumptions concerning the disturbing influence of potentially confounding variables.

I suggest that the way to approximate the model of disciplined inference in research concerning nonlaboratory social processes is to adopt a quasi-experimental approach. The pages that follr · outline one type of quasi-experiment, the interrupted, time-series design.[18] I strongly urge the use of this design as an alternative to the ex post facto designs that utilize matching and partial correlation as control techniques. In matching one attempts to select observations so that they are as similar as possible on potentially confounding variables. This is central to the "most similar systems" design in comparative inquiry as elaborated by Przeworski and Teune and advocated by Naroll under a different label.[19] In partial correlation, one attempts to build the potentially confounding information into the design so that one can assess its impact. Campbell and Stanley have discussed the problems involved in creating regression effects when using matched groups, partial correlations, and analysis of covariance in the attempt to hold constant the operation of potentially confounding variables.[20]

Meehl has illustrated additional problems: (1) the systematic "unmatching" of subjects on variables codetermined by or simply related to the variables on which matching was carried out; (2) the creation of unrepresentative subpopulations attributable to the biased selection of matched pairs.[21] This of course eliminates our basis for generalizing to the original population. These criticisms, as well taken as they are, seem to make quasi-experimental designs, especially those based on regression-discontinuity logics, relatively more attractive. The "quasi" in quasi-experimental reflects the recognition that such designs are compromises between the laboratory ideal and the world as it is given. In quasi-experimental designs we are led to focus on a limited number of variables where variation is demonstrated and where relationships are probed to see how well they stand up to a list of plausible rival hypotheses.

DESIGN

Outlined here is one of a class of quasi-experimental designs assembled by Campbell and Stanley (1963), the interrupted time-series design (see diagram below). This design is appropriate to data distributed over time (I refer to such a distribution as a series) and where there is theoretical reason to believe that some event should cause a change in the behavior of the series. Stated in more precise terms, this design involves (1) the periodic measurements or observations on some variable at equally spaced points in time, (2) the occurrence of an event (quasi-experiment) somewhere into the series, and (3) the assumption that the event occurs midway between selected measurement points. Finally, this design involves a critical evaluation of results in light of those hypotheses which pose the severest threat to the hypothesized relationship.[22] This design may be diagrammed as follows:

$$x_1, x_2 \cdots x_m, \underset{\underset{\text{event 1}}{\uparrow}}{x_{m+1}}, x_{m+2} \cdots x_n, \underset{\underset{\text{event 2}}{\uparrow}}{x_{n+1}}, x_{n+2} \cdots$$

where x represents periodic observations on some variable over time and where events 1 and 2 represent two occurrences thought to have an effect on the behavior of the series.

The key question involved in this design is whether the occurrence of the events (experiments) in question had an effect on selected dependent variables or whether the behavior of the series after the events represents an undisturbed continuation of the series from its previous state. This is by no means a simple question and cannot be resolved by a simple visual inspection of plots of the data. Two questions are involved: One, did a nonrandom change occur in the vicinity of the experiment; two, is this change attributable to the occurrence of the experimental event? The resolution of the first question is the task of tests of significance used in conjunction with appropriate theoretical models. The second question is more a problem of the validity of interpretation. It thus involves untangling a variety of potentially operative causal factors and selectively eliminating those that are plausible but false.

Let us direct our attention to the first problem and see what a significant change might look like. Figure 6.1 illustrates a variety of possible patterns a series may assume. Suppose each of these lines represents the behavior of a dimension of integration over time. The vertical X represents the occurrence of some important event, such as the formation of the EEC, the acceptance of a landmark piece of legislation concerning agricultural policy, the elimination of tariffs, and so forth. If the EC is a system in the sense that it is composed of a set of coordinated social structures, then these events should have an impact on other variables. In figure 6.1, lines A, B, and C show no discernible effect, while lines D-G suggest that changes have occurred, though in different fashions. Let us look at these individually for a moment. Line A indicates no effect of X. It is true that the post-X values are higher than the pre-X values but the result is obtained by a simple extension of pre-X values and indicates no distinct effect of X. The line is said to contain a general (i.e., monotonic and in this case linear) trend, or increase over time. This kind of line is commonly at the basis of most positive growth systems. Line B represents a cyclic pattern where more or less regular crests and troughs are observed over fairly well-defined time intervals. Although it may appear that X had an effect here, it is clear that the post-X pattern again is predictable by an extension of the properties of the cycle before the occurrence of X. This interpretation becomes clearer once we have a fuller picture of the cycle. Suppose, however, that X occurred two observations earlier than it did in the figure, and suppose further that we only had information on a fragment of the cycle. The result is illustrated in figure 6.2 wherein line A is actually a temporal fragment of line B. If we observed only A it would appear that X forced an authentic change in the subsequent operation of A when in fact the increase in A is a function of the orderly continuation of the cycle.

The presence of a cycle is not always so clear-cut. It is not uncommon for several cycles to be present in the data simultaneously and to be nested in one another. Similarly, line C in figure 6.1 represents no true effect of X, although in this case this owes to random fluctuation in the variable, not to the presence of cycles. Random fluctuation becomes a threat to hypothesized interpretations when the behavior of a variable has a high standard deviation.

The other four patterns in figure 6.1 (D-G) represent true changes, although whether they owe to X is of course another matter. Line D represents the kind of change usually associated with static equilibrium. A disturbance variable causes a temporary shift in the behavior of the series after which the series returns to its normal (i.e., previous) behavior. Line E represents a dynamic equilibrium change where the introduction of X causes a change in the behavior of the series which becomes more or less permanently absorbed into the conduct of the series. The series reaches an equilibrium but it is at a new level. It is important to note that the form of the series does not change. Its slope has not changed but the level at which the series operates is higher. Line F, on the other hand, reflects a change in slope after X. That is, there is a change in the growth rate of the variable after X. Finally, line G represents both an intercept difference and slope change after X, indicating that the operation of the series is pushed up to a new level and, in addition, is characterized by a new growth function.

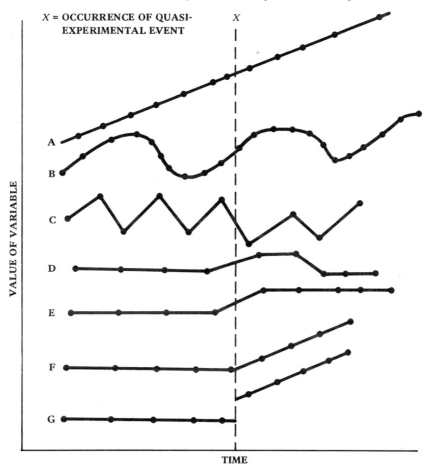

Fig. 6.1. Possible patterns of behavior of a time-series variable. SOURCE: Donald T. Campbell and Julian C. Stanley, *Experimental and Quasi-Experimental Designs for Research* (Chicago: Rand McNally, 1966), p. 38. It is reprinted with permission of the original publisher, the American Educational Association.

The discussion to now was concerned with the question "did a change occur?" Until a confident answer is given to this question there is no point in moving on to further analysis, which concerns itself with such questions as "what caused the change?" "what variables contributed?" "which are spuriously related?" and so on. The major substantive explanation of changes, when it is established that they have occurred, is the quasi-experimental variable in question. Since hypothesis testing is more than establishing positive associations but involves also creative attempts to falsify hypotheses through a careful exposure of the researcher's hypothesis to competing plausible interpretations, a checklist of trouble spots is useful. The following list is adapted from Campbell and Stanley with some modifications of my own.

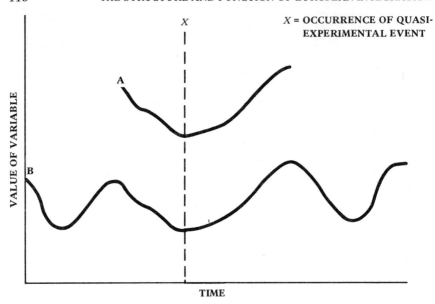

Fig. 6.2. Interpretation of a series based on fragmentary versus complete evidence.

PLAUSIBLE RIVAL HYPOTHESES

1. *Random instability.* A change found after a quasi-experimental event is attributable to random fluctuations in the data. Any distribution has a random error component in it owing to observational errors of a nonsystematic nature, sampling inaccuracies, and perhaps also, small, nonsystematic changes in the thing being studied. *Corrective:* Tests of significance are designed to inform us as to whether or not an observed value could have occurred by chance.

2. *Trends and other periodicities.* A periodicity is defined as any repeatable pattern in the series. A trend is defined as a special kind of periodicity, one characterized by an average increase or decrease, that is, a mean shift, in the behavior of the variable. Trends and periodicities are what Campbell means by "Maturation," that is, processes dependent upon the passage of time. *Corrective:* Solutions to the problem of trend (assuming that there is a theoretical basis for wanting to be rid of it) include trend-removal techniques,[23] adjustment in the interpretation of significance tests,[24] and corrections in the number of observations to take account of autocorrelation.[25]

3. *Other substantive variables (history).* These include all other events and/or processes that may appear coterminously with X or between X and its presumed effects, and which rival X as an explanation of the observed changes. *Corrective:* The only correctives here are good theory and imaginative use of control groups and matched groups. If, for example, dissolution of trade barriers is viewed as an alternative explanation of subsequent integration, one could select his units so that they were matched (i.e., similar) on trade barriers but different on the hypothesized variable.

4. *Scoring procedures.* It is possible that changes observed after X may be the result of changes in the way the variable is recorded after X, rather than to the effect of X itself. This is a prosaic matter but one that can greatly affect one's results. *Corrective:* If recording changes are made and one recognizes them, one can usually adjust for them (e.g., by adding or subtracting an appropriate constant).

5. *Irrelevant indicators.* While the change we observe may be a true change (i.e., nonrandom) and indeed it may be a response to X, it nevertheless may represent a response irrelevant to the concept with which we are dealing. For example, we may be interested in the impact of certain events on economic integration but our indicator (imports and exports) may be invalid indicators. We know that every indicator and index contains a good deal of variance that is independent of the concept in which we are interested. It may be that the change represents a response on the part of this component. *Corrective:* One can use a strategy of multiple operationism in which a variety of indicators are pooled to form a composite index. Hopefully this results in the cumulation of true concept variation and the canceling out of unwanted variance.

TESTS OF SIGNIFICANCE

It is presumably the function of tests of significance to estimate the probability that an observed point or distribution could have occurred by chance.

In our case we are specifically interested in whether some characteristic (e.g., the mean, the slope of a line, the value of a particular point, the value of an intercept of a line) of a distribution of points previous to a quasi-experimental event is significantly different from that characteristic in the distribution after the occurrence of the event. As has been pointed out,[26] however, there are some special problems in the application of tests of significance to time-series data. For example, a simple t-test assessing the difference between pre-X and post-X means would produce significant results if trend were represented in the series. Figure 6.3 illustrates this. The line from X to Y' probably has a mean significantly higher than the line from Y to X. This significance ignores the fact, however, that there is a general regression of both pre- and post-X distributions and that this regression obtains independently of the quasi-experimental event.[27] Techniques have been developed which first detrend the values in a series and then express "residualized" scores in terms of their departures from a general regression line. Presumably then, these residual scores could be utilized as the transformed data for appropriate tests of significance.

It is important to notice that we are not saying that there is no difference between the pre- and post-X distributions or that nothing has occurred to cause this difference. What we are saying is that the change in question is not peculiar to X but is a general property of the series. It must thus be explained by reference to the operation of more long-term, smoothly operating values. To put it another way, one must tie the language of inference and tests of significance to the underlying theoretical model.

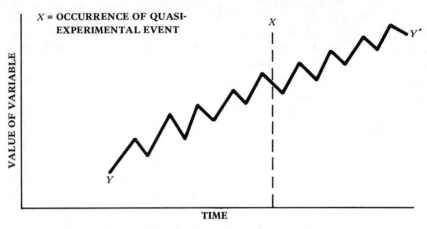

Fig. 6.3. Tests of significance where trend is involved.

Four tests of significance are utilized here and since the evaluation of the three quasi-experiments is based on an understanding of these tests they must be explained. Briefly, each of these tests is based on a calculation of the difference between expected and observed (or in the case of a double Mood, between expected and expected) values of points or distributions where expected values are based on some property of the regression line.

Single-Mood test. The single-Mood test is a *t*-test appropriate for assessment of the deviation of the first value after the occurrence of an event from a theoretical value predicted by an extrapolation from a linear fit of pre-X values. As pointed out elsewhere it is a simple line-fitting technique based on the least-squared criterion where the regression estimate of the pre-X data is used to predict the first observation after X.[28] This predicted value is then compared with the first observed value. The t statistic yields a value indicating the probability that the observed value could have occurred simply by extrapolating the line. The single-Mood test is suited for distributions of the type illustrated in figure 6.4.

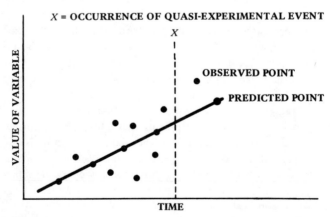

Fig. 6.4. Single-Mood test.

Double-Mood test. The double-Mood test simply extends the logic of the single-Mood test. It involves both a pre-X and a post-X linear fit and a comparison of the predictions by these two estimates of a hypothetical value lying midway between the last pre-X point and the first post-X point.[29] This test is appropriate primarily for the assessment of intercept differences.

Walker-Lev test 1. This statistic evaluates the hypothesis that a common slope fits both pre- and post-X data. This common slope condition may hold even if the occurrence of an event causes a change in the mean level at which the series operates, for example, a five-year plan may result in a shift in productivity to higher levels without affecting the rate of economic growth.

Walker-Lev test 3. This test yields an F statistic that tests the null hypothesis that a common regression line fits both pre- and post-X distributions. Separate regression estimates are calculated for both sets of data. These are subsequently compared to see if they could have been drawn from the same population.

EVALUATION OF THE QUASI-EXPERIMENTS: LIST OF DEPENDENT VARIABLES

Attention is now turned to the individual events of interest here. In all cases we are interested in whether the event had any effect on the subsequent operation of a selected set of system variables. Below is a list of these six variables and a brief explanation of each.[30] All the variables (with the exception of interest group formation) are expressed in T scores.[31]

1. *Interest group formation.* This variable represents the frequency of the establishment of associational interest groups at the European Community level. It includes all interest groups, agriculture, industry, specialized groups, and umbrella organizations, for the twenty-year period from 1950 to 1969.

Since this variable, and all others here, were coded quarterly, this yielded a total of eighty observations.

2. *Adjudication component.* This component of integration reflects the adjudicative activity of the European Court of Justice. It is a composite measure of three indicators of the Court's activities: communications of the Court; judgments of the Court; and new cases brought before the Court. These indicators were added on the basis of a factor analysis that indicated that they were all tapping the same dimension.

3. *Rule-making component.* This component represents the legislative capacity of the EC. It again is a composite measure of three indicators: parliamentary questions, Council regulations, and Commission regulations. All three of these indicators reflect the ability of the EC to formulate binding laws. Parliamentary questions are more tangentially involved but Council and Commission regulations are the core of this process. Council and Commission regulations have the status of Community laws, are binding in all respects, and are directly applicable to all member states. While their legal status is the same, Council regulations are more general in scope and concern the more political matters that face the member states.[32]

4. *Implementation component.* This component represents the administrative capacity of the Community institutions. Presumably it reflects the need to implement, enforce, and watch over the ever-growing body of Community law. It is a composite measure based on Commission directives and decisions.

5. *Trade exports.* This variable represents the total intra-Community exports for all classes of goods. It is based on a calculation of a ratio of intra-Community exports over total exports of Community members to outside countries.

6. *Trade imports.* This variable represents the total intra-Community imports for all classes of goods. It is based on a calculation of a ratio of intra-Community imports over total imports of Community members from outside countries.

Quasi-Experiment 1: Formation of the EEC

On January 1, 1958, the EEC came into existence. The Treaty of Rome set forth the goals of the EEC. These goals included not only the removal of internal tariffs and quotas and the establishment of a common external tariff but also the pursuit of common policies in a variety of areas, for example, agriculture, social affairs, and monetary affairs. The founding members of the EEC were interested not only in technical and economic cooperation but also in eventual political integration. Presumably the coming into effect of the Rome treaty was to set in motion the forces that ultimately were to lead to economic and political integration.

One of the ways of viewing integration is in terms of the expansiveness of the centers around which activity takes place and around which attitudes become organized. Thus one could ask to what degree key national interest groups have shifted their purposes, programs, targets, and tactics to a new, more comprehensive level. To what extent have national interest groups begun to make demands of regional political structures and to what extent have they come to see their fate as bound up with these structures? From this perspective, the formation of the EEC presents an interesting hypothesis: Did the establishment of the EEC act as a stimulus encouraging a shift in interest group activity to the European level? We can begin to answer this question by examining the pattern of interest group formation from 1950 to 1969.

Figure 6.5 presents a plot of the frequency of interest group formation from 1950 to 1969 with the data grouped at successive three-month intervals, or time points. From it, we can see that there is a marked rise of interest group activity in the vicinity of the formation of the EEC in 1958. This activity sustains itself for fourteen time points (three and one-half years) past the formation itself. This would seem to indicate not only that the formation of the EEC had an effect but that the effect was more than a momentary one. Before moving on to tests of significance it is important to notice one more important feature of this plot, besides the sharp increase in the formation activity after 1958, notably the sharp upswing during the last two quarters of 1957. It is a phenomenon that may recur and to which I referred earlier: the tendency (in cybernetic systems) for responses to occur before the official occurrence of the stimulus itself. That is, the response is in anticipation of an event.

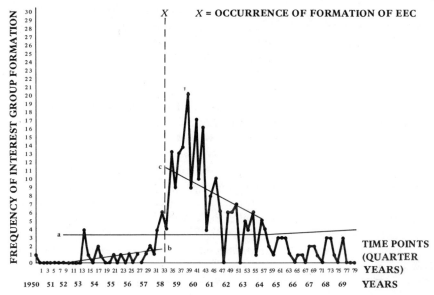

Fig. 6.5. Effect of formation of EEC on interest group formation in Western Europe. *a*, total (i.e., pre-*X* and post-*X*) regression line; *b*, pre-*X* regression line; *c*, post-*X* regression line.

Table 6.1 shows the results of the four tests of significance and attests to the validity of the visual interpretation.

TABLE 6.1

QUASI-EXPERIMENT 1: FORMATION OF EEC

Variable	Pre-[a] N	Post-[a] N	*t*-value Single Mood	*t*-value Double Mood	Significance Level[b] Single Mood	Significance Level[b] Double Mood	Significance Level[b] Adjusted Double[c] Mood	Lag 1 Auto-correlated Error[d]
Interest group formation	32	52	1.47	7.46	yes (.10)	yes (.001)	yes (.01)	.11

[a]Pre-N and post-N refer to the number of observations occurring before and after the event, namely, the formation of the EEC.

[b]Significance levels are reported for one-tailed tests for values lying between .001 and .10. Values above .10 are not taken to be statistically significant.

[c]This refers to the interpretation of the double-Mood test corrected for the amount of autocorrelated error in the distribution.

[d]Autocorrelated error is reported here for the two segment, separate pre-test, post-test, detrended series. That is, we are interested here in the autocorrelation of observations after the regression lines for the pre-N and post-N groups have been separately removed.

SOURCE: The tables on which the adjusted double Mood were made are provided in Joyce Sween and Donald T. Campbell, "The Interrupted Time Series Quasi-Experiment: Three Tests of Significance," Northwestern University (August 1965), mimeo.

The single-Mood test yields a value of 1.47 which is significant at the .10 level. This indicates that the frequency of interest group formation in the first quarter of 1958 could not have been expected on the basis of random fluctuations in the series. The double-Mood value is much larger (7.46) and is significant at the .001 level. This gives us confidence that the establishment of the EEC actually had an impact on interest group activity and indeed this view agrees with the conventional wisdom of a number of European observers. Lindberg points out that by late 1961 there were 222 economic interest groups organized at the European level, of which all but a few had been created since 1958.[33] Similarly the *Bulletin der Europäischen Wirtschaftsgemeinschaft* noted as early as 1961: "The emergence of a European consciousness in the different branches of the economy and in the growing interdependence of the markets of the six countries is especially obvious in the great number of occupational associations in industry, agriculture, trade, handicrafts and the free professions which have been established since the ratification of the Treaty of Rome."[34]

Now let us see if we can move beyond the test of significance and assess how well these results stand up to rival interpretations. One possibility is that a general trend in the series is responsible for the increase in interest group activity after formation. This interpretation is not plausible in that there is a general absence of group activity before 1958, with the exception of the last months of 1957. Since negotiations concerning the establishment of the EEC were going on since 1955 it is not surprising that many interest groups were adapting to the new situation even before it formally materialized. In addition, the plausible hypothesis of trend is neutralized since, even controlling for it in the interpretation of the double-Mood *t*-value, the results are still significant. The other rival hypotheses are more difficult to cope with. History, or the occurrence of other events than the establishment of the EEC, does not seem a serious threat since it is difficult to suggest other important events occurring at that time which reasonably could have had an effect. Scoring procedures also present no problem since the data were collected in one standard reference,[35] and since there were no visible recording changes in the period under consideration. Finally, the rival hypothesis that interest group activity is a poor indicator of political integration is difficult to treat systematically here since we do not have additional indicators occurring far enough before 1958 to submit them to test. Thus the kind of multiple operationism that can increase our confidence in an indicator will have to wait until additional indicators of interest group activity are available.

We should also note that in addition to the formation of the EEC having an impact on the level of subsequent interest group activity, it also seems to have introduced a change in the growth rate in that activity. In this regard we are particularly interested in whether there is a significant difference between the slope of the regression line before and after the establishment of the EEC. Walker-Lev test 1, which tests the null hypothesis that a common slope is suited to pre-n and post-n distributions, is extremely significant, yielding an F-value of 32.67 with 80 degrees of freedom. Also Walker-Lev test 3, which tests the null hypothesis that a common regression line fits both distributions, yields a value of 72.27 with 81 degrees of freedom. Both of these are significant at the .01 level. This is convincing evidence that both the level at which interest group formation occurred and its rate of growth are significantly different after the establishment of the EEC.

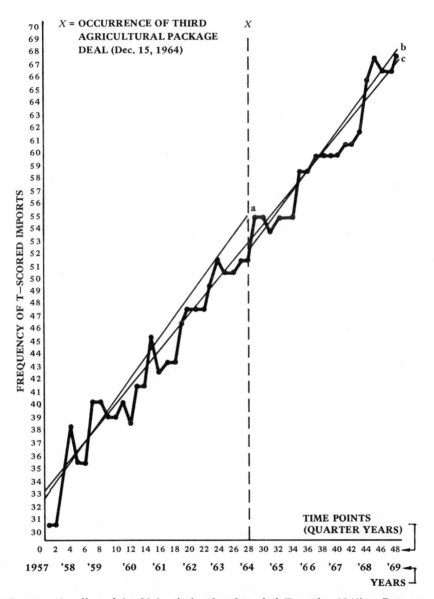

Fig. 6.6a. The effect of the third agricultural package deal (December 1964) on European import integration. *a*, pre-X regression line; *b*, post-X regression line; *c*, total (i.e., pre-X and post-X) regression line.

Quasi-Experiment 2: The Third Agricultural Package Deal,
December 15, 1964

The adoption of the Commission proposals by the Council of Ministers on December 15, 1964, was the third installment in the formulation and implementation of the common agricultural policy. The regulations adopted climaxed the end of a long marathon session in which the question occupying center stage was that of a common price level for Community cereals. After tendering several unsuccessful proposals the Commission submitted a package to the Council at 5 A.M. Sunday morning.[36] The basic points of agreement in this proposal were the following: (1) an agreement on the Community price for nondurum wheat (425 Deutsches Marks per metric ton); (2) West Germany agreed to the ceiling suggested by the Commission for compensation as well as the principle of regressive graduations in compensation; and (3) all agreed to make July 1, 1967, the date for the entry into force of the common price.[37] The importance of this decision for Germany was outlined in a speech by Ludwig Erhard to the Bundestag on December 2, 1964: "The grain price has become the key to further progress in European integration . . . I know that this step poses grave problems for German agriculture. We take this road with the intention of achieving a breakthrough for Europe, and of making a further important contribution towards the consolidation of Franco-German relations."[38]

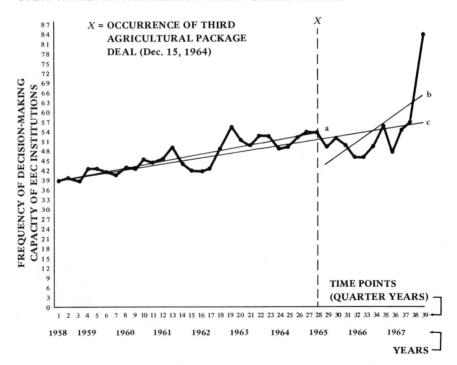

Fig. 6.6b. The effect of the third agricultural package deal (December 1964) on the decision-making capacity of European institutions. *a*, pre-*X* regression line; *b*, post-*X* regression line; *c*, total (i.e., pre-*X* and post-*X*) regression line.

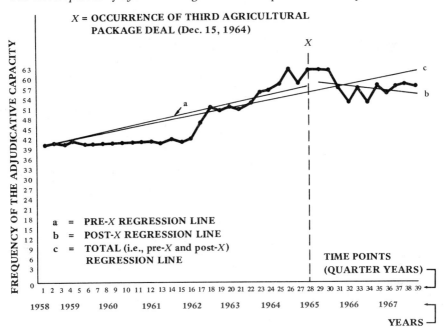

Fig. 6.6c. The effect of the third agricultural package deal (December 1964) on the adjudicative capacity of European institutions. *a*, pre-*X* regression line; *b*, post-*X* regression line; *c*, total (i.e., pre-*X* and post-*X*) regression line.

But the importance of these decisions was not limited to Germany. From July 1, 1967, the date when the common price was to come into effect, the matter of price policy was to be out of the hands of the separate national administrations. What if any effect did these decisions have on a variety of variables representing economic and political integration? First, let us examine plots of three dependent variables as shown in figures 6.6*a*, 6.6*b*, and 6.6*c*. The visual interpretation of these plots reveals several things. First of all the import variable (fig. 6.6*a*, p. 125) is dominated by a strong upward growth trend. There are of course fluctuations around the trend line but, for the most part, they do not appear significant. The decision-making component (fig. 6.6*b*) and the adjudication component (fig. 6.6*c*) also show an upward growth although the slopes of these two lines are neither as steep nor as smooth as the line for exports. Also, for both of the latter variables, there appears to be a small drop in the level of activity after December 15, 1964. Whether this drop is significant or not is another question that is answered later.

Table 6.2 presents the results of the tests of significance for the five variables. None of the variables was significant on the single-Mood test. All of the variables with the exception of the adjudication component were significant on the double-Mood test. All of these values held up when they were corrected for autocorrelation.

TABLE 6.2
QUASI-EXPERIMENT 2: THIRD AGRICULTURAL PACKAGE

Variable	Pre-N	Post-N	t-value		Significance Level			F-value		Significance		Lag 1
			Single Mood	Double Mood	Single Mood	Double Mood	Adjusted Double Mood	Walker-Lev Test 1	Walker-Lev Test 3	Test 1	Test 3	Auto-correlated error
t-scored imports	28	20	1.24	4.08	no	.001	.001	48.63	19.05	.05[a]	.05[a]	.40
Implementation	28	11	1.26	2.53	no	.01	.01	.15	12.30	no	.05	.19
Decision making	28	11	1.66	3.02	no	.01	.01	8.77	1.97	.05	no	.33
Adjudication	28	11	1.00	.13	no	no	no	13.34	5.05	.05	.05	.73
Interest group formation	60	24	1.02	3.04	no	.005	.01	3.25	25.54	no	.05	.60

[a]The tables on which these F-values were checked for significance are calculated to yield critical values at the .05 level. These values are large enough to be significant at a much higher level of confidence.

TABLE 6.3
QUASI-EXPERIMENT 3: THE AGRICULTURAL CRISIS

Variable	Pre-N	Post-N	t-value		Significance Level			F-value		Significance[b]		Lag 1
			Single Mood	Double Mood	Single Mood	Double Mood	Adjusted Double Mood	Walker-Lev Test 1	Walker-Lev Test 3	Test 2	Test 3	Auto-correlated error
t-scored imports	30	18	.88	2.24	no	.025	.05	.57	4.53	no	.05	.18
t-scored exports	30	18	3.16	5.24	.005	.001	.01	24.61	40.56	.05	.05	.51
Implementation	30	9	1.55	2.27	.10	.025	.05	.08	8.35	no	.05	.31
Decision making	30	9	1.39	3.69	.10	.001	.01	17.78	.83	.05	no	.08
Adjudication	30	9	1.31	2.77	no	.005	.05	1.84	25.21	no	.05	.72

[a]The tables for the adjusted double-Mood are based on critical values for .01 and .05.
[b]F-values assessed for significance on tables where only the .05 level of significance is given. See Hubert M. Blalock. Social Statistics (New York: McGraw-Hill Book Co., 1960).

The interpretation of the *F*-values presents a different picture and presents strong evidence against the hypothesis that adoption of the agriculture package had a strong, positive effect. The slope change after December 1964 was significant in three out of the five cases but in the wrong direction. In all three cases—imports, adjudication, and decision making—there was actually a decline, and a significant one at that, in the subsequent rate of growth. Of course there are strong rival explanations as to why this occurred. One possible explanation is that the institutional system of the Community had reached a kind of saturation point and found it difficult to keep up the old rate of growth. Countervailing pressures and dampening effects normally come into operation to act as checks on almost all growth systems sooner or later. Boulding has pointed out that many social and economic variables are of the ogive form, displaying little or no growth in the early stages, then showing strong spurts and sustained periods of sharp growth, and finally leveling off and perhaps even declining.[39] This is a good characterization of many of our variables but particularly the political ones. Another possible interpretation however, is that it was not December 1964 but June 30, 1965, that precipitated the decline. The events of June 30 of course initiated the agricultural crisis in the EEC and it is plausible that the effects of December 1964 and June 1965 are so commingled as to make an independent assessment of their effects impossible. In any case I think we can conclude with some confidence that the adoption of these decisions did not produce a sustained positive effect.

Quasi-Experiment 3: Onset of the Agricultural Crisis of June 1965

The agricultural crisis of 1965, which lasted for more than six months, was the most severe test for the European Economic Community up until that time. The immediate cause of the crisis concerned some rather technical details related to the financing of the common agricultural policy. The underlying causes, however, had to do with the proposals of the European Commission that the European Parliament be given increased powers and that the Commission be supplied with an independent source of revenue so as not to be tied to the individual states. Additional factors may also have played an important part, for example, the impending majority voting, which was to come into effect by the first of the year, and the emerging role of the Commission as a diplomatic actor.

The crisis involved the walkout of Couve de Murville, then the French representative in the Council of Ministers, as well as of other representatives of Community institutions where member states are directly represented. They did not return until the end of January 1966, when after two sets of meetings an agreement to disagree was adopted, and the French representatives returned. During this time the five remaining states attempted to conduct the routine business as best they could. Most observers agree that the crisis was both a symptom and a cause of a decline in European integration. This assumes of course that there was a measurable decline in the first place. Our task here is to assess how deeply the crisis affected Community behavior on a number of variables.

Figures 6.7*a* and 6.7*b* plot the imports and exports. The plots indicate that both series (imports and exports) are dominated by a positive trend component. Each plot seems fairly smooth and is characterized by a strong upward movement. The autocorrelation coefficients, which are measures of serial dependence in the data, are .99 for imports and .98 for exports. In addition, there is no noticeable visual effect for imports in the general region of the onset of the crisis. In the case of exports among Community members, however, something seems to have occurred. There is a drop-off in the region of crisis from 56.24 to 54.44 (these data are measures in *T* scores as discussed previously), then back up to 56.00 and to 58.00. Then there comes a more sustained decrease where it takes two and one-quarter years to get back up to the 58.00 level.

As the visual interpretation suggests the single-Mood *t*-value for imports is only .88 (table 6.3), which is not significant. The *t*-value for exports, however, was 3.16, which is significant at the .005 level. The double-Mood values for imports and exports (2.24 and 5.24, respectively) were significant at the .025 and .001 levels, respectively.

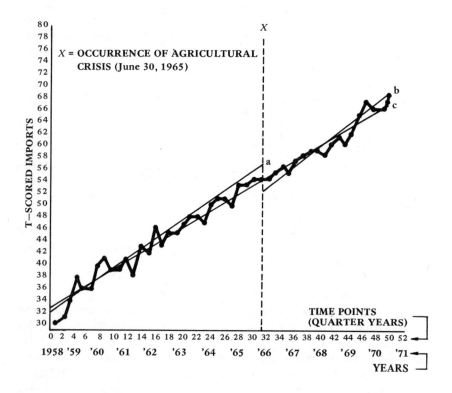

Fig. 6.7*a*. The effect of the agricultural crisis (June 1965 to February 1966) on European import integration. *a*, pre-*X* regression line; *b*, post-*X* regression line; *c*, total (i.e., pre-*X* and post-*X*) regression line.

The slopes for imports and exports also provide some interesting information. The slope of the import distribution actually increases from .750 to .802
for the post-*X* observations. Although this is counter to the direction we would
hypothesize it is not enough of a change to be significant (the Walker-Lev value
for test 1 is .57). On the other hand, there is substantial decrease in the slope for
the export data, from .996 for the pre-*X* observations to .531 for the post-*X*
observations. Also it is clear from an inspection of the post-*X* part of the plot
that the slowest part of this growth occurs in the first nine to ten time points
(two and a quarter to two and a half years). After the tenth point the growth
rate appears to pick up considerably. The *F*-value for test 1 is 24.61 which is
well above the significance level. Similarly, the *F*-values for Walker-Lev test 3 are
4.53 and 40.56, both significant at the .05 level.

Also, these results are not substantially affected by the presence of trend
in the data. The autocorrelation of .18 does reduce the significance of the
double-Mood for imports from .025 to .05 while the autocorrelation of .51 for
exports reduces the confidence level from .001 to .01. Although the size of these
reductions is substantial the important feature is that the results still lie well
within the zone of significance.

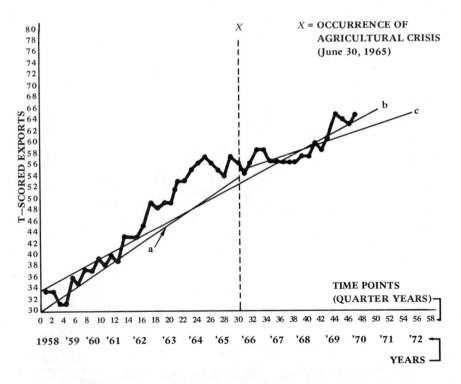

Fig. 6.7*b*. The effect of the agricultural crisis (June 1965 to February 1966) on European
export integration. *a*, pre-*X* regression line; *b*, post-*X* regression line; *c*, total (i.e., pre-*X* and
post-*X*) regression line.

Figures 6.8*a,* 6.8*b,* and 6.8*c* show the effect of the crisis on the three political variables—political implementation, decision making, and adjudication. The plots again suggest visually that there is something operating on the system in the region of June 30, 1965. All three variables drop off in the time periods after June 30. The implementation variable dropped from 52 to 50, 51, 51, 50; the decision-making component from 54 to 52, 48, 48, and 52; and the adjudication variable from 61 to 56, 52, 56, and 52. These changes, while perhaps not dramatic, are substantial and, what is more important, they are consistent. This lends strong support to the hypothesized interpretation by rendering implausible the rival explanation of indicator eccentricity. Here is visible convincing evidence of convergence in the results of three indicators of political integration. Still, however, the impressions are visual. What are the results of tests of significance? In table 6.3 the results of the single-Mood test are again extremely consistent: 1.55, 1.39, and 1.31 for implementation, decision making, and adjudication, respectively. The first two of these are significant at the .10 level while the adjudication values are not quite large enough to qualify. In light of the fact that the largest drop-off occurs in the adjudication variable this may seem surprising. It should be borne in mind, however, that it is not the departure from the last observed, pre-*X* value in which we are interested but the departure of the first post-*X* value from the extrapolated pre-*X* regression line.

The results of the double-Mood test present much the same interpretation. These values are 2.27, 3.69, and 2.77 for implementation, decision making, and adjudication, respectively. These values are all significant at the stated levels. Again, if we consider how widely these double-Mood values can fluctuate, it is remarkable how closely the results come out.

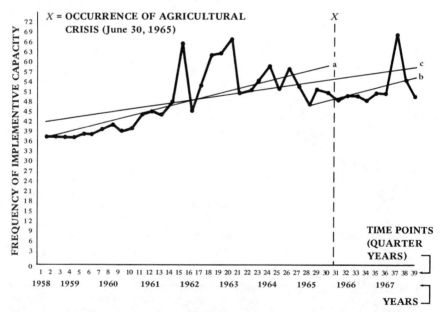

Fig. 6.8a. The effect of the agricultural crisis (June 1965 to February 1966) on implementive integration. *a,* pre-*X* regression line; *b,* post-*X* regression line; *c,* total (i.e., pre-*X* and post-*X*) regression line.

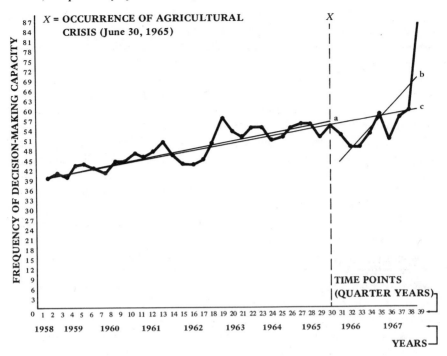

Fig. 6.8*b*. The effect of the agricultural crisis (June 1965 to February 1966) on decision-making integration. *a*, pre-*X* regression line; *b*, post-*X* regression line; *c*, total (i.e., pre-*X* and post-*X*) regression line.

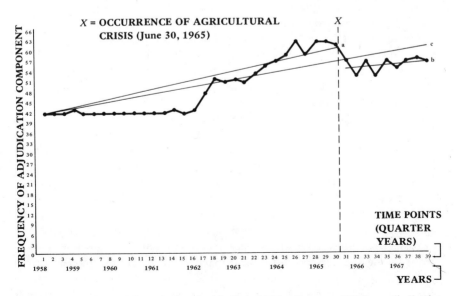

Fig. 6.8*c*. The effect of the agricultural crisis (June 1965 to February 1966) on adjudicative integration. *a*, pre-*X* regression line; *b*, post-*X* regression line; *c*, total (i.e., pre-*X* and post-*X*) regression line.

What do the slopes of the lines show after the crisis? The key question here is whether or not the crisis had any effect in slowing down the rate of growth of a variety of Community variables. Consider export integration first. The F-value for Walker-Lev test 1 is 24.61, indicating there is a marked shift in the slope for the postcrisis observations. The slope of the line after the crisis is .531 compared with .996 before the crisis. It is important to interpret these results in conjunction with a visual inspection of the plot (fig. 6.7b). We see that there is a very low growth rate for the first nine observation points following the crisis, that is to say, for approximately two and a quarter years after the crisis the Community showed no appreciable increase in the rate of export integration. If one considers that the first seven and a half years reflect a period of nearly undisturbed growth this flattening out of export integration appears all the more remarkable. The fact that the slope after the crisis is as high as it is reflects the extremely sharp increase in export trade in the last quarter of 1967, an increase that is sustained in the remainder of our data, right up to the end of 1969. One interpretation is that by this time the crisis had worn off and the Community became susceptible to new influences. The merging of the Community institutions on July 1, 1967, may have been a factor in this increased integration or the impending completion of the customs union in July of 1968 may similarly have had a triggering effect.

Confidence in the effect of the crisis on economic integration would be increased if the crisis brought about significant changes in other economic indicators. Unfortunately there is no significant slope difference for the postcrisis observations on the import indicator. In fact, although the F-value for test 1 is a nonsignificant .57, the slope after the crisis is actually higher (.802) than before the crisis (.750).[40] However, Walker-Lev test 3, the test of the null hypothesis that one regression line fits both pre- and post-change data, is significant. We can see from the two regression lines that although the slopes are nearly identical (figs. 6.7a and 6.7b), the intercept of the postchange distribution is lower than that for the prechange distribution.

The results for the Walker-Lev tests for the three political integration variables (implementation, decision making, and adjudication) present an even more difficult problem for interpretation. Table 6.3 shows that there is a significant slope change only for the decision-making variable and that the sign of this change is not in the predicted direction. That is, there is an increase in the slope from .548 for the pre-X group to 3.083 for the post-X group. Again, we must stress that it is crucial to interpret these tests in light of the plot of the variable itself (see fig. 6.8b). Notice that there is a decline and then a lull in the decision-making capacity of the Community for four time points (one year) after June 1965. The values drop from 54 for the last value prior to the crisis to 52, 48, 48, and 52. After this lull the Community seems to become reinvigorated and surpasses its former levels of activity. The important feature is this. The increased slope after the crisis is to a large extent a function of the low values from which the postchange distribution starts out. The gradual attenuation of the effects of the crisis and the consequent normal resumption of the system's growth pattern, makes the slope that much steeper. To put it more concisely, and at the same time more generally: if the intercept is not the same or higher for the postchange regression line, it is difficult and probably fallacious to interpret a higher post-X slope as evidence of a true, positive effect of some event.

The slope tests for the implementation and adjudication variables, while not statistically significant, are nevertheless in need of further interpretation. Again, although there is very little difference between pre-X and post-X slopes (.746 and .983, respectively), it should be observed that for a year and a half after the crisis occurred the Community in its administrative capacity operated at a very low level (fig. 6.8a). To some extent this trend may have been under way before the crisis occurred. In any case the slope value is as high as it is only because of these initially low values. Finally, the adjudication variable shows a sharp drop after the crisis (fig. 6.8c) but again picks up slightly as time goes on. The slope actually does decrease from .830 for the precrisis series to .283 for the postcrisis series. But this decrease is not significant. It is interesting to see (table 6.3) that the F-value for Walker-Lev test 3 is 25.21, a value that is significant well beyond the .05 level. The reason for this high value is evident if we note that the intercept in the postchange group is well below that for the prechange group. A similar interpretation could be made for the significance of test 3 on the implementation variable. The intercept for the postcrisis group is substantially below that of the precrisis series.

The results of the F tests can be summarized in two ways. First, significant results were obtained in six out of ten cases and in several cases these results were fairly dramatic. Second, we can say with some confidence that it seems to be much more difficult for an event to force a change in the subsequent slope of a series as opposed to a change in intercept. In terms of substantive theory, this is equivalent to saying that the occurrences of events in the EC have impacts that are generally short-term and limited to affecting the *level* of *intensity* at which a variable operates, rather than long-term and influencing the rate of growth of these variables. To put the matter still a different way, changes occurring in the EC seem to affect other variables but are then absorbed by them. They do not seem to have an effect that is cumulative and self-sustaining. In short, while the level of growth and system activity is affected, its growth rate generally is not. Velocity may be easier to alter than acceleration.

For those cases where the plausible rival hypothesis of random instability has been eliminated (that is, those results that are statistically significant) let us inquire further to see how well they stand up to additional threats to validity. The presence of autocorrelation does not affect any of the t- or F-values to such an extent as to make any of them insignificant. In all cases the probability level for the double-Mood values is decreased: imports (from .025 to .05), exports (from .001 to .01), implementation (from .025 to .05), decision making (from .001 to .01), and adjudication (from .005 to .05). The effect of this adjustment for autocorrelation, however, is not to push these values outside the acceptable significance levels. In addition, there do not seem to be any serious *substantive* explanations that compete with the crisis as an explanation of the changes in the vicinity of 1965-66. One possibility, raised peripherally by Miriam Camps in 1966, is that both the crisis and the stagnation of European integration from

1965 to 1968 were the result of the unresolved differences between the French and the other five member states over the form and desirability of political integration. The French advocated a loose, confederal scheme along the lines suggested by the Fouchet negotiations whereas the five had something more supranational in mind. The reason that the year 1965 was so significant is that by this time the Community had gone a long way toward completing what has been called negative integration.[41] In other words, the Community had been mostly occupied with removing tariffs and internal barriers to the flow of goods and services. In addition, much of the activity occurring during this period was essentially implementive in nature and involved merely the administration of steps that were already carefully defined by the Treaty of Rome. Finally, by 1965 the key decisions had been taken toward the establishment of the common agricultural policy, for example, the financing of the policy, the key aspects of the controversy relating to the uniform price system and to the market organizations, had been resolved by late December 1964. Although much remained to be done, for example, in monetary matters, transport, social affairs, the Community had run out of steam in those areas in which there was basic agreement at the time the Rome treaty was signed. Therefore, as Camps observes, by 1965 the EEC had reached a watershed in which it was forced to tackle more controversial issues, issues whose resolution had uncertain political effects. The French were very reluctant to become involved in the formulation of economic policies which might involve political integration.

While this interpretation of the crisis is convincing it does not really affect the validity of the interpretation that the crisis had an influence on subsequent Community integration. It merely puts these events in a proper developmental sequence, that is, from political disagreement to crisis to Community disintegration. A rigorous test of this is beyond the scope of this book. Essentially it would require holding constant or "partialling out" the effects of the crisis. If the postcrisis disintegration (or lull in integration) still obtained, the conclusion might be that these underlying political disagreements caused the crisis and disintegration.

Finally, a word should be said about the rival hypothesis of irrelevant indicators. Community regulations, decisions, directives, and a variety of additional, official Community acts have been used essentially to indicate the level of decision making in the EC. A convincing argument is offered that although the EC kept up the pace of its activity its style after the crisis was considerably more timid and its autonomy considerably more restricted. In place of the previously bold Commission initiatives is now substituted a petty bargaining mentality (un esprit du marchandage) and a shift in the locus of power to the Committee of Permanent Representatives, the delegate body of the nationally oriented Council of Ministers.[42] If we were to take this argument seriously, and I think it merits serious consideration, it would add confidence to the interpretation that the crisis did have a serious impact on the level and development of subsequent integration. It would indicate that the indicators at work here are not as sensitive as they might be. We would thus be in the position of confirming through use of the "hard case." The argument could then be made that confirmation could be more dramatically made through indicators that got at the autonomy and forcefulness of the Commission in the decision-making process.

ASSESSMENT OF THE MODEL AND REFORMULATION

The original model on which this analysis was carried out was based on the assumption of nonindependent, temporal observations. In the model, change was assessed by using the criterion of series discontinuity in the region or after the region in which an important event occurred. A true change in this model is reflected in some value (or values) of a variable that depart significantly from an actual or projected regression line. It should be emphasized that the model makes no assumptions about the time required for the event to register an effect or for the relative weight of impact of an event on the beginning, end, or any other point in the series. It is assumed that once the event registers its effects, its impact is felt uniformly throughout the series. There is thus no provision in the model for wearing-off effects or for the gradual erosion of an event's impact over time.[43] There is, in addition, no provision for curvilinear effects or for other complex functional relationships. An evaluation of the results of the analysis and a suggestion as to how their interpretation stimulates a reformulation of the model follow.

The first conclusion to draw is that, on the basis of the limited analysis, the European Community appears to be a moderately well-integrated system. There is, over a fairly broad, nontrivial range of indicators, a reasonably well-developed set of linkages. These results are seen as partly superseding those presented elsewhere.[44] To summarize the results: most of the dependent variables examined reacted (i.e., were sensitive) to the three events: the formation of the EEC; the agricultural package deal of 1964; and the agricultural crisis of 1965-66. There were, however, significant variations in these patterns of response. The single-Mood statistic was significant in four out of eleven cases and the test for common slope (F test 1) in only five out of ten cases. By contrast the double-Mood and test for the null hypothesis of a common regression line (F test 3) were significant in ten out of eleven and eight out of ten cases, respectively. What this means in substantive terms is that in most cases the occurrence of an important event had no immediate effect and in only half the cases was there a significant change in the form of the relationship. Yet, there is overwhelming evidence to suggest that pre-X and post-X distributions are significantly different. The double-Mood test and Walker-Lev test 3, both of which are based on comparisons of regression lines, provide strong, convergent evidence for this.

One reason why the test for slope significance failed to be significant more often may become clear once we recognize the typical response of a variable to the occurrence of an event. Take the case of the effect of the agricultural crisis on decision making in the European Community (see fig. 6.8b). After the crisis there is a marked decrease that lasts for approximately one year. After that time the Community seems to resume its course. Consider for a moment the effect of this type of behavior on the interpretation of the slope test. The predicted direction of the slope change is of course negative, that is, the rate of growth of decision making is expected to be less after the crisis. As a matter of fact, the slope is steeper as can be seen by examining the regression lines drawn in figure 6.8b. My interpretation of this is straightforward. The crisis did have a predicted (negative) effect, but it was not a permanent one. If one examines the slope for the first four or five time points after the crisis, one does find a negative slope. The effect of the crisis seems to have lasted for about one year after which time the Community resumed its normal, decisional growth pattern. By normal I mean normal with respect to an altered base line. Thus it is assumed that the crisis was permanently absorbed into the operation of the decision-making variable in the form of a lower level or frequency of operation even though the negative growth rate seems to have completely eroded after one year.

An Alternative Model

The utilization of a theoretical model has several advantages. Setting forth theoretical expectations provides a set of baselines useful in interpreting interesting substantive results. Second, by establishing (before data analysis) a fairly simple and explicit set of functions to which the data should conform, some restraint is placed on opportunistic and ad hoc curve fitting. Third, and most important here, by announcing what the expectations of the model are, we have clear standards in terms of which to assess unexpected results. These unexpected results are responsible for announcing defects and inadequacies in the original model thereby making reformulations and improvements possible.

The general properties of the reformulated model would have to include at a minimum: (1) no specification of immediate effect after an event, allowing for the joint possibilities of delayed effects or anticipated effects; and (2) a temporary effect, lasting typically one or two years and then eroding, possibly by becoming extinguished or possibly by being absorbed by the system.

These kinds of expectations are paralleled very closely (though in a much more formalized fashion) by a type of stochastic model formulated by Box and Tiao[45] and labeled the "integrated moving average process." The core of this model is that of a system (or variable) subjected to periodic random shocks, a proportion of which are absorbed into the level of the series.[46] An additional property of the model is that the further one moves away from the event the less the behavior of the distribution is a function of the event.[47]

In terms of substantive theory, this process most closely resembles something lying about midway between what Boulding calls the equilibrium and cumulative processes.[48] This process is one in which a disturbance variable forces an adjustment by the system after which equilibrium is restored. The equilibrium, however, is at a new position, having incorporated a trace of the disturbance into its permanent behavior.

A final word may be said about integration in Europe, as growth and as coordination. All the variables examined, with the exception of interest group formation, are increasing and have been increasing for the past ten years. Thus the European Community could be conceptualized as a positive growth system, displaying impressive increases across a broad range of variables. But the coordination of these components, as measured by the sensitivity of selected system variables, is somewhat less impressive, though by no means negative. Nevertheless, the assessment at this point is that the growth component is the dominant one. This should not be cause for disappointment. As mentioned, it is good strategy for a young system to avoid excessive centralization and coordination since there is likely to be tension between growth and coordination. Growth rests on a niche-filling strategy, an ability to probe and respond to the demands of a changing environment. It thus requires a large measure of freedom to stumble, to find and exploit the proper opportunities. Seen from this perspective, the loose haphazard way in which Community structures sometimes interrelate is one of its strongest features.

CHAPTER SEVEN

The External Relations of the European Community

The traditional view of international relations as the interaction of foreign policies among cohesive, neatly contained nation-states has given way to a more complicated picture where a plurality of units, some subnational, others regional and global, mingle in a common environment.[1] In the eighteenth and nineteenth centuries nation-states interacted with one another through fairly regularized, official channels. Diplomats, more or less carefully instructed, met one another as gladiators in the interstate arena. For a variety of reasons, including the lack of well-developed communications and transportation systems and the low level of social mobilization, it was impossible for other groups to engage in the interstate diplomatic process.

The picture today is quite different. The process of social mobilization which has involved more and more groups in the political process has hacked away at the underpinnings of the nation-state, loosening up and making porous its once nearly hermetic boundaries. Rosenau points out how the United States plays a part in the determination of the defense budget of the Federal Republic of Germany each year. Jean Monnet, often called the father of European integration, frequently flew to Washington after World War II and had a large voice in one of the major postwar policies of the United States, European recovery. Al-Fatah, an Arab guerilla organization, resembles a state within a state and negotiates with foreign powers in ways similar to nation-states. The Viet Cong sit at the Paris negotiations even though they are not formally a state. Local governmental units in Berkeley, California, discuss the possibility of negotiating a peace treaty with North Vietnam, and rich oil men from Texas attempt to arrange for the release of American prisoners of war in North Vietnam. The emergence of the multinational corporation further erodes the usefulness of the distinction between domestic and international politics. British and Dutch Unilever and the host of American companies in Europe confuse the international accounting process, making it exceedingly difficult to determine who gains and who loses. To be sure revenues for investing firms increase and profit margins may soar, but the gains are not so one-sided. Jobs are provided by the investing companies as well as accessibility to otherwise unobtainable products. European states have

141

resented United States investment, as is indicated by the immense success of Servan-Schreiber's book *Le Défi Américain*. Even so, most European countries, particularly Belgium, have offered very attractive subsidies to United States firms in forms of cash grants, tax exemptions, low-interest loans, and free buildings. Finally, to illustrate the ultimate confusion in the transformation of international society and, correspondingly, the degree to which we have moved away from an exclusive state-as-actor approach, we can note that not only have foreign firms penetrated domestic markets but they have done this on a variety of levels. The state of Illinois, for example, is the largest exporting state in the U.S. and Europe is its single, largest customer. Thus, in 1968, Illinois set up an office in Brussels to promote trade, to attract European business into Illinois, and to exploit the facilities of the largest inland seaport in the United States, the Great Lakes. All told, there are more than fifty subsidiaries of Illinois-based firms in Belgium.[2]

The nation-state is bursting its old seams, its neat, older contours yielding to messier, more variegated forms of expression. A century of structural specialization and social mobilization has spawned a bewildering variety of groups. Interests, organized or not, which previously made themselves felt only through the official organs of the state, or not at all, now find that they can do much better on their own. Developments in communications and technology have decreased the cost of time and space so that someone like Arafat can become an international figure with some bargaining power. As Kissinger argues, in today's age, the radio transmitter may bring advantages unobtainable with nuclear weapons.[3]

On a more fundamental level what we are witnessing is an inevitable consequence of a triple evolution of forces unleashed in the nineteenth century and brought to fruition in the twentieth. These three processes, (1) the pervasive structural specialization that gave rise to differentiated economic, political, and social institutions, (2) the demise of traditional authority, and (3) the widespread process of social mobilization, have operated together to produce profound changes in our forms of social and political organization. The first process, structural differentiation, resulted in a proliferation of social groupings, each equipped with a task expertise suited to its function. With specialization came a loosening of social controls, the rise of professional universalistic norms, and increased autonomy for the system's parts. It is interesting to note that Parsons describes the process of differentiation as one involving "emancipation from ascriptive bonds."[4]

The second process, the demise of traditional authority, has had less obvious effects. Previously, social, political, and economic institutions existed and acquired legitimacy from tradition. Aristocracies could claim continuous lineage from the Middle Ages. Society was cut up into a series of clearly graded. hierarchies allowing for little vertical mobility. This kind of social structure encouraged deference among the masses and professionalism among rulers. Neither demagogues nor popular controls on elite activity was possible. Gradually traditional authority declined and was replaced by rational-legal authority. Rulers and institutions came to be assessed on the basis of their ability to fulfill popular needs. If a ruler did not rule well, he could be removed from office. If a social institution did not perform up to standards, it could be changed. The effect was to undermine the pillars of a society based on birth, privilege, and ascription. The new pillars were those of functional rationality, achievement, and instrumental legitimacy. This demanded new social forms, interest groups, political parties, elections, representative institutions, and the like. It was the task of these structures to channel social demands to appropriate decision-making centers, to supply them with information, and to monitor their behavior. This led directly to the third process, social mobilization. If institutions were to acquire legitimacy by justifying their activity to public clients, these clients had to awaken themselves from slumber of the Middle Ages and articulate their demands. In many ways this process has made its greatest strides since World War II.

The cumulative impact of these three processes was to weaken the nation-state and to set in motion a search for alternative forms of social and political expression. The pluralization of interest groups weakened the nation-state at the extremities, made its boundaries more elastic, more porous. The passing of traditional authority and the process of social mobilization unleashed a torrent of demands to which the nation-state could not fully respond. Since national institutions were no longer sacred they were sometimes simply bypassed in favor of regional and global structures.

It is in this context that one must try to understand the EC in international relations since it is to these forces that it has responded. Its role in external affairs mirrors the weaknesses of national systems in dealing with certain ranges of problems. Yet the EC is not merely another, yet larger billiard ball but, in a much more complicated way, an additional layer in an already confusing global system.

Several questions guided the following discussion. In what ways is the EC a unit with respect to its environment? Can it fruitfully be characterized as a partial international subsystem or a regional subsystem? How and to what extent do other units (particularly other states and international organizations) interact with the EC? Do they recognize a supraordinate unit or do they orient to and interact with the EC's component structures? Are there distinct institutions and structures that represent the EC and act on its behalf and over what range of issues do these function?

THE EUROPEAN COMMUNITY IN INTERNATIONAL RELATIONS

Since its inception in 1958 the EC has been involved in international relations in a variety of ways. The Treaty of Rome itself empowered the Community to negotiate on the level of tariffs with third countries during the transitional period. The Community was also allowed to sign association agreements with countries that desired less than full membership. On July 9, 1961, July 20, 1963, and September 12, 1963, important agreements were signed by the Community and Greece, the independent states of Africa, and Madagascar and Turkey.[5] Between 1963 and 1967 the Commission negotiated the Community viewpoint at the Kennedy Round of tariff negotiations. More recently, in July 1970, the Buenos Aires declaration brought together twenty-two Latin American states of diverse interests in their expressed wish for closer links to the Community. India and Pakistan have been incorporated into a scheme of generalized preferences which they have gratefully acknowledged. Great Britain, Northern Ireland, Norway, and Denmark, twice refused membership, have now won admission (with Norway excluded) and have assumed their roles in the Common Market. Many other countries, Spain, Austria, Israel, and Japan among them, have sought special arrangements and accommodations with the Community. The specter of a large Europe is frightening to some, especially the Soviet Union. Ralf Dahrendorf poses the possibility of a sprawling regional Community:

> Sometimes the picture is drawn of a European Community which, along with the countries linked to it under preferential arrangements, already has a majority in the General Agreement on Tariffs and Trade (GATT) and which, after the entry of Britain, Denmark, Ireland and Norway, is heading for a majority in the United Nations. There would be ten members, six remaining EFTA Countries with still unclear links with the Community, eighteen African states associated under the Yaoundé Agreement and three under the Arusha Agreement, plus at least eight English-speaking countries in Africa after the entry of Britain, currently seven, and soon maybe thirteen, Mediterranean Countries with preferential agreements—making a total of fifty-eight states already. Are we faced here with the emergence of an almost coherent regional bloc from the Arctic Circle to the northern frontier of South Africa?[6]

A Community with a core in Western Europe would certainly be a formidable force in interstate politics but a Community as large as sketched by Dahrendorf would not be a monolith. In fact it would have very little cohesiveness at all. But the Europe of the Six or nine is itself an impressive grouping. Jean Deniau, former Commission member in charge of external affairs, notes that the Six, as an importer of foodstuffs and raw materials, accounts for 31 percent of world trade as opposed to 16 percent for the United States and 18 percent for the United Kingdom. It also accounts for 31 percent of the exports in world trade compared with 20 percent for the U.S. and 16 percent for the U.K. Thus the Community represents the world's largest outlet or market for raw materials and agricultural products, a fact of importance to developing countries, and is as well the source of a large portion of the world's exports.[7]

Although the Community is definitely a powerful economic area few see it as an emerging superpower capable of entering into the power calculations of the United States and the Soviet Union. If a European diplomacy exists it is, in Hartley Clark's words, "a business-suit diplomacy"[8] suited more to technical questions of tariffs, agricultural surpluses, and balance of payments than to talk of national security, defense, missiles, and German reunification. It is the task of these men to dismantle the tariff and protectionist structures among the six member states and to coordinate trade policies during and after the transition period.

The Treaty of Rome establishes a legal basis for external relations powers. This is unique in that, as Werner Feld observes, powers traditionally ascribed to nation-states are now transferred to a regional institution. But it is primarily in the more technical and economic domains that these powers apply.[9] When the focus of international involvement becomes more political, decision making passes either to national capitals or, more likely, to carefully instructed Community officials. In the Kennedy Round of tariff negotiations, negotiating power was vested in the supranational Commission operating under a restrictive mandate issued by the Council of Ministers. In the more political negotiations concerning British accession negotiations were conducted by the Council of Ministers.

Finally, the Community is the focus of substantial diplomatic activity. By May 15, 1960, seventeen nonmember states had already asked and received permission to establish diplomatic relations with the Community. The number of countries had increased to sixty-nine by February 1967 and to approximately eighty-five by 1973. There are few countries that do not recognize the Community today, the Soviet Bloc aside, and this recognition appears to be closely tied to the Community's internal development. This constant stream of diplomatic activity is, as Gordon Weil observed, "the surest sign that 'Europe' already exists in the eyes of the outside world."[10]

Given the range of activities in which the EC engages, it is not surprising to see a considerable variety of responses to it. The Community has been characterized as an embryonic superbloc, an international version of industrial and finance capitalism, and, on the other hand, as a diluted free trade area. It has been viewed as an exclusive arrangement, given to eliminating internal obstructions to the movement of goods, but protectionist and discriminating toward the outside world. Conversely its champions argue it possesses an essential expansiveness and openness toward the world. Finally, the EC are sometimes characterized as an aggravation to the Cold War, the economic counterpart to NATO, while others see the EC as an independent force, evidence of an emerging multipolarity. By growing in economic strength and attempting to separate itself from Atlantic (and more particularly U.S.) ties, the Community provides the Third World countries an alternative to the United States and the Soviet Union. Some feel that perhaps a detente between the superpowers could best be achieved by actively fostering a multipolar world in which the increased diffusion of responsibility would soften the competitiveness and zero-sum feelings characteristic of the present system.

VARIETY OF LEVELS ON WHICH THE COMMUNITY ENGAGES IN EXTERNAL RELATIONS

The Community engages in external relations and evokes a multitude of responses, but the interface between the Community and its environment is not at all simple. As with most other aspects of the European unification process the contact points between the EC and the world are complicated by a variety of levels and varying interaction patterns over different content areas. The first level of activity is at that of the nation-state. Many of the bilateral and multi-lateral negotiations between the Six and the world take place strictly on a nation-state basis. The institutional trappings of the EC may be used, meetings may be held in Brussels in Community buildings, but no supranational rules govern the behavior. This level includes the summit meetings, for example, the Hague Conference in December 1969 at which individual heads of state partici-pated as well as the meetings of foreign ministers concerning the decision on British entry. Actually, many of the regular meetings of the Council of Ministers attended by the foreign ministers of the member states are difficult to distin-guish from multilateral meetings of separate nation-states.

On a second level the EC confronts its environment as a unit. It signs commercial treaties, receives ambassadors, and formulates policies toward developing countries. On this level the EC is treated as a distinct international person, with autonomy from its parent states, and the ability to enter into the international political arena on its own. It is this level that most concerns the nation states.

On a third level domestic groups enter into foreign relations by bringing their demands directly to Community institutions. In an earlier chapter it was pointed out that industrial, agricultural, and commercial groups engage supra-national officials in the formulation of policies. Thus domestic interest groups may have an impact—however indirect—on international politics.

Finally, the EC acts in external relations through its contacts with and membership in international organizations, both global and regional. The Six have participated in the General Agreement on Tariffs and Trade (GATT), the Organization for Economic Cooperation and Development (OECD), most of the specialized agencies of the United Nations, and the European Free Trade Association (EFTA). Moreover, unlike the United Nations, the Community is a recognized subject under international law and can bring legal action against the International Court of Justice.

To sum up, the EC is a significant actor in global politics but the ways in which it interacts are highly complicated. This multiplicity of contacts mirrors an internal fluidity, a condition where internal structures are far from perfectly crystallized. The Community's lack of internal coherence gives it a flexible, almost double-jointed quality in external affairs. It is capable of acting as a unit, as in the Kennedy Round, or as a loose collection of sovereign nation-states, as in the negotiations for British entry, or as an intermediary between domestic interest groups and foreign publics. While this lack of structure is seen by those who promote the development of firm political institutions as a symptom of institutional weakness, it can be a source of strength. It gives the Community a good deal of maneuverability and enhances its niche-filling capacity, a capacity that ruthlessly exploits opportunity to grow in many directions.

Thus, the EC is seen as penetrating and being penetrated by other entities in a variety of ways. Its policies have an impact on the rest of the world. They are also a response to forces in that world. Von Geusau points out that the initiation and takeoff of the process of European integration were rooted in the international environment of the late forties.[11] Similarly the crises and stagnation of European integration in the sixties reflect the muted bipolarity and emerging detente in the international system.[12]

A SYSTEMIC PERSPECTIVE

One way to cope with this bewildering variety of behavioral levels is to extend the systems perspective set forth in earlier chapters. Such a viewpoint allows us to achieve an overall perspective while still retaining a focus on component processes as these processes relate to the operation of the larger system. In other words, a systems perspective permits one to grasp the large picture and at the same time to focus on detail as it systematically relates to the larger functional problems of the system.

The general systems model provides a set of related and potentially helpful concepts: openness, variety, pattern-matching, and constraint. The model relies heavily on the notion of the complex, adaptive, variety-managing system outlined by Buckley, concepts of openness put forth by Bertalanffy and the idea of adaptive behavior as pattern-matching as set forth by Tolman and Brunswick and discussed by Campbell.[13]

Systems are open if they engage in constant interchanges with their environments, receiving inputs and discharging outputs. Generally the inputs are substances of high structure and potential energy whereas the outputs are products returned to the environment in a more degraded form. The interchange between system and environment is seen as essential for the persistence of living systems. Open systems are also variety-management systems. They elaborate structures designed to map or fit this environmental variety. The notion of elaboration is crucial since it is generally through the reassembly or creation of system parts that the system responds to increased environmental variety. That is, as Ashby states it in his "law of requisite variety," "only variety can destroy variety."[14] To put it another way a perfectly adaptive system is one in which for every distinguishable patterned difference in the environment there is a corresponding system structure to map it. Of course the subtlety, nuance, and richness of the environment are only approximately imitated and grossly oversimplified. Simon, in his *The Sciences of the Artificial,* has demonstrated how such oversimplifications are at the basis of the art of engineering.[15]

Finally, the notion of constraint is important. Constraint refers to the "relatively stable 'causal', spatial and/or temporal relations between these distinguishable elements or events. . . ."[16] It is the presence of such environmental constraint which makes adaptive behavior possible. Behaving adaptively, in other words, demands an environment populated by fairly stable relations, an environment that repeats itself, that shows consistent departures from chaotic activity. Ashby refers to this as "the recurrent situation" and points out that the greater the degree of environmental constraint, the greater the capacity of the system to specialize against it. Adaptive behavior involves fitting system form to environmental pattern. The environment and the system mirror each other, however presumptively and approximately. In the discussion that follows focus is placed on the shifts in environmental patterns insofar as they are responses to the EC. These shifts may provide clues to changes in form within the Community itself. The relationships between the evolving EC and the countries of the Council of Mutual Economic Assistance (COMECON) as well as the Kennedy Round of tariff negotiations are examined below. Then the Community is scrutinized from different perspectives. Several questions become apparent. Is an integrated Europe, particularly a politically unified one, likely to be an aggressive, militant force in global politics? Is it likely to lead to an economic fortress Europe and a further widening of the gap separating rich and poor countries or will its spread-out effects lead to general economic benefits? Finally, will a united Europe be a halfway house on the way to more comprehensive integration or is it likely to be a terminal station existing in complacent symbiosis with the nation-state?

The European Community and Eastern Europe

The evolution of relations between the EC and the Communist bloc countries of Eastern Europe presents an interesting case study of the linkages between two regional subsystems. Relations take place on a variety of levels and the bloc-to-bloc interaction is only one layer of behavior grafted on top of a series of others. The Soviet Union prefers bilateral negotiations, ignoring, at least officially, the supranational organizations. By the end of the transition period (1970), the Soviet Union was forced to deal with the EC as an entity since it was in charge of directing the common commercial policy. Subnational relations are important also and to a large extent, the Soviet Union has attempted to achieve its foreign policy objectives in Western Europe operating through the French and Italian Communist parties and Communist-dominated labor unions.[17] Finally, bloc-to-bloc and bloc-systemic level relations are important. It should not be forgotten that the European integration movement was launched in the face of an emerging bipolarity. By 1947 the hope for Soviet-American cooperation and for solving conflicts through the United Nations had given way to fear and suspicion. The political context of this change included the termination of lend-lease to the Soviet Union, the Western fear of Soviet presence in Eastern and Central Europe, the Communist movements in France and Italy, and the Greek Civil War.[18]

It is not often recognized that the process of European recovery and subsequent economic integration were part of a comprehensive Western response to the beginning of the Cold War. This response had three components. There was a political-strategic component, manifested in a containment policy; a regional security policy, represented by NATO; and an economic component, reflected in the Marshall Plan, and later, the ECSC and EEC.[19] Thus Europe was launched in response to political changes in the global environment and was subsequently to reflect changes in that environment.

It has always been difficult for Americans and Western Europeans to understand why the Soviet Union reacted so negatively to the EEC. After all, the EEC concerned itself mostly with economic and technical issues—tariffs, agricultural matters, transport rates. Therefore the Soviet and East European attitude could be written off as a typical xenophobic response. But while most West Europeans, accustomed to social systems in which the economic sector enjoys a good deal of functional autonomy, perceive the Common Market, NATO, and containment as distinct spheres of activity, the Soviet Bloc does not. The ideas of an economic community and a military alliance were both born and developed in the crucible of the Cold War and the Soviet Union sees these as inextricably interlinked. The EEC is the direct descendant of European recovery and the Coal and Steel Community. And it should not be forgotten that it is through the EEC that West Germany is being firmly cemented into the Western bloc.

This brings us to the central issue dividing Eastern and Western Europe, what is cryptically referred to as the German problem. It is, as Ronald Steel put it, "the last and most intractable remnant of the Cold War in Europe, the knot that impedes reunification of the Continent and prevents the detente from evolving into a wider settlement."[20] The division of Germany symbolizes the breakdown of Great Power agreement on the control of Central Europe. Germany's division, the establishment of Berlin as an enclave under four-power administration, the emergence of NATO and the Warsaw Pact, and the period of protracted tension and brinkmanship known as the Cold War all flow from the division of Germany.

What role, if any, does the EC play in this division of Europe? Several answers are possible to this question. It is sometimes argued that the European Community ties the economy of West Germany closely to the Western alliance and that it provides an economic undergirding for the military agreements. Further, by drawing the economies of the countries of Western Europe closer together, the EC encourages a similar reaction on the part of the Eastern European economies. Second, and perhaps more fundamentally, the absorption of Western Germany into the Western Bloc has made one condition for the termination of the Cold War nearly impossible to achieve: the unification and neutralization of Germany. As long as the Federal Republic is firmly anchored in the EC, Germany cannot be united on terms that are acceptable to the Soviet Union. If the Federal Republic is outside the EC, it cannot be reunited on terms acceptable to Western Europe and the United States. West Germany has a large market, especially for French agricultural products, and is the hub of the spectacular economic growth that has been occurring in Western Europe. West Germany is enmeshed more broadly in a web of trade relationships, capital flows, and technology transfers within Western Europe and the Atlantic area. It is inconceivable that Germany would want to leave, or that her economic partners would let her go.

The problems raised by the disengagement of West Germany from the EC are mirrored by the difficulties incurred in considering the inclusion of the German Democratic Republic in the Community. Overlooking for the moment the fact that the Soviet Union is not likely to allow this or the equally important fact that East Germany has evolved into a distinct society with its own identity now, there are still some vexing questions that remain unanswered. The most important of these is how the member states of the EC are likely to view a reunified Germany of approximately seventy-five million people. As Ronald Steel put it:

> Prosperous and democratic, a West Germany of 50 million people is on a par with France, Italy, or Britain, and can therefore be integrated in a West European community. But a reunified Germany of 75 million people, stretching from Alsace to the Polish border and with its capital in Berlin, would control, if not destroy, the Common Market, and perhaps dominate all Europe. It is with Bonn, not Europe, that Europe has been able to make peace. It is because of her division that Germany has acquired loyal allies in the West—allies she could not otherwise have attracted and who have no vital interest in her reunification.[21]

While accepting the bulk of Steel's argument it is important to add that the picture is not so one-sided. Western Europe is the center of those forces which foster interdependence, cooperation, and international pluralism. The specialization of interest structures, the growth of technocracy, and the elevation of the expert and manager to improved social status, the declining importance of ideology, all the things that work for the loosening of political controls are taking place in their most advanced form in Western Europe. Trade has increased between East and West Europe, capital has begun to flow, and the advantages of factor mobility and comparative advantage are making themselves felt. As Steel himself notes, the French have licensed their color television system to the Communist bloc and Fiat has set up an auto plant in the Soviet Union. If the political divisions of Europe are still as deep as ever, there is nevertheless a layer of economic and social cooperation grafted on top of this. And given our uncertain knowledge about the linkage between economic and political realms, there is no reason to believe that this bifurcation cannot be sustained indefinitely.

For a variety of reasons the Soviet Union and Eastern Europe opposed development in European integration. Politically and militarily, a revived EEC was viewed as a potential core of an aggressive NATO and a material base for revanchist Germany. Whether acting as an independent force along Gaullist lines or in concert with the U.S., the Soviet Bloc feels they have everything to gain by keeping Western Europe weak. Another objection is that a Western Europe that is economically strong will serve as a magnet for the states of Africa, Asia, and Latin America. It will serve as evidence that the decline of capitalism is at least not imminent and may offer an attractive alternative to the Soviet development model. Finally, the integration of Europe is seen as damaging to the trade of the Soviet Bloc. Eastern Europe is an exporter of raw materials and agricultural products. The progressive elimination of internal tariffs within Europe and gradual realization of self-sufficiency in certain sectors would damage the export position of many Eastern European countries.

In fact, the fears of the Soviet Bloc of being increasingly cut off from Western trade have not materialized. From 1953 to 1965 both imports and exports between the EC and the COMECON countries increased by nearly 400 percent.[22] The share of the EC countries in the trade of the COMECON states is much larger than the share of the COMECON in the trade in the EC countries. This is a simple reflection of the fact that the EC countries account for a much larger proportion of world trade than do the Soviet bloc countries.

Despite these fears the Soviet reaction to the formation of the EEC was extremely muted and confused. More attention was placed on fitting this development into Marxist doctrine than in fashioning concrete responses to it. On the one hand the formation of the Common Market was viewed as an internationalization of capitalism, a transnational extension made possible by the technical advances in the means of production. This new twist in the evolution of capitalist societies was an effort to prolong the life of a basically defective system while leaving untouched its basic problems. The concrete changes in COMECON came later, after the EC had proved itself, started to formulate policies, and attracted interest in membership by nonmember countries. It may be helpful to examine the COMECON responses on the hypothesis that these responses are attempts to adapt to important changes in the EC's becoming an international actor.

COMECON and the EC

On January 5, 1949, Bulgaria, Hungary, Czechoslovakia, Poland, Rumania, and the Soviet Union brought into existence COMECON,[23] an economic organization designed to increase internal trade and coordinate respective national economic policies. The political context for this decision includes the rejection of participation in the Marshall Plan, the creation of several European economic organizations, and the hardening of the Cold War represented by the containment doctrine and the impending formation of NATO.

COMECON played a very passive role during the first ten years of its existence. It served primarily as an intergovernmental clearing house where economic information was exchanged and where bilateral trade arrangements could be negotiated. The death of Stalin in 1953 and the Twentieth Party Congress of the Communist Party of the Soviet Union in 1956 unleashed centrifugal forces within the Soviet Bloc. These forces, along with the subsequent creation of the EEC, provide the basis for the reactivation of COMECON.

The creation of the EEC did not bring an immediate response, except at the ideological level. But events in 1960-61 brought forth more concrete responses. Korbonski notes that "a decision to strengthen COMECON seems to have been made in the 1960's"[24] and relates this decision to the British application for membership in the EEC. For different reasons, both Great Britain and COMECON were skeptical of the success of the EEC. With the British application in the summer of 1961 and the rapid advances in the formulation of the common agricultural policy in the winter of 1961 and the beginning of 1962, the COMECON countries were prompted to reassess the situation. As Korbonski points out:

> Several COMECON members depend on the Common Market
> as a source of supply of machinery and equipment and as an impor-
> tant customer for foodstuffs and other products. These countries

realized that once a common agriculture policy was agreed upon and a common tariff was established, they would be prevented from selling their traditional exports and would be unable to acquire machinery necessary for continuing their industrial expansion. One can speculate that closer integration of COMECON countries was intended to prepare them for this eventuality, and at the same time to induce them to search for alternative sources of supply and outlets for their exports both within and outside COMECON.[25]

Shulman marks the British application for membership as the beginning of a new phase in the relations between the EEC and COMECON.[26] This was the phase marked at the interbloc level by negotiations for expansion of EEC membership and the working out of the central components of a common agricultural policy. At the systemic level it was characterized by the Cuban missile crisis between the United States and the Soviet Union, an increased tempo in the arms race, and the Nassau Conference between Kennedy and Macmillan. The Soviet Union responded by exerting strong diplomatic pressure on Britain, Norway, Denmark, and Northern Ireland concerning the disadvantages of joining. Several of the COMECON countries (the Soviet Union, Poland, and Yugoslavia) discontinued their importation of Norwegian frozen fish. Austria's flirtation with the EEC, in terms of her attempts to achieve associate status, brought strong disapproval from the Soviet Union, who made it clear that any connection between Austria and the EEC would be interpreted as a violation of her neutral status. This was also the period in which the French and Italian Communist parties, during the Moscow Conference in September 1962, started to shift their views on how to respond to the EEC.[27] The EEC was now accepted as a reality in global politics. Consequently the COMECON countries should seek closer collaboration with it and attempt to mitigate its discriminatory features.

The final phase of COMECON's reaction can be dated from January 1963 when de Gaulle vetoed British entry application and subsequently (January 22, 1963) signed the Franco-German Friendship Treaty. The Kennedy-Macmillan meeting at Nassau convinced de Gaulle that he could not cooperate with the "Anglo-Saxons" that he would have to find the core of his independent force within continental Europe. Since the fears centering on a strengthened Common Market are in reality fears of a resurgent West Germany, this Franco-German rapprochement was viewed with deep concern. Previously, at a meeting of COMECON countries in June 1962, the Soviet Union offered a proposal for the reorganization of COMECON. The Polish delegate presented a counterproposal that called for a more tightly knit structure than the one proposed by the Soviet Union. Given the French-German rapprochement in early 1963, the Soviet Union would follow through in implementing the proposal. The adopted proposal set up an Executive Committee composed of a representative from each country. This committee was to act as a planning agency for the economic integration of the entire bloc.

One conclusion that seems obvious is that for COMECON members, the EEC was a significant other. Its development was responded to in a variety of ways, by consolidating and by remaining flexible enough to maintain contacts with Western European countries. Soviet leadership was caught in a dilemma. By not consolidating its economic hold on Eastern Europe it ran the risk of these countries gravitating toward the West. By overreacting it ran the opposite risk of pushing the Western countries closer together. Whatever the vicissitudes of a particular policy at any given moment, the upshot of the development of the EEC was to force the COMECON countries from a grudging acceptance of it to dealing with it as a significant actor. This is seen not only in the tightening of COMECON but also in the efforts of the Soviet Union to encourage participation by French and Italian Communists in the institutions of the European Community, especially in the European Parliament and the Economic and Social Committee. "Despite its ups and downs, the Common Market has resulted in profound modifications in Soviet ideas concerning contemporary capitalism and the present configuration of power; it has led to a radical revision of the Council of Mutual Economic Assistance (COMECON)—the Soviet counterpart organization for eastern Europe; and it has greatly complicated Moscow's leadership of the world communist movements."[28]

The European Community and the Kennedy Round

The Kennedy Round refers to a multilateral round of tariff negotiations that occupied the Council of Ministers and Commission of the EC for a four-year period, from 1963 to 1967. Several developments in the international system form the backdrop to the negotiations and were influential in bringing about these negotiations. The Kennedy Round was partly the result of the response of the United States to the growing economic power of the EEC. In late 1961 the EEC would implement the first large installment of its common external tariff. Also, the United States had a deep fear of the evolving common agricultural policy of the Common Market. Farm exports account for a third of all U.S. exports and a substantial share of them have their destination in Common Market countries. In this sense the Kennedy Round can be viewed as an effort on the part of the United States to persuade the Common Market to pursue a more liberal outward-looking trade policy. Also the fear of the failure of Great Britain to gain membership in the EEC may have played a role.[29] Western Europe has been an area of primary commercial importance to the U.S. and although every American president since World War II has been supportive of European integration, this support was always contingent upon the assumption that an integrated Europe would be an open, expansive concern rather than an exclusive club.

In terms of concrete policy the U.S. response was the passage of the Trade Expansion Act on October 11, 1962. This act gave the President broad powers to negotiate across the board 50 percent tariff reductions in a large number of areas. In contrast with the commodity-by-commodity reductions under the earlier Reciprocal Trade Agreements Act, this new legislation made possible tariff cuts on broad commodity groupings. Finally, while the previous multilateral tariff negotiations conducted under the GATT were concerned with lowering industrial tariffs, the Kennedy Round had as one of its goals also the inclusion of agricultural products.

It had been obvious from the beginning that the process of European integration was not taking place in a vacuum but rather was embedded in a complicated network of global relationships. An examination of the negotiations during the Kennedy Round offers a case study of several aspects of this emerging network and gives one a new vantage point for assessing the external behavior of the EC. In contrast with EC-COMECON relations, where interactions are characterized by mutual animosity and action-reaction processes, the Kennedy Round is of interest primarily because it permits us to examine the autonomy of a Community institution in an important foreign policy area.

The goals of the negotiations (50 percent tariff reductions over a wide range of commodities) were approximated enough to call them a success. The tariffs on 6,300 items were reduced by an average of 35 percent and the benefits of these reductions were to spread to more than eighty states as a consequence of GATT's most favored nation clause.[30] Agreement on a policy with regard to a world cereals price was not reached but an antidumping policy was formulated and accepted.

The difficulty the Commission had in conducting the negotiations in agriculture raises an interesting point. The capacity of the EC to negotiate effectively was related to its own internal development. Difficulties in the conduct of external negotiations were mirrored by internal difficulties. Discussions in the fall of 1964 were sluggish and offered little basis for optimism. The Commission argued that since there had as yet been no agreement on a common grain price, something which was to be achieved in December 1964, there was little point in carrying the discussions any further. The goals of the Kennedy Round with respect to agriculture were defined very early in the negotiations. The major goal was the "creation of acceptable conditions of access to world markets for agricultural products in furtherance of a significant development and expansion of world trade in such products."[31] The crucial problem, as von Geusau pointed out, is that this goal was in no way reconciled with "the equally legitimate demands of agricultural producers in the various producing countries regarding the improvement of agricultural prosperity and the establishment of a better social balance between the various social and professional categories within one and the same country."[32] As a result of these problems major agreements in agriculture eluded the Kennedy Round negotiations. Tariffs were reduced on some products and a common food aid policy was formulated but little or no progress was made toward the working out of integrated arrangements for world trade in cereals, dairy products, and other key agricultural commodities.

The role of the Commission as the representative of the Community viewpoint was extremely important. This is true especially insofar as its behavior reflects the supranational element in the Community decision-making process. The institutional complex through which the negotiations were conducted included the Commission, the Council of Ministers, and the Article 111 Committee. In effect, Article 111 of the Rome treaty, vested authority to conduct negotiations in the Commission in consultation with a special intergovernmental committee. This Committee would supply a mandate to guide the behavior of the Commision, monitor its day-to-day activities, and act as a watchdog for the

Council of Ministers and the individual national interests. The ambivalence of the member states seemed to be reflected in the bifurcated institutional structure designed to conduct negotiations. The member states recognized the necessity of delegating functions to some unified body which could present effectively the common viewpoint. As a check on the possibility that the Commission might attempt to push a Community viewpoint when one did not exist, a series of restraints were incorporated into the negotiating process. This at times made the negotiations awkward, for example, Commission members had to perform delicate balancing acts among national capitals, Brussels, and Geneva, and no doubt diluted the strength of the Community's position.

From the beginning it was evident that the Commission was going to function as more than a mouthpiece of the individual national interests. At an early stage of the negotiations the Commission took fairly strong positions with respect to the disparities issue,[33] the inclusion of nontariff barriers in the negotiations, and the form that a possible agricultural agreement might take.

Yet, on balance, the Commission exerted little independent initiative during the course of the negotiations, especially up to 1966. The activity of the Commission was watched closely by both the Council of Ministers and the Article 111 Committee. The Commission's mandate, issued in 1963, was re-evaluated several times and during such evaluations the negotiations were in abeyance. Jean Rey, the commisioner in charge of the negotiations, was severely circumscribed in his work by the need to shuttle between Brussels and Geneva where he reported on the progress of the negotiations and received new instructions.

During the fall of 1966 and the winter of 1967 the Council of Ministers held a number of key sessions where they evaluated the question of whether the Commission should receive a new mandate. A number of thorny issues related to disparities and nontariff barriers demanded increased flexibility for the Commission. On the basis of a long meeting on January 12, 1967, the Council of Ministers decided not to issue a new mandate but to tell the Commission to go ahead on the basis of the older one. The Commission was told to use its discretion in its search for possible solutions. There was much difficult negotiation ahead, particularly in the last several weeks preceding the agreement in May 1967, and the Commission acted with considerable independence during these meetings. As Coombes put it, although it is difficult to fix a specific date "it is clear that in the final stage of the negotiations the Commission's team of negotiators was able to take up a position in response to the situation in Geneva rather than looking over its shoulders to what was happening in the Council of Ministers in Brussels."[34]

To the extent that the Commission's activity is monitored closely by institutions standing in for the nation-state one can look upon its role as essentially bureaucratic. In this context the role of the Commission in the Kennedy Round is seen as one of doing a certain amount of legwork for the Council of Ministers. Most observers, however, felt that the Commission's role extended beyond this considerably. In a perceptive analysis of the European Commission David Coombes argues that this body performed several valuable functions during the Kennedy Round, all of which departed from its bureaucratic role. In the first place the Commission performed a valuable function in laying the groundwork for the conferences. Hallstein himself (president of the Commission at that time) went to Washington several times in 1962 ostensibly to give Kennedy encouragement to go ahead with his plans for the conference. Much of this work comes under the category of providing expertise and legwork in matters that national ministers do not consider sufficiently important; yet its importance should not be underestimated. When an institution acquires a position where it can provide information over a wide range of issues it has acquired the capacity to play an important role in the legislative process.

Second, the Commission played an important mediating role in the decision-making process, interposing itself at critical times, skillfully playing one interest off against another and using the internal political situation of the Community as a bargaining lever. It also took several important initiatives, not only in 1963 when the conference began but also in 1966 and 1967 when the contracting parties moved into the most intensive round of the negotiations. The Commission acquired more autonomy in this mediating role as the negotiations moved to their conclusion. Observers who emphasize the closeness with which Commission activities were supervised by the Article 111 Committee forget that national delegates representing individual countries were also watched carefully. The U.S. delegation took many trips back to Washington for renewed instructions and also had the composition of the negotiating team changed several times in response to domestic political considerations.[35] Perhaps what we see here is more a function of general historical currents that have been affecting the content of diplomacy than anything peculiar to the Kennedy Round. As a result of changes in technology and communications diplomats no longer have the autonomy in the field which they once enjoyed. While classical diplomacy provided the diplomat with a gross mandate it could not provide the detailed instructions to meet all contingencies and nuances that would be confronted. Today, when a negotiator is in doubt, or when flexibility is needed, he may simply get on the telephone or airplane. What is happening is that the focus of diplomatic activity is becoming less and less decentralized.

As the internal policies of the Community become more unified its supranational structure will have implications for its relations with the rest of the world. This is true for the implementation of the common external tariff (CET) as well as for the establishment of common policies in agriculture, industry, social affairs, and transport. The internal negotiations conducted for the common agricultural policy brought this out well. Until the EC's partners knew whether they were dealing with six separate price systems or one, no progress could be made. The agricultural package deal adopted on December 15, 1964, eliminated a huge obstacle to the negotiations. In short, when Europe became an entity, it was treated as a reality by other countries. In terms of the general systems theoretic orientation the EC represented novelty or variety in the environment. The states in the global system responded by mapping this variety, through the elaboration of existing structures (e.g., sending diplomats to the

Community) and dealing with the Community as an independent entity during the negotiations. If Europe was not born at Geneva, as one source suggests, at least it represented the first installment of its coming to grips with the problem of how it was to fit into the global system.[36]

THE EUROPEAN COMMUNITY AS AN EXTERNAL ACTOR: SOME NORMATIVE CONSIDERATIONS

The evolution of the Community's role in the world evokes several important normative questions.[37] Two of these seem to be particularly relevant. First of all, will an integrated Europe be open toward its neighbors, cosmopolitan in its relations with them, or will it be an exclusive, protectionistic, and autarkic Europe? Will it be easier or more difficult for Europe to build bridges and establish contacts with the countries of Africa, Asia, Eastern Europe, and Latin America with a united Europe or with a series of individual European nation-states? Will a united Europe provide a convenient stepping-stone on the way to world government or will it be a permanent island, a club of rich, advanced industrial nations, more self-sufficient than before and increasingly reluctant to dilute its strength by joining others? Second, will a united Europe, should it achieve political unity, become a more militant center than before? How would the Soviet Union and Eastern Europe respond to a politically unified Europe? Would the possibility of detente, of the waning of the Cold War, be increased by the existence of a third pole or would a strong Europe be seen as the stalking horse of the United States on the Eurasian continent?

Europe: Cosmopolitan or Provincial?

Pointing to the difference between regional and global integration Mitrany had this to say:

> A central, and vital difference is inherent, and ineradicable, in their very nature: the U.N. has internationally a *unifying* role (however imperfectly achieved so far), whereas the EEC or any other regional union while having a unifying role *locally* has of necessity a *divisive* role internationally. In fact, the more effective the first, the sharper the second. [Regarding] "the twin human predicaments of war and poverty," the EEC might contribute something towards the second, but regionalism as such, has nothing to contribute towards the nuclear nightmare, much less towards the new space problem.
>
> Beyond a certain point the comparison between an egocentric regional unit and the grand limitless purpose of a universal body becomes meaningless. The "actor roles" become so different and distant in scope that they no longer belong to the same world of organization and policy—and of possibilities. One can admire the EEC, but as students we cannot overlook that, internationally speaking, its limits are also its limitations.[38]

E. H. Carr, speaking in the context of the League of Nations experience, expressed a somewhat different view:

The lure of universality has had since 1919 a dangerous fascination for promoters of international order. The universality of any world organization almost inevitably tends to weaken its appeal to particular loyalties and particular interests. It was probably a weakness of the League of Nations that its commitments were general and anonymous: it imposed the same obligations on Albania as on Great Britain, and the same obligation on both to defend the independence of Belgium against Germany and that of Panama against the United States. These generalities could be justified in terms of pure reason but not translated into terms of concrete policy, so that the whole structure remained abstract and unreal . . . A world organization may be a necessary convenience as well as a valuable symbol. But the intermediate unit is likely to be the operative factor in the transition from nationalism to internationalism.[39]

Is a united Europe at odds with a potentially united globe? Are the bonds that lace Europe together of one cloth with those that set her apart from states outside? Will Europe become an island of wealth, closed off from the rest of the world, freed from any internal restrictions on factor mobility but insulated from the world by its common external tariff? Or will it be an open regionalism, extending its benefits to other countries and providing a lever for movement to more comprehensive integrative schemes? Mitrany has pointed out what should be painfully obvious, namely, that: "The argument about the need of an intermediate step is obviously only valid if the regional unions are to be open unions; whereas if they are to be closed and exclusive unions, the more fully and effectively they are integrated the deeper must in fact be the division they cause in the emergent unity of the world."[40]

The important question is whether Europe is a closed or open region. For some scholars integration is by definition a process of growing exclusiveness. Professor Deutsch looks upon integration as the process whereby certain areas become more dense in transactions than others. Since transactions are measured in terms of proportions (e.g., the extent that a collection of entities interact with one another as a proportion of their interactions with other members of the system), any given group of nations can integrate only at the expense of other actors. This share-of-the-pie model embodies competitive assumptions that are useful in some contexts but not in others.[41] One of the advantages of adopting a model with variable sum assumptions is that the problem of whether a region is integrating at the expense of others becomes an empirical question. One could ask whether in fact trade with countries within the EEC has progressed at the expense of trade with countries outside. One could also ask if attitudes favorable to European integration compete with attitudes toward institutions at other levels. The answer to these questions is not so simple as I suggest here. The argument over what factors to control (e.g., inflation, population growth, internal productivity, increases in the total trade of the international system) is by no means settled. If we accept for purposes of argument, however, that it is legitimate to use absolute trade figures—preferably controlled for inflation—then we can at least examine the external trade relations of the EEC in an exploratory way.

TABLE 7.1

GROWTH OF EEC IMPORTS AND EXPORTS,
SELECTED YEARS, 1953-1965
(DOLLAR AMOUNTS IN BILLIONS)

				Compound Annual Rate of Increase (Percent)	
Type of Trade	1953	1958-59	1965	1955 to 1958-59	1958-59 to 1965
Total imports from members	4.0	7.4	20.4	12.2	17.0
Total exports to members	4.0	7.5	20.8	12.3	17.1

SOURCE: This table is adapted from Lawrence B. Krause, *European Economic Integration and the United States* (Washington, D.C.: The Brookings Institution, 1968), p. 21. It is reprinted here with the permission of the Publisher.

TABLE 7.2

EEC IMPORTS FROM NONMEMBERS,
SELECTED YEARS, 1953-1965
(DOLLAR AMOUNTS IN BILLIONS)

				Compound Annual Rate of Increase (Percent)	
Type of Trade	1953	1958-59	1965	1953 to 1958-59	1958-59 to 1965
Total imports from nonmembers	11.2	16.2	28.6	7.1	9.2
Total exports to nonmembers	10.3	16.5	27.1	9.0	8.0

SOURCE: Adapted from Lawrence B. Krause, *European Economic Integration and the United States* (Washington, D.C.: The Brookings Institution, 1968), p. 21. This table is reprinted here with the permission of the Publisher.

The first fact to note is that trade among EEC members has increased at fantastic speeds since the early 1950s. From 1953 to 1965 both imports and exports quintupled among EEC members. Table 7.1 gives a picture of this increase for selected years. This dramatic increase in trade is often pointed to as evidence of the success of European integration. How did trade with other states fare while this rapid internal growth of the EEC was transpiring? An examination of table 7.2 indicates that during a comparable period, trade with nonmembers almost tripled. The absolute, dollar increases in trade are impressive as are the growth rates representing the EEC's increase in imports and exports with nonmember states. The fact that these growth rates lagged behind the growth rates for member states is not evidence that nonmembers might have fared better without an integrated Europe. That inference would neglect the effect of integration on the total amount of trade carried out by the EEC. Although the evidence is inconclusive, there is a strong possibility that removing obstacles to the flow of trade may have generated forces resulting in an increased productivity and an increased amount of total trading carried out by EEC members.

This picture holds up when we go beneath the gross trade patterns and examine particular countries as well as regions outside of the EEC. One particularly important region is made up of the eighteen associated African states and Malagasy, a group of former French colonies that are linked to the EEC through Article 131. Article 131 of the Treaty of Rome provided for the first legal ties between the EEC and this group of states who were former colonies of the European states. As Okigbo notes, the objectives of the association were to "promote the economic and social development of the countries and territories and to establish close economic relations between them and the Community as a whole."[42]

In the years immediately following the initiation of the EEC the majority of these associated states acquired independence from the former colonial powers. Since both the EEC and the majority of African states wanted to continue the association, negotiations commenced. The result of these negotiations was the first Yaoundé Convention which came into full operation in January 1964.[43] It is a controversial question as to whether the association has acted, as one observer has it, "to contractualize and institutionalize links between a group of imperialist countries and a number of third world countries"[44] or to promote and foster development and trade in one segment of the developing world.

TABLE 7.3

EEC TRADE WITH SELECTED COUNTRIES AND REGIONS
(MILLIONS OF DOLLARS)

Type of Trade	1958	1960	1961	1962	1963	1964	1965	1966
Imports from U.S.	2,808	3,830	4,054	4,458	5,051	5,438	5,693	6,021
Exports to U.S.	1,164	2,242	2,232	2,447	2,563	2,849	3,425	4,097
Imports from Yaoundé Associates	914	952	941	930	939	1,150	1,146	1,319
Exports to Yaoundé Associates	712	603	673	666	726	821	828	847
Imports from African nonassociated countries and Nigeria	524	664	674	704	802	909	987	1,111
Exports to African nonassociated countries and Nigeria	364	527	538	543	596	625	751	767
Imports from Central and South America	1,647	1,870	1,892	2,223	2,268	2,465	2,615	2,731
Exports to Central and South America	1,604	1,693	1,860	1,783	1,567	1,676	1,706	1,905

SOURCE: Adapted from Werner Feld, *The European Common Market and the World* (Englewood Cliffs, N.J.: Prentice-Hall, 1967), pp. 96 and 121. Reprinted with permission of the Publisher.

Table 7.3 gives some idea of the development of trading ties among the EEC and the United States, the eighteen African states associated with the EEC through the Yaoundé Convention, the nonassociated African countries and

Nigeria, and Central and South America. If we examine these trade figures we can see that U.S. imports and exports to and from the EEC more than doubled, exports from the Yaoundé Associates rose about 45 percent, while imports of the Yaoundé members from the EEC increased by 18 percent.[45] Ironically, the nonassociated African states and the Latin American countries, who had expressed some fear that their trade positions would be harmed by the associated African states, actually experienced a much greater trade increase with the EEC. EEC imports from Central and South America increased by 65 percent whereas exports increased by approximately 29 percent. At the same time both imports and exports linking the EEC states to the nonassociated African states increased by more than 100 percent. It is true that in terms of pure volume of trade exchanged between the African states and members of the EC, there has been a substantial increase. Yet such an undifferentiated measure of volume is so crude as to invite more detailed examination and several observations of a more critical nature. First, it should be noted that the increases of the Yaoundé Associates (45 percent for exports and 18 percent for imports) are much lower than the corresponding increases for the advanced nations. For the United States these figures were somewhere between 200 percent and 300 percent whereas for the industrialized European countries the increases were often between 300 percent and 500 percent. This fact becomes all the more remarkable and important when we remind ourselves that the baseline from which these increases are calculated, that is, the actual volume of trade, is very low for the African countries.

Another factor of some importance has to do with the composition of goods traded. For the most part the European states provide the finished, manufactured goods while the African states are suppliers of foods, primary products, and raw materials. And it is probably not through any malicious, calculated design that this is the case. It is more likely the consequence of a free trade ideology applied to unequals. African industry, crafts, and textiles simply cannot compete with the products of the highly mechanized, large-scaled manufacturing methods of European and American products. It is only by developing a protectionist position that the economies of the African states will become more diversified. The EC has encouraged just the opposite of diversification. When the Yaoundé Convention (establishing continuing relations between the EEC and the Associated African States) became effective it eliminated tariffs on a broad range of primary products exported by the Eighteen, including: pineapples, coconuts, coffee, tea, cloves, nutmeg, pepper, vanilla, and cocoa.[46] As Jalée notes, these are all raw products that do not require any domestic processing.[47]

This dependence on a limited range of exportable goods leads directly to another difficulty for countries of the developing world, namely the declining terms of trade. The developing countries acquire less money for their exports while the industrialized countries acquire more and more. This seems to be a result of the fact that most primary products go more directly into consumption while manufactured goods are more removed. As a result, primary products such as foodstuffs as well as textiles and raw materials have a low income elasticity and thus lag behind the income increases of the developed countries.[48]

The EEC did not stop with granting tariff concessions to the associated African countries. The member countries also actively undertook to stimulate economic and social development projects "including the building of roads, ports, schools, hospitals, and the prevention of soil erosion."[49] A European Development Fund (EDF) was created to administer development schemes. This fund itself allotted $581 million over the first five-year period (1958-1963). The principal recipients of this program are the former French colonies.[50] Although the impact of the EDF has not yet been assessed, it seems fair to conclude at this point that there has been no radical change in the pace of economic development in these countries. And the program is probably not without negative consequences. A large portion of the funds is earmarked for improving infrastructure, transport facilities, ports, and so on. One consequence is that economically relevant hinterlands are brought into closer touch with former colonial rulers. This is effected through the ease in exporting primary products once the transport costs from field to port are cut down. Thus the creation of enclaves attached to the metropolitan power and the increased dependence on the production of primary commodities are two possible consequences of the program that need to be examined carefully and critically.

It is difficult to make any summary statement concerning the effect of the European Community on the Associated African States. There are simply too many points of contact and examination of the full implications has only begun. There are sporadic outbreaks of tension between the EC and the Associated States that lead one to reflect. One of the more recent of these outbreaks occurred in October 1972 and concerned a conflict between Italy and the Eighteen over importation of African fruits and vegetables into the EC. Italy happens to produce many of the same products that are produced by the African states, for example, peas, beans, sweet pimentos, eggplant, gourds, celery, and melons. As a result Italy wanted to prevent the unfettered import of these products from Africa, so that she could export more of her own products to the member countries. While such conflicts are regrettable it must be kept in mind that normally African products enjoy duty-free entry into the EC and in fact the EC has allocated some of her development funds in behalf of the development of the African fruit and vegetable industry. Compared with the protectionist inclinations of most nation-states the EC seems very open indeed.[51]

While the overall picture of the EC's effects on Africa is blurred several dangers are readily highlighted: the increased dependence on the former colonial powers, the retardation of industrial growth and economic diversification, the declining share of world trade of less-developed countries, and the reluctance to trade with their fellow African countries because of the broader range of products offered by the economically diversified European countries. All are very real dangers that need to be weighed carefully by the Associated States. The ultimate tragedy would be, as Ali Mazrui has indicated, if the African chose short-term tariff concessions above long-term political autonomy and industrial expansion.[52]

The darkest spot in the external orientation of the EEC is its relations with the Communist states of Eastern Europe. Despite the fact that EEC imports and exports with these states almost tripled between 1958 and 1966 the development of the EEC engendered hostility on the part of the Soviet bloc countries. The initial reaction to the formation of the EEC was one of cautious indifference.[53] This phase lasted from 1958 to July 1961 when Prime Minister Macmillan announced that Britain would attempt to join the EEC. The deeper the interest of nonmember states in joining the EEC, the more intense the Soviet resistance. Khrushchev attempted to cast the EEC alternatively as the latest adaptation of the capitalist system and as a new form of colonialism designed to retain access to the raw materials of Asia and Africa.[54]

The development of the EEC has resulted in more than ideological responses from the Soviet Bloc. It led to a tightening of relationships within COMECON and to increasing integration of the countries of East Europe into the Soviet Union's orbit. "From its founding in 1949 until recently, COMECON was a loosely organized and relatively ineffective coordinating body for eastern Europe. Since the Common Market came into being, COMECON has become transferred into an instrument through which the states of eastern Europe are being absorbed into the Soviet economic complex and are being moved in the direction of political merger."[55]

It would seem that pressures exist for both the EEC and COMECON members to turn inward and for each bloc to become as independent as possible. It would also seem that, to the extent that political institutions emerge which are capable of coordinating and controlling the activity of member states, the freedom of each state to engage in independent foreign policy initiatives leading to the establishment of contacts with respective blocs will decline.

Let us accept for the moment that trade between the EEC and a variety of nonmember states has increased significantly. It is still quite possible that the emergence of regional groupings is perceived by the people as competitive. One could argue that trade may increase at the same time that mutual hostility increases. It could also be argued that, to the extent the people focus their attention and loyalty on European institutions they detract from the loyalty and attention they could direct to other levels, whether this be national, local, or global. As with trade, two conceptual models are implicit here. The first is a competitive or constant-sum model where increases in loyalty for one set of institutions detract from the amount of loyalty for other institutions. Different institutions thus compete with each other for a fixed amount of loyalty. The second model is more elastic. It views loyalties as indefinitely expandable to cover many different institutional arenas. The question of which model is correct is a difficult one. Mitrany suggests that regional unions would set up loyalty commitments that would serve to define further and distinguish given geographical areas: "To build up a cohesive loyalty national movements have often had to disinter or invent all sorts of historical, social and emotional affinities, above all to keep alive the fear of some common external danger. Regionalism, starting with more differences than affinities, would have to go even further in that."[56]

To provide an answer to the question of which model is more appropriate we must draw on information about attitudes and opinions of people in regional blocs. Ronald Inglehart has conducted work in this area. He has provided us with interpretable data and a provocative theoretical argument. Analyzing data from samples of youth in four countries (the Netherlands, Federal Republic of Germany, France, and the United Kingdom), Inglehart found an empirical compatibility between Europeanism and broader forms of cosmopolitanism and internationalism. While the strength of this relationship varied from country to country, Inglehart's smallest space analysis indicated that Europeanism was positively related to a global outlook.[57] In another article Inglehart sets forth the theoretical basis for these findings.[58] He sees cognitive mobilization, part of the continuing process of the modernization of Europe, as lying at the basis of this relationship. As more and more people become absorbed into the communications infrastructure opinions and loyalties previously dormant now become activated. If conditions are such as to cast the role of European institutions in a favorable light, positive loyalty may develop without eroding at all the position of the nation-state. As new institutions and policies become salient for people, new loyalties emerge and attach to them. Since to a large extent the respective institutional and policy areas of the EEC and the nation-states are either complementary or symbiotic—and not competitive—it may be hypothesized that loyalties will also not be competitive.

There is one final way in which we can assess the compatibility of European regionalism and globalism and that is by examining the fit or harmony between regional institutions themselves and global institutions such as the United Nations or the GATT. Although the U.N. made formal constitutional provisions for regional organizations, the political context of the evolution of European-United Nations relations has been strained at times. There is a regrettable tendency, for example, for regional organizations to export many of their serious problems to the United Nations.[59] According to Claude's perceptive analysis, the kinds of issues dealt with by regional organizations represent a limited version of all possible issues, conflictual issues being omitted. A functional differentiation of labor emerges where global institutions deal with conflict-laden matters while regional institutions are preoccupied with cooperative matters. In the long run this would be damaging to the development of global institutions by making them appear weaker and less competent than they really are. European institutions have been seen as antagonistic to global organization for other reasons. Historically, the development of the United Nations has been associated with a process of decolonization, a process that was in many ways coextensive but not identical with the decline of Europe's position in the world. The United Nations, with its emphasis on problems of the Third World, particularly global development programs, rapidly became a symbol of the shift of the center of world politics away from Europe. As Claude put it: "If the League was in some sense a European regional institution, symbolic of the Europe-centeredness of the political world, the United Nations has been from the beginning, and has become increasingly with the passing years, a world organization, symbolic of the de-Europeanization of the political world."[60]

The economic counterpart to this problem concerns the relationship between the EC, seen as an economic unit, and GATT. One could ask whether a regional economic union is compatible with a more global one in terms of both historical and theoretical considerations.[61] The historical conditions concern the evolution of EEC economic policy, particularly its common external tariff; theoretical considerations turn mostly on the question of whether an economic union fosters trade creation or trade diversion.

Even before the EEC was formally inaugurated the potential for its conflicting with GATT was recognized. As far back as 1965, the contracting parties of GATT, at their eleventh session, took up the question of their possible future relationship with the EEC.[62] The most obvious source of conflict stems from Article 1 of the GATT treaty, setting forth the "most favored nation" clause. Essentially, Article 1 states that any tariff or trade concession granted to any country must be extended to all the other contracting members. In other words tariffs could not be lowered on a discriminatory basis unless certain conditions were met. In Article 24 of GATT, it was specified that tariffs could be reduced on a regional basis provided "the duties and other regulations of commerce . . . shall not on the whole be higher or more restrictive than the general incidence of the duties and regulations of commerce applicable in the constituent territories prior to the formation of such union."[63]

The theoretical argument for or against a free trade area or customs union is generally made in terms of its trade-creating versus trade-diverting aspects. Trade creation occurs

> . . . when, as a result of the removal of trade barriers within a customs union, a member country replaces its own high-cost (formally protected) production by imports from another member of the union. Trade diversion occurs when, as a result of the removal of trade barriers within a customs union, a member country replaces its imports from a low-cost non-union source, by a higher cost source within the union. The shift is caused by the newly created tariff discrimination favoring union members.[64]

It was Jacob Viner's argument that the welfare impact of a customs union should be assessed in terms of the differential between trade creation and diversion. The greater the creation and the less the diversion of trade, the more beneficial the customs union. The question now becomes one of determining which kinds of custom unions are likely to produce a high level of trade creation. Viner offers the following guidelines in helping to answer this question: a customs union is likely to have a beneficial impact if (1) the economic area covered by the custom union is large, thus allowing room for a comprehensive specialization of labor; (2) the average tariff level on imports coming from countries outside the customs zone is low compared with what those tariffs would be in the absence of the union; and if (3) there is a large differential in unit costs for protected industries of the same kind in different areas within the customs union.[65] Kreinin presents evidence to indicate that the EC compares favorably with most other commercial areas in terms of these three criteria. A high volume of trade occurred among the Six before the Community was formed thus cutting down on the possibility of trade diversion. Also the common tariff toward nonmember countries is very low in most cases, especially after the Kennedy Round. In some cases, the Six extended reductions in its own tariffs to all outside countries in order to avoid charges of discrimination. Finally, there is much evidence to indicate that unit costs differ widely from country to country within the Community and that an elimination of tariffs will lead to comparative advantages through elimination of protected industries.[66]

A Third Bloc and Militancy Between Regions

Consider a world in which Western Europe becomes the core of an economically, politically, and militarily powerful region. German industry becomes linked effectively to an efficient French agriculture. Great Britain's admission has added stature to Europe's advanced technologies in computer industries and aerospace. A common currency has been adopted and common policies have been set up in agriculture, industry, transport, labor, and social affairs. Finally, owing to her internal unity and the fact that she faces the world as a unit, Europe adopts a common foreign policy and defense policy. De Gaulle's dream of an effective French force de frappe becomes a European reality, as jointly, Britain, France, and Germany produce a formidable finite deterrent system.

How would such a Europe affect the global political system? What kind of force would it be? Granted that presently Europe is a long way from the condition described in the scenario, now is the time to assess its potential impact.

On balance the legacy of World War II highlighted the dangers of nationalism. Somehow loyalties to the nation-state had to be checked and made to dovetail into some larger scheme of political and social unity. The optimistic globalism of the immediate postwar period gave way to a proliferation of regional units. Their institutions were to create partial zones of peace that would serve as bridges between blocs. For many, if not most Europeans, regional integration was an expedient. It was unrealistic to expect the countries of Western Europe, Asia, Africa, and Latin America to unite. Thus temporary halfway houses would be created. This argument is stated well by Denis de Rougement: "Everything . . . singles Europe out to foment the antibodies that will render mankind immune to some of the viruses Europe alone was propagating. In saving itself by federation (an arrangement far older than its nationalism), it can offer the world the recipe and the model of a fruitful transcendence of the national framework."[67]

While some saw Western Europe as the beginning of a global integration process others saw it as the incipient formation of another powerful bloc, potentially more militant than the separate states. Beneath this argument was the notion that the powerful were destined to be militant, that powerful states were likely to play an imperial role, and that expansive capabilities meant expansive intentions. Still others were not willing to grant an independent role to regional unions and interpreted them as extensions of Cold War power politics. In many ways the function of military alliances in the post-World War II era is to formalize spheres of influence.

These questions are important and complicated and call for a much more detailed analysis than can be given here. But the problem can usefully be examined briefly from three perspectives: (1) the relationship between power and militancy; (2) the relationship among numbers of actors, systemic uncertainty, and propensity to war; and (3) the relationship among numbers of actors, crosscutting cleavages, and conflict.

Power and Militancy

Why do not Belgium, Luxembourg, and Portugal perceive the Soviet Union as a threat in the same way the United States does? Why are they not willing to shoulder larger proportions of the defense budget within NATO? One quick answer is that they do not worry since the United States is responsible for checking the Soviet Union. But this begs the question of what it is that makes the United States responsible. Another response is that they simply cannot afford to play a military role. But the matter goes beyond this. Ethical positions are inexpensive. Why do not more Western European countries take up a moral position condemning the Communists in Vietnam? Also, most countries in Western Europe do not perceive Vietnam as one of their vital interests whereas the United States does (or has). Not to be able to shoulder the expense of a war is one thing; not to feel the war is necessary is another.

One attempt to explain this is embodied in the "Great powers must become imperial" thesis. Robert Tucker presents the case for power creating its own interests.[68] The greater the power the more expansively the state defines its own interests until finally national interests become coterminous with imperial ones. The difficulty with this argument is that it essentially recapitulates the problem in different words. Rather than explanation it offers a definition.

Olson and Zeckhauser start from a deductive theory (rather than with an examination of history) and draw certain conclusions for burden sharing in alliances, particularly in NATO.[69] The authors distinguish between public and private goods, public goods being available to all if they are achieved and cannot be denied to individual members (e.g., deterrence for an alliance). Private goods are specific to individuals. They can be given to some individuals and denied others (e.g., money, property, tax credits). The authors demonstrate that with public goods, the rational incentive to pay is dependent upon the perception of the probability of the actor that its contribution will help to achieve the goal. The less wealthy, powerful, and large a state is, the more it will perceive its contribution as futile. This works toward the adoption of an attitude of resignation. Larger powers perceive the probelm in exactly the opposite way. If the United States pays half the cost for the NATO deterrent its decision not to contribute will mean no deterrent. Luxembourg's one-half of one percent will matter little. Surely the logic of this argument applies to perceptions of interest in international politics in general and is not limited to sharing burdens within alliance blocs.

One can conceptualize the problem in the following way. The global system can be viewed as a collection of alliances, even if they are only latent.

That is, alliances need not be defined by some formal pact but by a common-ality of interest and some recognition that nations are jointly pursuing similar goals. A small state with an interest in containing a large power is likely to have its behavior affected by the presence of another state whose policy is to check that power. These two states are linked in an alliance where a process of mutual adjustment[70] stabilizes their behavior toward the third power. In those cases of common interest where the interest (goal, good) is public, in the sense used here, it becomes rational for a state to play a role calculated on the basis of the effect of its contribution. Developments in the global system, particularly in tech-nology, communications, and weapons systems, are making more and more of the goals of states public. The transition from defense to deterrence as the prime component of military policy has made it difficult to protect certain allies but not others. Kissinger argues that de Gaulle recognized that in NATO the dif-ference between a committed ally and a neutral is that the neutral does not pay. They both receive the benefit of the nuclear shield of the United States.[71] This is also why the McNamara Doctrine caused so much dissension within NATO. By proposing a more discriminating nuclear strategy it raised the specter of deter-rence becoming a private commodity, to be enjoyed by some nations (perhaps the United States, Canada, and Great Britain) and denied others. The fear of Europeans was that Europe would become a battlefield for conventional war while the United States' deterrence would be retained exclusively for less periph-eral clashes.

What are the implications of this theory for a united, politically strong Europe? According to the power and militancy hypothesis a stronger Europe might want to play a more influential role in Eastern Europe. It might decide to revive the former French influence in North Africa or increase its presence in the Mediterranean or the Middle East. Pinder and Pryce, in presenting the case for a united Europe, argue that the weakness of each individual nation-state in Europe is the reason for its inability to deal effectively with the Soviet Bloc.

> For a long time the German policy was to offer the Russians detente as a prize for allowing German reunification—or, more exactly, to resist almost any measure of detente on the grounds that it might freeze the division of Germany. This proved barren because in conditions of East-West tension no prize seems big enough to the Russians to justify their allowing East Germany to rejoin West Germany, short perhaps of West Germany agreeing to join the Soviet Bloc.[72]

> ... the Gaullist idea of a Franco-Russian guarantee for a reunified but neutralized Germany was an empty one. For France is so much weaker than Russia that the French part of the "guarantee" is meaningless ... The fact is that France, like Germany, is a medium-sized state, and as such has nothing to offer the Russians that would lead them to change their posture in a matter they regard as vital to their security.[73]

It is clear that Pinder and Pryce see the problem of Europe's lack of global influence as stemming from its weakness. Detente with the Soviet Bloc is seen as a problem of having bargaining leverage, something to give in return for Soviet concessions. A strong, united Europe would, in their view, play an active role. It could offer economic incentives, such as credits, payments arrangements, and trade conditions that would be attractive to Eastern Europe. It could foster cooperation in science and advanced technologies and it could act as a forum for arms control and perhaps eventual American disengagement from Europe. But the incentives Pinder and Pryce offer are those derived from bargaining from situations of strength: "A federal Europe could both provide a counterweight to Russia in conventional defense and offer the Russians and East Europeans powerful economic and political incentives for detente . . . a European Political Community, integrating the conventional forces of the member countries, could counterbalance Russia, even if the Americans were to withdraw their troops."[74]

The authors present a good case for an expanded European role, a role that would be based on its newly founded strength-through-unity. Although this active role aims at peaceful relationships (detente) it is clearly a detente based on dissociative rather than associative policies.[75] That is, in spite of the comprehensive program of economic cooperation envisioned, there is more than a hint of hegemony in the relationship and the proposal for an integrated defense can only be perceived as a threat by the Soviet Bloc. If peace would be fostered it would probably be owing to a stalemate rather than to positive cooperation. In view of the way the Soviet Bloc has responded to European integration in the past, even when it concerned only relatively minor economic and technical questions, it must be assumed that they will respond to a militarily united Europe with outright alarm.

I have not argued here that Europe should not unite, or that a united Europe would not play a positive role in global politics, or even that the fears of the Soviet Bloc are well founded in resisting a stronger Europe. I have simply tried to speculate on possible reactions. Below I want to assess several arguments for the effect of a united Europe on the stability of the international system.

Multipolarity, Uncertainty, and Europe

If Europe were to emerge as a first-rate power, on the same plane as the United States and the Soviet Union, a multipolar global system will have emerged. Each of the three blocs would then be characterized by a bloc leader, a set of allies (or satellites; this depends upon the degree of hierarchical control in the bloc) and a second-strike nuclear capability. What effect will this emerging multipolarity have on the stability of the international system?

The literature on international systems offers some theoretical cutting points. The traditional writings on balance of power stress the cynical but moderate nature of diplomacy and the frequent but limited use of violent conflict. Balance of power systems seem to involve frequent-though-small conflicts. One source of conflict is the uncertainty in the system which in turn is partly linked to the number of major national actors (or more precisely, to the number of possible combinations among these actors). Any one state will have a difficult time in determining the strength of response to any given action since in an

n-actor system, $\frac{n(n-1)}{2}$ possible dyads could form. A high level of indeterminacy characterizes the contemplation of aggressive actions in this type of system. Thus some wars occur because the reaction to an aggression is underestimated or in some cases (e.g., insecurity over the potential intentions of future coalition) overestimated. The latter type of miscalculation usually manifests itself in a preemptive war.

The most sophisticated argument for this position is made by Kenneth Waltz who sees the "stability of a bipolar world" as having its source in its lack of uncertainty, in the clarity with which rewards and punishments are structured. The obsession of the United States and the Soviet Union with each other may be a source of tension but it is also a source of stability, a deterrent to the actual outbreak of war. In a global system without peripheries (i.e., gray areas are not clearly within one or another bloc) stability would be greatest; no uncertainty would exist; no gambles would be encouraged; no miscalculations should occur.[76]

On close examination this argument raises several problems. Aside from the fact that war arises from a number of conditions besides uncertainty there is the more pressing question of source of uncertainty. Three obvious candidates are: (1) the number of potential combinations of actors, (2) the presence or absence of peripheries, and (3) the ability to assess capabilities. It is only the first that favors the bipolar system. There is nothing inherent in the bipolar system which makes for the absence of peripheries. It may occur just as easily in a multipolar system. It is much more a function of the geographical scope of the interests of the major actors than the number of actors itself. For example Kaplan argues that risky behavior and willingness to go to war are related to the uncertainties of the loose bipolar system but here it is not bipolarity that is important but the looseness of which Kaplan speaks,[77] a looseness that could just as easily be a characteristic of a multipolar world. Systemic uncertainty is a function of the perception of the probability of alternative responses to aggressive moves. In game theoretic terms it is associated with ambiguity of certain outcomes in a payoff matrix or ambiguity concerning the structure of the matrix itself. Although the present bipolarity removes alliances as a source of uncertainty, several others remain. Indeed, to talk about the world in bipolar terms strikes me as being "great-power-centric." It is to view the world from Washington and Moscow. The poles themselves have never been as internally homogeneous as we have imagined. Western Europe has been less concerned about Southeast Asia and Cuba and more concerned about Suez, Algeria, and North Africa in general. That the United States could not make its nuclear guarantee equally credible to all situations introduced uncertainty into the strategic picture, an uncertainty that was only aggravated (in European eyes) by the evolution of the McNamara Doctrine. In this sense an emerging multipolarity might introduce more certainty by providing Western Europe with a nuclear capability of her own, a capability that would credibly be used in a variety of subnuclear situations where the utilization of the United States force is questionable.

International Pluralism, Multipolarity, and Europe

There is yet another way in which a strong, united Europe might have a beneficial impact on the global system. The argument is that a strong European bloc will reduce the sense of competition between the Soviet Union and the United States. If multipolarity emerges the two existing blocs will soften; members of one bloc will occasionally dislodge themselves and take positions along with members of another bloc. A system of crosscutting cleavages will emerge which will dampen interbloc conflict.

This pluralistic model of global politics is set forth by Karl Deutsch and J. David Singer. Their basic argument is that, to the extent conflict positions are superimposed or reinforcing, positive feedback is strengthened and self-correcting feedbacks are weakened.

> Thus, if all clashes and incompatibilities in the system produce
> the same divisions and coalitions—if all members in class Blue line up
> *with* one another and *against* all or most of those in class *Red*—the
> line of cleavage will be wide and deep, with positive feedback operat-
> ing both within and between the two classes or clusters. But if some
> members of class Blue have some incompatible interests with others
> in their class, and an overlap of interest with some of those in Red,
> there will be some degree of negative or self-correcting feedback,
> both within and between the two classes.[78]

The argument over the relation between actors and interaction opportunities is generalized and given fresh insight by Johan Galtung's conceptualization of entropy in the global system. A high entropy system would be characterized by a large number of units interacting freely with one another. There would be no pockets of dense interactions, no states with high interactions contrasted with states with low interactions. In an entropic system one could expect many small conflicts but the conflicts themselves would be depolarized in the sense of not occurring over the same issues for a given number of actors. Since very little pattern exists in this system, indeed, since in a perfectly entropic system interactions would be uniformly (more precisely, randomly) distributed across units, there would be little opportunity for cumulative hostility to build. "In a high entropy system the world is more complicated, more 'messy' as we have expressed it. The possibilities at any point in the system are *more* numerous indeed but their consequences are slight.[79]

If one extends the line of reasoning implicit in the Deutsch-Singer-Galtung argument it seems that the greater the number of systems actors the lower the possibility of large, uncontrollable conflicts. Galtung makes this point explicitly and adds that the chances for an associative peace are maximized by a multiunit setting. For the most part these arguments seem convincing, with one reservation. Whereas a multipolar system would be more flexible and would not promote the pitting of one bloc against another in all-out war, the other side of the coin would seem to be increased risk taking and uncertainty. Morton Kaplan notes that

One of the factors that inhibited League of Nations intervention in the disputes of the 1930's was that axis advances did not constitute polarized threats against any particular or specific European or American nation. The vital difference in 1950 in Korea stemmed from the fact that only the United States could respond and that the failure to respond by the United States would have had a direct impact upon its national security of a visible kind that was not equally apparent to France or England in the 1930's in the Ethiopian case or in the Manchurian affair.[80]

How are we then to assess the impact of the emergence of Europe as an independent force in the global system? We could expect the diminishing of tension between the two extant blocs, a decline of the action-reaction process that characterizes their relations (and that becomes most explicit in arms races), and an increase of interactions. We could also expect, and here experimental results from Brody's simulation bear us out, a greater tendency for communications between the North Atlantic Treaty Organization and the Warsaw Pact countries as well as a loosening of within-bloc relations within these two alliances. This loosening of alignments might also be accompanied by an increase in the perception of threat from members within the bloc.[81] Finally, as the literature on international aspects of civil strife points out, one line of evidence suggests that the level of intervention in the internal affairs of states is a function of the form of the international system. Intervention is maximized in unipolar and tight bipolar systems and minimized in multipolar systems.[82]

In the final analysis there is no conflict between Waltz's argument for the stability of a bipolar world and the Deutsch-Singer-Galtung thesis that peace is most likely to come about after the emergence of a plurality of global actors. The kind of peace of which Waltz speaks is dissociative peace based on states placing their power against one another. It is a standoffish kind of peace based on a threat system. The kind of peace of which Galtung speaks, and presumably also Deutsch and Singer,[83] takes on more positive aspects, being based on interactions—cooperative and conflictual—over a broad range of issues. It is much more a working peace in Mitrany's sense.

ASSESSMENT AND CONCLUSION

The European Community is engaged in a bewildering variety of functions having to do with external affairs. The Community plays a strong role in the formulation and guidance of foreign commercial policy as the Kennedy Round indicated; it is also recognized as an independent entity by most countries and regions of the world. Hopefully, the examination of the behavior of the Community during the Kennedy Round and the survey of EC-COMECON relations, has shed some light on this focus. One could also have looked at relations with the African world, particularly as they have developed through the Yaoundé Convention as well as the development aid administered through the European Development Fund (EDF). Whether this association is beneficial or "a typical neo-imperialist pact"[84] is debatable but the EC clearly has had an impact, at least if we are to judge by the interest that Africans show in its development.

The difficult question is whether, in matters of external concern, the Community is system or subsystem dominant. Are the formulation and control of external behavior functions of institutions uniquely organized at the supra-national level or do they issue from a concert of independent nation-states? These are the polar extremes, of course, and the truth may lie anywhere in between. In general, however, we may conclude that in matters concerning important political questions (such as the admission of a new member), the individual nation-states retain a predominant role and negotiations tend to be bilateral. In more technical, less controversial matters supranational institutions enjoy more autonomy and a loosely monitored delegation of responsibilities is likely to take place.

The orientation adopted here suggests that one can learn much about a system by examining its environment, and vice versa. This approach embodies more than the trivial suggestion that system affects environment and vice versa. It suggests that we view system and environment as part of a unified field, an integral behavioral matrix. System and environment do more than affect each other; they also *reflect* each other, displaying a remarkable purpose-like fit for their respective forms and functions. If we take this position not as a cause for rejecting traditional system-environment distinctions but as an insight stimulating the search for interdependencies, it has good effects. The focus is not on the impact of specific environmental events but on the form (morphology, structure) of the environment and the consequences this bears for the system.

Let me state the model more explicitly. Social systems are viewed as tension-oriented, variety-managing, structure-elaborating systems. Such systems thrive on stress often introduced through environmental variety. The emergence and development of the EC represented a source of increased variety for the global system to which it responded in a number of ways but primarily through the elaboration of new structures. Thus adaptation for complex social systems is seen as a process of pattern matching, of finding fit through the creation or differentiation of new structures.

The central importance of the notion of variety for adaptive behavior in complex social systems is discussed by Ashby in his "law of requisite variety." Essentially, this law states that any environmental disturbance (variety) on a system must be regulated by the system through an effort to map it through structural elaboration.[85] Buckley states the relationship in the following way: "In effect, complex adaptive systems reduce the randomness of environmental variety by 'harnessing' the tension generated through the development of new structures. Constraint is increased—and with it a more complex system structure —by mapping the environmental variety into employable form."[86]

Since the formulation offered here leans heavily on the shape of the environment it would be helpful to establish the dominant forms the environment can assume. Relying heavily on an earlier formulation by Emery and Trist,[87] I attempt to establish a typology of environments below. Keep in mind that we are considering the EC as the environment and the remainder of the world as the system. Searching for changes in the global system should provide a key to changes in the EC.

1. *Random environment.* In this environment Europe would be characterized by entropic interactions—no clear structure or pattern. Efficient response or mapping in this kind of environment would be impossible. Since it is characteristic of social systems to structure their activities into definite patterns this type has a low empirical probability of occurring. Therefore this category is introduced only as a base line. Adaptation requires some departure from chaos, some repeatability in the environment; it is what Ashby calls "the recurrent situation" and what Campbell refers to as "stable discontinuities." The system's response to this kind of Europe would be purely random, the optimal strategy being "the simple tactic of attempting to do one's best on a purely local basis."[88]

2. *Clustered-decentralized environments.* In this environment the behavior impinging on the global system starts to hang together in definite configurations. The environment assumes form, pattern, although the form is such that interactions are much denser within units than between them, and regulation, to the extent it occurs, is a function of the basic components of the system (states) rather than an overarching organization. This environment is best illustrated by the classical balance of power system composed of relatively autonomous nation-states.

Systemic responses to the emergence of the clustered-decentralized environment are appropriate, that is, they have adaptive value. These responses must be of a special kind, being limited essentially to ad hoc, bilateral relationships. Thus concrete responses to this type of environment will include recognition of units, sending and receiving ambassadors, intergovernmental collaboration, and bilateral diplomacy. The fluid nature of this environment and the absence of structure at the systemic level preclude adaptation based on more structured, multilateral processes. In Ashby's terms the absence of environmental disturbance at the systemic level precludes globally systemic responses. All the variety to be mapped lies within the component units.

3. *Clustered-centralized environment.* If Western Europe were to evolve toward a hierarchical form of federal union, much as the nation-states formed historically, this category would be fulfilled. Such a development would be a disturbance to which the global system would have to respond. These responses, or variety-management processes, might include (*a*) awareness of the EC as a cognitive reality and an affective one, that is, a distinct set of European political institutions, policies, and leaders would be perceived and positive or negative significance attached to them; (*b*) the establishment of diplomatic contacts at the European level; (*c*) commercial relations with the emergent level playing its own role; and (*d*) the development of exchange and threat systems in which the community would relate to the world.

4. *Clustered, centralized-decentralized environment.* This is the "causal texture" of the environment I believe the EC most closely approximates today. Hierarchically it is a mixed system. Rather than neat layers' being superimposed one on top of another this environment is like a marble cake characteristic of cooperative federalism in the United States.[89] In this category, form and function blend together in confused—though discernible—patterns. National,

supranational, and subnational forces fuse in the processing of any given issue. Structurally, this system is marked by interpenetration as evidenced for example by the roles of the foreign ministers, Committee of Permanent Representatives, and the General Directorate of External Affairs in the Kennedy Round and in the negotiations for British entry. It is also characterized by delegation of power from national to supranational authorities, a delegation that rests on a presumed distinction between administrative and political tasks.

It is difficult to respond adequately to a system of this type. Traditional bilateral contacts are inadequate and organized multilateral responses are too presumptive in the amount of systemic structure they assume exists at the European level. What is needed here as a response is a strategy of multilevel contact, but more important, a strategy of flexibility, of niche-filling. It demands a good deal of experimental probing and of trial and error behavior until satisfactory fits are found. It also requires the ability to learn the difference between a political body and its delegate vehicle.

In the development of its internal policy the Community assumed a coherent structure that caused external actors to respond to it (in some respects) as a unit. In turn the Community was forced to adopt unified positions when confronting its environment. The subsequent attempt by the EC to find its place in the world is very much an extension of this process of mutual adjustment.

Conclusion:
Models and Regional Integration

One of the goals of writing this book was to provide a conceptual map for the study of regional integration in Western Europe. The key tools used in this effort have been provided by structural functional analysis as it has been elaborated in the political development literature. I confess that when I began this book I started with the assumption that the European Community was an imperfect microcosm of a fully developed nation-state and that parallels between the process of nation building and the process of supranational integration were insightful and productive even if not always strictly accurate. It now seems clear that this strong version of the analogy of regional integration as a larger process of nation building and state building is inadequate.

Many of the shortcomings of the model became clear while research on European integration was in progress. Reconceptualization therefore took place during the research process itself. Thus, there is no chapter in this book on the political socialization of Europeans where originally such a chapter was intended. I have come to view the construction of European loyalties that are in any sense akin to national attachments as irrelevant to regional integration. Similarly, there is very little treatment of the autonomy of the European Community's emerging political institutions from national authorities. I believe that this gap is also for a good reason, viz., that regional integration, at least to the extent that it has occurred in Western Europe, is not taking place at the expense of the nation-state. Rather as Lindberg and Scheingold note, there is a good possibility that regionalism and nationalism enjoy a symbiotic relationship.[1]

Recently, Donald Puchala has written an article that simultaneously details many inadequacies of past models of regional integration and sets forth an alternative model. He dubs this new model of integration the "Concordance System" and carefully distinguishes its characteristics from the nation-state. This model is defined as follows: "A 'Concordance System' by my definition is an international system wherein actors find it possible consistently to harmonize their interests, compromise their differences and reap mutual rewards from their intereactions."[2]

The Concordance System is marked by a pragmatic bargaining style, a high degree of mutual sensitivity among actors, the presence of actors from several levels (subnational, national, transnational, and supranational), and a certain level of legitimacy for Community institutions.[3] As a descriptive model for capturing the essential patterns of the international integrative process this is a satisfying model. Much of what this model implies is of course not inconsistent with the approach and details of my own analysis, for example, the emphasis on the pragmatic style of interest groups, the existence of nonnational actors in the interest-articulation and external relations processes, the limited legitimacy and authority of Community institutions. Still, Puchala's article makes it clear that the differences between regional integration and the formation of nation-states need to be spelled out. I believe there are at least three important differences.

One, nationalism was and is a process of the emergence and growth of deep-seated loyalties both to an ascriptively defined group, for example, a language, racial, religious, or territorial group, and to commonly evolved cultural and historical communities. These loyalties are deep-seated in the sense that the nation-state provides the fundamental orientation points for the identification of the individual. One is identified as a national, his education is national in scope and content, and decisions are made concerning one's economic welfare and military security by national authorities; even definitions of morality are decided by national institutions when a violent act is interpreted differently if committed privately inside a state as opposed to the same act committed publicly (i.e., with the sanction of public institutions) against members of another nation-state. National loyalties are very diffuse, partly nonutilitarian, and they often emerge through a series of rapid, discontinuous social transformations. In contrast with this, loyalties toward European Community institutions are specific, very utilitarian in the sense of being organized around the expectation of an economic payoff, and these loyalties have emerged rather quietly and incrementally.

A second difference is that nation building is a process accompanied by profound social transformation including the breakdown and disruption of many traditional social structures. This is true whether one contemplates the emergence of nationalism in England and France (where in the former case strict limitations were placed on the monarchy and in the latter the monarchy was completely abolished) or in more recent examples of modernizing societies in Africa and Asia. Nationalism traditionally involves large-scale changes in the economic and social composition of society—the decline of the aristocracy, the rise of the third estate and the idea of democracy, the movement from ascription to achievement, the ferment among artists and intellectuals. Professor Kohn captures the pervasiveness of nationalism in the changes of the educational structure in France: "The French Revolution established the first comprehensive system of national education to raise new generations of virtuous and patriotic citizens. Education was for the first time regarded as a duty and chief interest of the nation. Only a common education, it was felt, could realize the unity of the fatherland and the union of its citizens. The emphasis shifted from the classics and the humanities to patriotic songs and history. . . ."[4]

When compared with these radical changes, European regional integration appears as a ripple on the surface. To be sure, integration has involved some important societal changes in the scale of production, greater rationalization of the use of resources, the embourgeoisement of the worker, the growth of the importance of technocrats and economic managers. Still these changes are not of the magnitude of those accompanying the emergence of nation-states.

A third difference between the processes of nation building and regional-community formation is that feelings of nationalism were closely tied up with the desire for autonomous political expression, that is, a nation generally wanted to form its own independent state. There seems to be no comparable desire for a sovereign state at the European Community level. Neither is regional integration eroding the power of the nation-state.

If regional integration is not best understood as an international extension of the nation-building process, how are we to approach it? I suggest that Puchala's notion of the "Concordance System" is an excellent place to start. I would like to add to and elaborate his ideas by positing four characteristics of the regional integration process in Europe: limited institutional autonomy; limited scope of policy making; limited support for European Community institutions; and limited institutional variety.

The European Community is not just an international concert in which agreements are reached through multilateral diplomatic negotiation. It is also a political system that possesses many of the functional characteristics of domestic political systems. The structures performing these functions, however, have limited independence in carrying out their activities. Their revenue base is very small and at the mercy of national governments and their autonomy to make decisions is limited by the threat of the national veto. In short, the range and sheer quantity of Community activity is impressive but the key control centers lie at the national level. Second, while the scope of the European Community's activities is fairly extensive it is limited in the sense of being removed from some of the most important political functions, for example, conduct of foreign policy, defense, public order, and civil liberties. Third, the European Community has only limited support for its activities both in terms of feelings that have penetrated mass and elite levels as well as of the restricted scope of issues to which supportive attitudes apply. The European Community requires limited, issue-specific support and this support is tendered very cautiously and with the understanding that the minimum interests of the actors will be preserved. Nothing approximating the diffuse reservoir of support for national political institutions exists. That is what makes it so difficult to go beyond the present system where interest groups play so important a part. Finally, the European Community does not possess the full range of political institutions required to effectively discharge its functions. There are no political parties and no representative legislature. There is a Council of Ministers, resembling both executive and legislature, which is made up of national officials who essentially moonlight at the supranational level. The Commission, whose hybrid status was discussed in detail, is by far the most energetic and innovative of the European Community's institutions but is politically not responsible to the people.

These limitations are closely interrelated. The limited scope of policy making makes it possible for the European Community to deal with issues sector by sector, and to make whatever compromises need to be made within a sector. This removes the need to treat issues within a comprehensive framework where separate interests must barter and compromise with one another. Consequently, the European Community can get by without having to face the difficulties of piecing together coalitions but in so doing it is forced to rely heavily on interest groups. This in turn puts the focus on narrow pressure-group claims and encourages solutions at the technocratic rather than at the political level. The final consequence is a limitation on the buildup of legitimacy of Community institutions and a destruction of political accountability. The former is hampered because of the narrow, hedonistic policy-making calculus in the European Community. There are many demands made of Community institutions but these lack programmatic appeal, ideological coherence, and underlying principles of any sort. Accountability suffers because the initiators of policy making, the interest groups, are so numerous, fractionated, and devoid of broad political programs as to make their consequences, taken individually, virtually invisible and hence uncontrollable. The Commission, the only real European policy-making institution, does not have the power to transform and significantly reshape group demands. Instead, it reluctantly parcels out authority to individual groups.

It follows from the above that the European Community is neither a superstate nor an emergent nation. It is not a superstate because it lacks the significant qualities of a state—legitimacy, autonomy, sovereignty—and lacks a certain level of capability including the financial and military resources to provide for the welfare and security of its population. It is not a nation because the loyalties, expectations, and sentiments of the populations of the member states are organized around individual nation-states.

Whatever name one gives to it, the European Community is an important new layer of experience grafted onto the original nation-states. Within stated limits, it is a political system that legislates, administers, adjusts conflicts, and responds to the demands of organized groups. To be sure the power exercised by Community institutions is delegated power, given by national authorities and closely monitored by them. This delegated power is somewhat unusual since it is delegated upward. It represents administrative centralization rather than decentralization. In the final analysis, this delegation is based on the tenuous distinction between policy making and administration. Perhaps the European Community, truly a creature of the individual member states, will one day prove too difficult for its parents to control.

References

Alger, Chadwick F. "Comparison of Intranational and International Politics." In R. Barry Farrell (ed.), *Approaches to Comparative and International Politics.* Evanston: Northwestern University Press, 1966. Pp. 301-328.

———. "Problems in Global Organization," *International Social Science Journal,* 22, 4 (1970), 691-709.

Alker, Hayward R., and Bruce M. Russett. *World Politics in the General Assembly.* New Haven: Yale University Press, 1965.

Allen, James Jay. "The European Common Market and General Agreement on Tariffs and Trade: A Study in Compatibility," *Law and Contemporary Problems,* 26, 3 (1961), 559-571.

Almond, Gabriel A. "A Comparative Study of Interest Groups and the Political Process." In David Apter and Harry Eckstein (eds.), *Comparative Politics: A Reader.* New York: Free Press, 1963. Pp. 397-408.

———. "Interest Groups and the Political Process." In Roy C. Macridis and Bernard E. Brown (eds.), *Comparative Politics: Notes and Readings.* Rev. ed. Homewood, Ill.: Dorsey Press, 1964. Pp. 131-139.

———. Introduction. In Gabriel A. Almond and James S. Coleman (eds.), *The Politics of the Developing Areas.* Princeton: Princeton University Press, 1960. Pp. 3-64.

———. "Political Development: Analytical and Normative Perspectives," *Comparative Political Studies,* 1, 4 (1969), 447-469.

Almond Gabriel A. and James S. Coleman (eds.). *The Politics of the Developing Areas.* Princeton: Princeton University Press, 1960.

Almond, Gabriel A. and G. Bingham Powell, Jr. *Comparative Politics: A Developmental Approach.* Boston and Toronto: Little, Brown and Co., 1966.

Almond, Gabriel A. and Sidney Verba. *The Civic Culture.* Boston: Little, Brown and Co., 1965.

Angell, Robert C. *Peace on the March: Transnational Participation.* New York: Van Nostrand Reinhold Co., 1969.

Apter, David E. *The Politics of Modernization.* Chicago: University of Chicago Press, 1965.

Aron, Raymond. *The Great Debate.* New York: Doubleday and Co., 1965.

———. *Peace and War.* New York: Praeger Publications, 1968.

Ashby, W. R. "Adaptation in the Multi-Stable System." In F. E. Emery (ed.), *Systems Thinking.* Middlesex, England: Penguin Books, 1969. Pp. 230-240.

———. "Self-Regulation and Requisite Variety." In ibid., pp. 110-124.

Bachrach, Peter and Morton S. Baratz. "Decisions and Nondecisions: An Analytical Framework," *American Political Science Review.* 57 (Sept. 1963), 632-642.

———. "Two Faces of Power." In Roderick Bell, David V. Edwards, and R. Harrison Wagner (eds.), *Political Power.* New York: Free Press, 1969. Pp. 94-110.

181

Bentley, Arthur. *Inquiry into Inquiries: Essays in Social Theory.* Boston: Beacon Press, 1954.

Blalock, Hubert M. *Social Statistics.* New York: McGraw-Hill Book Co., 1960.

Bliss, Howard. Introduction. In Howard Bliss (ed.), *The Political Development of the European Community.* Waltham, Mass.: Blaisdell Publishing Co., 1970. Pp. 1-23.

Boulding, Kenneth E. "Toward a General Theory of Growth," *Canadian Journal of Economic and Political Science,* 19, 3 (Aug. 1953), 326-340.

———. *A Primer on Social Dynamics.* New York: Free Press, 1970.

Box, G. E. P., and George C. Tiao. "A Change in Level of a Non-Stationary Time Series," *Biometrika,* 52, 1, 2 (1965), 181-192.

Brickman, Howard J. "Conceptual Frameworks for the Study of Integration." Evanston: Northwestern University (May 1969). Mimeo.

Brody, Richard H. "Some Systemic Effects of the Spread of Nuclear Weapons Technology: A Study through Simulation of a Multi-Nuclear Future," *Journal of Conflict Resolution,* 7 (Dec. 1963), 633-753.

Buckley, Walter. *Sociology and Modern Systems Theory.* Englewood Cliffs, N.J.: Prentice-Hall, 1967.

Campbell, Donald T. "Common Fate, Similarity and Other Indices of the Status of Aggregates of Persons as Social Entities." In J. David Singer (ed.), *Human Behavior and International Politics.* Chicago: Rand McNally and Co., 1965. Pp. 85-95.

———. "Pattern-Matching as Essential to Distal Knowing." In K. R. Hammond (ed.), *The Psychology of Egon Brunswick.* New York: Holt, Rinehart and Winston, 1966. Pp. 81-106.

Campbell, Donald T. and Robert A. Levine. *Ethnocentricism: Theories of Conflict, Ethnic Attitudes and Group Behavior.* New York: John Wiley and Sons, 1972.

Campbell, Donald T. and Julian C. Stanley. *Experimental and Quasi-Experimental Designs for Research.* Chicago: Rand McNally and Co., 1966.

Caporaso, James A. "Theory and Method in the Study of International Integration," *International Organization,* 25, 2 (1971), 228-253.

———. *Functionalism and Regional Integration: A Logical and Empirical Assessment.* Beverly Hills, Calif.: Sage Publications, 1972.

Caporaso, James A. and Alan Pelowski. "Economic and Political Integration in Europe: A Time-Series, Quasi-Experimental Analysis," *American Political Science Review,* 65, 2 (June 1971), 418-433.

Carr, E. H. *Nationalism and After.* London: Macmillan, 1945.

Cartou, Louis. "Le Rôle de la Commission." In Pierre Gerbet and Daniel Pepy (eds.), *La Décision dans les Communautés Européennes.* Brussels: University of Brussels Press, 1969. Pp. 3-11.

Clark, W. Hartley. *The Politics of the Common Market.* Englewood Cliffs, N.J.: Prentice-Hall, 1967.

Claude, Inis, Jr. "European Organization in the Global Context." Lectures given on March 15-17, Brussels: Free University of Brussels, 1965.

Coombes, David. *Politics and Bureaucracy in the European Community.* London: George Allen and Unwin, 1970.

———. *Toward a European Civil Service.* Political Economic Planning Publication, European Ser. 7. London: Chatham House, March, 1968.

Cosgrove, Carol Ann and Kenneth J. Twitchett. "Merging the Communities: A Milestone in West European Integration," *ORBIS,* 13, 3 (Fall 1969), 848-862.

Dahl, Robert. *Who Governs?* New Haven: Yale University Press, 1961.

Dahlberg, Kenneth. "The Common Market Commission and the Politics of Integration." Ph.D. dissertation. University of Colorado. Ann Arbor: University Microfilms, 1966.

Dahrendorf, Ralf. "Possibilities and Limits of a European Communities Foreign Policy," *World Today,* 27, 4 (April 1971), 148-161.

Demerath, N. J. and Richard A. Peterson (eds.). *System, Change and Conflict.* New York: Free Press, 1967.

Deniau, J. F. "The External Policy of the European Economic Community," *Law and Contemporary Problems*, 26, 3 (Summer 1961), 364-380.

Deutsch, Karl W., Sidney A. Burrell, et al. *Political Community and the North Atlantic Area.* Princeton: Princeton University Press, 1957.

Deutsch, Karl W., J. Lewis Edinger, et al. *France, Germany and the Western Alliance.* New York: Charles Scribner's Sons, 1967.

Deutsch, Karl W. and William J. Foltz (eds.). *Nation-Building.* Chicago: Aldine-Atherton, 1963.

Deutsch, Karl W. and J. David Singer. "Multipolar Power Systems and International Stability." In David V. Edwards (ed.), *International Political Analysis: Readings.* New York: Holt, Rinehart and Winston, 1970. Pp. 344-359.

Durkheim, Emile. *The Division of Labor in Society.* Trans. George Simpson. New York: Free Press, 1933.

Eisenstadt, S. N. "Breakdowns of Modernization." In Jason L. Finkle and Richard W. Gable (eds.), *Political Development and Social Change.* New York: John Wiley and Sons, 1966. Pp. 573-591.

Emerson, Rupert. "The Atlantic Community and the Emerging Countries." In Francis O. Wilcox and H. Field Haviland, Jr. (eds.), *The Atlantic Community: Progress and Prospects.* New York: Praeger, 1963. Pp. 110-130.

Emery, F. E. and E. L. Trist. "The Causal Texture of Organizational Environments." In F. E. Emery (ed.), *Systems Thinking.* Middlesex, England: Penguin Books, 1969. Pp. 241-257.

Emery, F. E. (ed.). *Systems Thinking.* Middlesex, England: Penguin Books, 1969.

Etzioni, Amitai. "The Epigenesis of Political Communities at the International Level," *American Journal of Sociology*, 68, 4 (Jan. 1963), 407-422.

———. *Studies in Social Change.* New York: Holt, Rinehart and Winston, 1966.

Etzioni, Amitai, and Eva Etzioni (eds.). *Social Change: Sources, Patterns and Consequences.* New York: Basic Books, 1964.

Feibleman, J. and J. W. Friend. "The Structure and Function of Organization." In F. E. Emery (ed.), *Systems Thinking.* Middlesex, England: Penguin Books, 1969.

Feld, Werner. "The Association Agreements of the European Communities: A Comparative Analysis." In Carol Ann Cosgrove and Kenneth J. Twitchett (eds.), *The New International Actors: The United Nations and the European Economic Community.* London: Macmillan and Co., 1970. Pp. 237-253.

———. *The Court of the European Communities: New Directions in International Adjudication.* The Hague: Martinus Nijhoff, 1964.

———. *The European Common Market and the World.* Englewood Cliffs, N.J.: Prentice-Hall, 1967.

———. "External Relations of the Common Market and Group Leadership Attitudes in the Member States," *ORBIS*, 10, 2 (1966), 564-587.

———. "National Economic Interest Groups and Policy Formation in the EEC," *Political Science Quarterly*, 81, 3 (Sept. 1966), 392-411.

———. "National-International Linkage Theory: The East European Communist System and the EEC," *Journal of International Affairs*, 22, 1 (1968), 107-120.

Finkle, Jason L. and Richard W. Gable (eds.). *Political Development and Social Change.* New York: John Wiley and Sons, 1966.

Fischer, Fritz. *The Development of Interest Groups in the European Economic Community.* Memoire Presented for the Diploma of the College of Europe. Bruges, Belgium, July, 1963.

———. *Die Institutionalisierte Vertetrung der Verbände in der Europäischen Wirtschaftsgemeinschaft.* Hamburg: Hansischer Gildenverlag, 1965.

Friedrich, Carl J. *Europe: An Emergent Nation.* New York and Evanston: Harper and Row, 1969.

Friesema, H. Paul. *Metropolitan Political Structure: Intergovernmental Relations and Political Integration in the Quad-Cities.* Iowa City: University of Iowa Press, 1971.

Fruchter, Benjamin. *Introduction to Factor Analysis.* Princeton: D. Van Nostrand Co., 1954.

Galtung, Johan. "On the Future of the International System," *Journal of Peace Research,* 4 (1967), 305-333.

———. "Entropy and the General Theory of Peace," *Proceedings of the International Peace Research Association: Second Conference.* Oslo, Norway, 1967. Pp. 3-37.

Gerbet, Pierre. "La Préparation de la Décision Communautaire au Niveau National Français." In Pierre Gerbet and Daniel Pepy (eds.), *La Décision dans les Communautés Européennes.* Brussels: University of Brussels Press, 1969. Pp. 195-208.

Gerbet, Pierre and Daniel Pepy (eds.). *La Décision dans les Communautés Européennes.* Brussels: University of Brussels Press, 1969.

Greer, Scott, David McElrath, David Minar, and Peter Orleans (eds.). *The New Urbanization.* New York: St. Martin's Press, 1968.

Grodzins, Morton. "Centralization and Decentralization in the American Federal System." In Robert Goldwin (ed.), *A Nation of States.* Chicago: Rand McNally and Co., 1961. Pp. 1-23.

Haas, Ernst, R. *Beyond the Nation State: Functionalism and International Integration.* Stanford: Stanford University Press, 1964.

———. "International Integration: The European and the Universal Process." In *International Political Communities: An Anthology.* New York: Doubleday and Co., 1966.

———. "Technocracy, Pluralism, and the New Europe." In Stephen Graubard (ed.), *A New Europe.* Boston: Houghton Mifflin, 1964. Pp. 62-88.

Haas, Michael. "A Functional Approach to International Organization." In James N. Rosenau (ed.), *International Politics and Foreign Policy.* Rev. ed. New York: Free Press, 1969. Pp. 131-141.

Halpern, Manfred. "The Revolution of Modernization." In Roy C. Macridis and Bernard E. Brown (eds.), *Comparative Politics: Notes and Readings.* 3d ed. Homewood, Ill.: Dorsey Press, 1968. Pp. 512-520.

Hanrieder, Wolfram. "Compatibility and Consensus: A Proposal for the Conceptual Linkage of External and Internal Dimensions of Foreign Policy," *American Political Science Review,* 61, 4 (Dec. 1967), 971-982.

Hazlewood, Leo A. "Informal Penetration, Systemic Constraints and Political Violence." Florida State University (1971). Mimeo.

Henig, Stanley and John Pinder (eds.). *European Political Parties.* Political and Economic Planning Publication. London: George Allen and Unwin, 1969.

Hertzfeld, Jeffrey. "COMECON and the Western Trade of COMECON Countries," *Common Market,* 8, 1 (Jan. 1968), 309-312.

Hinshaw, Randall. *The European Community and American Trade.* New York: Praeger, 1964.

Hoffman, Stanley. "European Process at Atlantic Cross-Purposes," *Journal of Common Market Studies,* 3, 2 (Feb. 1965), 85-101.

———. *Gulliver's Troubles, or the Setting of American Foreign Policy.* New York: McGraw-Hill Book Co., 1968.

———. "Obstinate or Obsolete? The Fate of the Nation-State and the Case of Western Europe." In Joseph S. Nye, Jr. (ed.), *International Regionalism: Readings.* Boston: Little, Brown and Co., 1968. Pp. 177-230.

Holt, Stephen. *The Common Market: The Conflict between Theory and Practice.* London: Hamish Hamilton, 1967.

Hughes, Barry B. "Transaction Data and Analysis: In Search of Concepts," *International Organization,* 26, 4 (Autumn 1972), 659-680.

Hughes, Barry B. and John E. Schwarz. "Dimensions of Political Integration and the Experience of the European Community," *International Studies Quarterly,* 16, 3 (Sept. 1972), 263-294.

Huntington, Samuel P. "Political Development and Political Decay." In Roy C. Macridis and Bernard E. Brown (eds.), *Comparative Politics: Notes and Readings.* 3d ed. Homewood, Ill.: Dorsey Press, 1968. Pp. 521-538.

Inglehart, Ronald. "Cognitive Mobilization and European Identity," *Comparative Politics*, 3, 1 (1970), 45-70.

——. "An End to European Integration?" *American Political Science Review*, 61 (March 1967), 91-105.

——. "The New Europeans: Inward or Outward-Looking?" *International Organization*, 24, 1 (1970), 129-139.

Ionescu, Ghita. "The New Politics of European Integration," *Government and Opposition*, 6, 4 (1971), 417-421.

Jacob, Philip E. and Henry Teune. "The Integrative Process: Guidelines for Analysis of the Bases of Political Community." In Philip E. Jacob and James V. Toscano (eds.), *The Integration of Political Communities*. Philadelphia: J. B. Lippincott Co., 1964. Pp. 1-45.

Jacob, Philip E. and James Toscano (eds.). *The Integration of Political Communities*. Philadelphia: J. B. Lippincott Co., 1964.

Jalée, Pierre. *The Pillage of the Third World*. New York: Modern Reader Paperbacks, 1968.

Kahneman, D. "Control of Spurious Association and the Reliability of the Controlled Variable," *Psychological Bulletin*, 64 (1965), 326-329.

Kaplan, Morton A. "International Politics and International Security." Paper delivered at the Midwest Workshop on National Security Education, Chicago (Spring), 1971. 1-9.

——. *Macropolitics*. Chicago: Aldine Publishing Co., 1969.

——. *System and Process in International Politics*. New York: John Wiley and Sons, 1957.

Kissinger, Henry A. *American Foreign Policy*. New York: W. W. Norton and Co., 1969.

——. *The Troubled Partnership*. New York: Anchor Books, 1966.

Kohn, Hans. *The Idea of Nationalism*. New York: Macmillan Co., 1948.

——. *Nationalism: Its Meaning and History*. Princeton: D. Van Nostrand Co., 1965.

Korbonski, Andrez. "COMECON," *International Conciliation*, 549 (Sept. 1964), 3-62.

Kothari, Rajni. *Politics in India*. Boston: Little, Brown and Co., 1970.

Krause, Lawrence. *The European Economic Community and the United States*. Washington: The Brookings Institution, 1968.

Kreinin, M. E. "The 'Outer Seven' and European Integration," *American Economic Review*, 50, 3 (1960), 370-386.

Kuhn, Thomas. *The Structure of Scientific Revolutions*. Chicago: University of Chicago Press, 1962.

Lambert, John. *Britain in a Federal Europe*. London: Chatto and Windus, 1968.

Lindberg, Leon N. "The European Community as a Political System: Notes toward the Construction of a Model," *Journal of Common Market Studies*, 5 (June 1967), 344-387.

——. "Interest Group Activities in the EEC." In Paul A. Tharpe, Jr. (ed.), *Regional International Organizations: Structures and Functions*. New York: St. Martin's Press, 1971. Pp. 11-20.

——. *The Political Dynamics of European Economic Integration*. Stanford: Stanford University Press, 1963.

Lindberg, Leon N. and Stuart A. Scheingold. *Europe's Would-Be Polity: Patterns of Change in the European Community*. Englewood Cliffs, N.J.: Prentice-Hall, 1970.

Lindbloom, Charles E. *The Intelligence of Democracy: Decision Making through Mutual Adjustment*. New York: Free Press, 1965.

Lowi, Theodore. "The Public Philosophy: Interest Group Liberalism." In Edward V. Schneier (ed.), *Policy-Making in American Government*. New York: Basic Books, 1969. Pp. 320-354.

McNemar, Quinn. *Psychological Statistics*. 3d ed. New York: John Wiley and Sons, 1962.

Macrae, Norman. "How the EEC Makes Decisions," *Atlantic Community Quarterly*, 8, 3 (Fall 1970), 363-371.

Martindale, Don. "The Formation and Destruction of Communities." In George K. Zollschan and Walter Hirsch (eds.), *Explorations in Social Change*. Boston: Houghton Mifflin Co., 1964. Pp. 61-87.

Masters, Roger D. "World Politics as a Primitive Political System." In James N. Rosenau (ed.), *International Politics and Foreign Policy.* Rev. ed. New York: Free Press, 1969. Pp. 104-118.

Mayne, Richard. *The Institutions of the European Community.* Political and Economic Planning Publication Ser. 8. London: Chatham House, 1968.

Mazrui, Ali. "African Attitudes to the European Economic Community." In Lawrence B. Krause (ed.), *The Common Market: Progress and Controversy.* Englewood Cliffs, N.J.: Prentice-Hall, 1964. Pp. 121-135.

Meehl, Paul R. "Nuisance Variables and the Ex Post Facto Design." In Michael Radner and Stephen Winokur (eds.), *Analysis of Theories and Methods of Physics and Psychology,* Minnesota Studies in the Philosophy of Science, 4. Minneapolis: University of Minnesota Press, 1970. Pp. 373-402.

Meynaud, Jean. *Les Groupes de Pression Internationaux.* Études de Science Politique, no. 3. Lausanne: M. Meynaud, 1961.

Meynaud, Jean and Dusan Sidjanski. "L'Action des Groupes de Pression." In Pierre Gerbet and Daniel Pepy (eds.), *La Décision dans les Communautés Européennes.* Brussels: University of Brussels Press, 1969. Pp. 133-147.

———. *Groupes de Pression et Coopération Européenne.* Recherches no. 14. Paris: Fondation Nationale des Sciences Politiques, 1968.

Miller, James G. "The Nature of Living Systems," *Behavioral Science,* 16, 4 (1971), 277-301.

Mitrany, David. "Delusions of Regional Unity." In Bart Landheer (ed.), *Limits and Problems on European Integration: Conference of May 30-June 2, 1961.* The Hague: Martinus Nijhoff, 1963. Pp. 37-46.

———. "The Functional Approach to World Organization." In Carol Ann Cosgrove and Kenneth J. Twitchett (eds.), *The New International Actors: The United Nations and the European Economic Community.* London: Macmillan and Co., 1970. Pp. 65-75.

———. "The Prospect of Integration: Federal or Functional?" In Joseph Nye, Jr. (ed.), *International Regionalism: Readings.* Boston: Little, Brown and Co., 1968. Pp. 43-74.

———. *A Working Peace System.* Chicago: Quadrangle Books, 1966.

Moore, Wilbert E. *Social Change.* Englewood Cliffs, N.J.: Prentice-Hall, 1963.

Moore, Wilbert E. and Robert M. Cook (eds.). *Readings on Social Change.* Englewood Cliffs, N.J.: Prentice-Hall, 1967.

Myrdal, Gunnar. *The Challenge of World Poverty.* New York: Vintage Books, 1971.

Naroll, Raoul. "Some Thoughts on Comparative Method in Anthropology." In Hubert M. Blalock and Anne Blalock (eds.), *Methodology in Social Research.* New York: Mc-Graw-Hill Publishing Co., 1968.

Newhouse, John. *Collision in Brussels: The Common Market Crisis of 30 June 1965.* London: Faber and Faber, 1967.

Nielsen, Terkel T. "Aspects of the EEC Influence of European Groups in the Decision-Making Processes: The Common Agricultural Policy," *Government and Opposition,* 6, 4 (1971), 539-558.

Noel, Emile. "Comment Fonctionnent les Institutions de la Communauté Européenne," *Les Documents Communauté Européenne* (Paris: Bureau of Information des Communautés Européennes), 51 (Dec. 1968), 1-14.

———. "The Committee of Permanent Representatives," *Journal of Common Market Studies,* 5, 3 (1967), 219-251.

———. "How the European Economic Community's Institutions Work." In Howard Bliss (ed.), *The Political Development of the European Community: A Documentary Collection.* Waltham, Mass.: Blaisdell Publishing Co., 1970. Pp. 77-90.

Noel, Emile and Henri Etienne. "Quelques Aspects des Rapports et de la Collaboration entre le Conseil et la Commission." In Pierre Gerbet and Daniel Pepy (eds.), *La Décision dans les Communautés Européennes.* Brussels: University of Brussels Press, 1969. Pp. 33-55.

———. "The Permanent Representative Committee and the 'Deepening' of the Communities," *Government and Opposition*, 6, 4 (1971), 422-447.

Nordlinger, Eric A. "Political Sociology: Marx and Weber." In Eric A. Nordlinger (ed.), *Politics and Society*. Englewood Cliffs, N.J.: Prentice-Hall, 1970. Pp. 1-20.

Nye, Joseph S., Jr. "Comparative Regional Integration: Concept and Measurement," *International Organization*, 22, 4 (1968), 864-871.

Olivetti, Marco M. "La Préparation de la Décision Communautaire au Niveau National Italien." In Pierre Gerbet and Daniel Pepy (eds.), *La Décision dans les Communautés Européenes*. Brussels: University of Brussels Press, 1969. Pp. 209-227.

Olson, Mancur, Jr. and Richard Zeckhauser. "An Economic Theory of Alliances." In Bruce M. Russett (ed.), *Economic Theories of International Politics*. Chicago: Markham Publishing Co., 1968.

Parsons, Talcott. "A Functional Theory of Change." In Amitai Etzioni and Eva Etzioni (eds.), *Social Change: Sources, Patterns and Consequences*. New York: Basic Books, 1964. Pp. 83-97.

———. "On the Concept of Political Power." In Talcott Parsons, *Sociological Theory and Modern Society*. New York: Free Press, 1967. Pp. 297-354.

———. "Order and Community in the International Social System." In James N. Rosenau (ed.), *International Politics and Foreign Policy*. New York: Free Press, 1961. Pp. 120-129.

———. "Polarization of the World and International Order." In ibid. Pp. 466-469.

———. *The Social System*. New York: Free Press, 1951.

———. *The Structure of Social Action*. Vol. 1. New York: Free Press, 1937.

Parsons, Talcott, and Neil J. Smelser, "The Primary Sub-Systems of Society." In N. J. Demerath and Richard A. Peterson (eds.), *System, Change, and Conflict*. New York: Free Press, 1967. Pp. 131-140.

Pertejo, J. "Le Thème Européen dans les Élections Présidentielles Françaises des 5 et 19 Décembre 1965." Paper presented to a seminar conducted by Professor Sidjanski. Geneva: Institut D'Études Européennes, May, 1967.

Pinder, John and Roy Pryce. *Europe after de Gaulle*. Middlesex, England: Penguin Books, 1969.

Puchala, Donald. "International Transactions and Regional Integration," *International Organization*, 24, 4 (1970), 732-763.

Przeworski, Adam and Henry Teune. *The Logic of Comparative Social Inquiry*. New York: John Wiley and Sons, 1970.

Rabier, M. Jacques-René. *L'Information des Européens et l'Intégration de l'Europe*. Brussels: Free University of Brussels Press, 1965.

———. *L'Opinion Publique et l'Europe*. Brussels: Free University of Brussels Press, 1966.

Rehwinkel, Edmund. "Das Misstrauen der Westdeutschan Landwirtschaft gegen der Wirtschaftspolitik der heutigen Bundesregierung," *Agrapolitik in Umbruch der Zeit*. 1966.

Rose, Richard. *Politics in England*. Boston and Toronto: Little, Brown and Co., 1964.

Rosenau, James N. (ed.). "Compatibility, Consensus and the Emerging Political Science of Adaptation," *American Political Science Review*, 61, 4 (1967), 983-988.

———. *Linkage Politics*. New York: Free Press, 1969.

———. "Pre-Theories and Theories of Foreign Policy." In R. Barry Farrell (ed.), *Approaches to Comparative and International Politics*. Evanston: Northwestern University Press, 1966. Pp. 27-93.

Rudolph, Lloyd. *The Modernity of Tradition*. Chicago: University of Chicago Press, 1967.

Schattschneider, E. E. *The Semi-Sovereign People*. New York: Holt, Rinehart and Winston, 1960.

Scheinman, Lawrence. "Some Preliminary Notes on Bureaucratic Relationships in the European Economic Community," *International Organization*, 20, 4 (1966), 750-774.

Schmitter, Phillippe C. "Central American Integration: Spill-Over, Spill-Around or Encapsulation?" *Journal of Common Market Studies*, 9, 1 (1971), 1-48.

———. "Three Neo-Functional Hypotheses about International Integration," *International*

Organization, 23 (Winter 1969), 161-166.

Schutzenburger, M. P. "A Tentative Classification of Goal-Seeking Behaviors." In F. E. Emery (ed.), *Systems Thinking.* Middlesex, England: Penguin Books, 1969. Pp. 205-213.

Scott, Andrew M. *The Revolution in Statecraft: Informal Penetration.* New York: Random House, 1965.

Shanks, Michael and John Lambert. *Britain and the New Europe: The Future of the Common Market.* London: Chatto and Windus, 1962.

Shulman, Marshall D. "The Communist States and Western Integration." In Francis O. Wilcox and H. Field Haviland, Jr. (eds.), *The Atlantic Community: Progress and Prospects.* New York: Praeger, 1963. Pp. 131-144.

Sidjanski, Dusan. *Dimensions Européennes de la Science Politique.* Paris: Librairie Générale de Droit et de Jurisprudence, 1963.

——. "The European Pressure Groups," *Government and Opposition,* 2, 3 (1967), 397-416.

——. *L'Originalité des Communautés Européennes et la Répartition de Leurs Pouvoirs.* Paris: Éditions A. Pedone, 1961.

Sidjanski, Dusan and David Handley. "Aperçu des Sondages d'Opinion sur l'Intégration Européenne, 1945-1969," *Méthodes Quantitatives et Intégration Européenne,* 13, 4 (1970), 118-139.

Simon, Herbert. *The Sciences of the Artificial.* Cambridge: Massachusetts Institute of Technology, 1969.

Singer, J. David. *A General System Taxonomy for Political Science.* New York: General Learning Press, 1971. Pp. 1-22.

Smith, Anthony D. *Theories of Nationalism.* New York: Harper and Row, 1972.

Snyder, Louis L. *The New Nationalism.* Ithaca: Cornell University Press, 1968.

Spinelli, Altiero. *The Eurocrats: Conflict and Crisis in the European Community.* Baltimore: Johns Hopkins Press, 1966.

Steel, Ronald. *Pax Americana.* Rev. ed. New York: Viking Press, 1970.

Sween, Joyce and Donald T. Campbell. "A Study of the Effect of Proximally Autocorrelated Error on Tests of Significance for the Interrupted Time-Series Quasi-Experimental Design." Evanston: Northwestern University (1965). Mimeo.

Teune, Henry. "Integration of Political Systems." Paper prepared for delivery at Annual Meeting of the International Studies Association, San Juan, Puerto Rico, 1971.

Thistlethwaite, Donald L. and Donald T. Campbell. "Regression-Discontinuity Analysis: An Alternative to Ex Post Facto Experiment," *Journal of Educational Psychology,* 51, 6 (Dec. 1960), 309-317.

Tiryakian, Edward A. (ed.). *Sociological Theory, Values and Sociocultural Change.* New York: Harper and Row, 1963.

Tolman, F. C. and E. Brunswick. "The Organism and the Causal Texture of the Environment," *Psychological Review,* 42 (1935), 43-77.

Tucker, Robert. *Nation or Empire?* Baltimore: Johns Hopkins Press, 1960.

Viner, Jacob. *The Customs Union Issue.* London: Carnegie Endowment for International Peace, 1950.

von Bertalanffy, Ludwig. *General Systems Theory.* New York: George Braziller, 1968.

von Geusau, Frans A. M. Alting. *Beyond the European Community: The Case of Political Unification.* Belgium: Heule Publishers, 1968.

——. *Economic Relations after the Kennedy Round.* Leiden: A. W. Sijthoff, 1969.

——. "Les Sessions Marathon du Conseil des Ministres." In Pierre Gerbet and Daniel Pepy (eds.), *La Décision dans les Communautés Européennes.* Brussels: University of Brussels Press, 1969. Pp. 99-107.

von Vorys, Karl. "Toward a Concept of Political Development," *Annals of the American Academy of Political and Social Science,* 358 (March 1965), 14-19.

Vredeling, H. "The Common Market of Political Parties," *Government and Opposition,* 6, 4 (Autumn 1971), 448-461.

Waltz, Kenneth. "The Stability of the Bipolar World." In David V. Edwards (ed.), *International Political Analysis: Readings*. New York: Holt, Rinehart and Winston, 1970. Pp. 318-342.

Weber, Max. *The Theory of Social and Economic Organization*. Trans. A. M. Henderson and Talcott Parsons. New York: Oxford University Press, 1947.

Weil, Gordon L. "The European Community: What Lies Beyond the Point of No Return?" *Review of Politics*, 29, 2 (1967), 160-179.

——. "From External Relations to Foreign Policy: The Community and the World," *European Community*, 9 (Sept. 1968), 13-15.

Weiner, Myron. "The Politics of South Asia." In Gabriel A. Almond and James S. Coleman (eds.), *The Politics of the Developing Areas*. Princeton: Princeton University Press, 1960. Pp. 153-246.

Wilson, Godfrey and Monica Wilson. *The Analysis of Social Change*. Cambridge: Cambridge University Press, 1968.

Wimmer, Hans. "Must the Ministers Endure Those All-Night Marathons?" *European Community*, 7 (Jan. 1970), 9-10.

Zeller, Adrien. *L'Imbroglio Argicole du Marché Commun*. Paris: Calmann-Levy, 1970.

MISCELLANEOUS PUBLICATIONS

Agence Europe, Daily, Agence Internationale d'Information Pour la Presse, Brussels.

"The Righteous Dumpers." *Agenor*, 16 (March 1970), 55-56.

"Die auf der Ebene Sechs Zusammengefassten Berufsverbände und die Gemeinschaft." *Bulletin der Europäischen Wirtschaftsgemeinschaft* (Brussels: Commission Secretariat), n.v. (April 1961), 12-15.

"Agriculture." *Bulletin of the European Economic Community*, 2 (Feb. 1960), 38.

"Two-Way Traffic: State Offices in Brussels." *The Bulletin: The Belgian Weekly in English*, 26 (July 1970), 16.

"Economic Advance-Political Retreat." *Common Market*, 3, 6 (1963), 104-107.

"Communication à la Presse." Document 969/65 (ag 272). Brussels (July 1965), 1.

"The Common Agricultural Policy." *Community Topics* (EEC Information Service), 28 (July 1967), 1-3.

"Les Organisations Professionnelles Agricoles et la CEE." *Documentation Européenne*. Brussels, 1969.

"Preparation for Entry Talks." *European Community* (Washington, D.C.), March 1970, p. 16.

"Summit Revives European Spirit." *European Community* (Washington, D.C.), Jan. 1970, p. 3.

"Unity: A Probe of European Attitudes." *European Community* (Washington, D.C.), 139 (Oct. 1970), p. 16.

First General Report on the Activities of the Community. Brussels: European Economic Community Commission, May 1959.

Germany in Europe. New York: German Information Center, n.d.

Les Groupes de Pression dans la C.E.E. Amsterdam: Europa Institut, 1965.

"Le Marché Commun et L'Agriculture." *Livre Blanc des Organisations Professionnelles Agricoles*. COPA, Oct. 1962.

Memorandum of the Commission on the Action Programme of the Community for the Second Stage. Brussels, Oct. 1962.

Memorandum on the Reform of Agriculture in the European Economic Community. Supplement 1. Brussels: Commission of the European Communities, 1969.

"Les Entreprises Américaines Installées en Europe Jouissent Souvent de Privilèges Fiscaux Exorbitant." *Le Monde*, June 23, 1970, p. 1.

"Common Market Curb on Produce Angers 18 African Countries." *The New York Times,* Oct. 18, 1970, p. 10.

La Politique Industrielle de la Communauté. Memorandum de la Commission au Conseil. Brussels: Commission des Communautés Européennes, 1970.

"Position du COPA sur les Propositions de la Commission Concernant la Fixation des Prix pour les Produits Agricoles." COPA Assembly. Brussels, July 22, 1969, Document A (69), p. 4.

Répertoire des Organismes Communs dans le Cadre des Communautés Européenes. Brussels: Services des Publications des Communautés Européennes, 1969.

"L'Europe Européenne: Est-Elle Née à Genève?" *Revue du Marché Commun,* 102 (May 1969), 283-284.

Seventh General Report on the Activities of the Community. Brussels and Luxembourg, Commission of the European Communities, 1964.

Treaty Establishing the European Economic Community and Connected Documents. Brussels: Publishing Services of the European Communities, n.d.

Notes

CHAPTER ONE

1. See S. N. Eisenstadt, "Breakdowns in Modernization," in Jason L. Finkle and Richard W. Gable (eds.), *Political Development and Social Change* (New York: John Wiley and Sons, 1966), pp. 573-591; and Samuel P. Huntington, "Political Development and Political Decay," in Roy C. Macridis and Bernard E. Brown (eds.), *Comparative Politics Notes and Readings*, 3d ed. (Homewood, Ill.: Dorsey Press, 1968), pp. 521-539. Although this literature is much too large to effectively summarize, the following works are a useful beginning: Gabriel A. Almond and James S. Coleman (eds.), *The Politics of the Developing Areas* (Princeton: Princeton University Press, 1960); David E. Apter, *The Politics of Modernization* (Chicago: University of Chicago Press, 1965); Gabriel A. Almond and G. Bingham Powell, Jr., *Comparative Politics: A Developmental Approach* (Boston: Little, Brown and Co., 1966); Samuel P. Huntington, *Political Order in Changing Societies* (New Haven: Yale University Press, 1969); Lucien W. Pye, *Aspects of Political Development* (Boston: Little, Brown and Co., 1966); and Albert O. Hirschman, *The Strategy of Economic Development* (New Haven: Yale University Press, 1958).

2. Again, this literature is already voluminous. Some of the more important contributions are: Karl Deutsch, Sidney Burrell, et al., *Political Community and the North Atlantic Area* (Princeton: Princeton University Press, 1957); Ernst B. Haas, *The Uniting of Europe: Political, Social and Economic Forces 1950-1957* (Stanford: Stanford University Press, 1958); Ernst B. Haas, *Beyond the Nation-State* (Stanford: Stanford University Press, 1964); Leon N. Lindberg, *The Political Dynamics of European Economic Integration* (Stanford: Stanford University Press, 1963); Leon N. Lindberg and Stuart A. Scheingold, *Europe's Would-Be Polity* (Englewood Cliffs, N.J.: Prentice-Hall, 1970); Philip E. Jacob and James V. Toscano (eds.), *The Integration of Political Communities*, (Philadelphia: J. B. Lippincott Co., 1964); Joseph S. Nye, *Peace in Parts: Integration and Conflict in Regional Organization* (Boston: Little, Brown and Co., 1971); and Amitai Etzioni, *Political Unification: A Comparative Study of Leaders and Forces* (New York: Holt, Rinehart and Winston, 1965).

3. See for example, Wilbert E. Moore, *Social Change* (Englewood Cliffs, N.J.: Prentice-Hall, 1963); Wilbert E. Moore and Robert M. Cook (eds.), *Readings on Social Change* (Englewood Cliffs, N.J.: Prentice-Hall, 1967); Edward A. Tiryakian (ed.), *Sociological Theory, Values, and Sociocultural Change* (New York: Harper and Row, 1963); N. J. Demerath and Richard A. Peterson (eds.), *System, Change, and Conflict* (New York: Free Press, 1967); Amitai Etzioni and Eva Etzioni (eds.), *Social Change: Sources, Patterns and Consequences* (New York: Basic Books, 1964); and Amitai Etzioni, *Studies in Social Change* (New York: Holt, Rinehart and Winston, 1966).

4. This analogy views nation-states as hard, impenetrable entities that interact with other nation-states only through official diplomatic representatives. See for example, James N. Rosenau (ed.), *Linkage Politics* (New York: Free Press, 1969); Wolfram Hanrieder, "Compatibility and Consensus: A Proposal for the Conceptual Linkage of External and Internal Dimensions of Foreign Policy," *American Political Science Review,* 16, 4 (Dec. 1967), 971-982; and James N. Rosenau, "Compatibility, Consensus and the Emerging Political Science of Adaptation," in ibid., pp. 983-988. This move away from the "state as actor" has also been incorporated by Paul Smoker into the International Processes Simulation (IPS) at Northwestern University in the form of multiple, nongovernmental actors. The utility of this focus has also been recognized by scholars in the field of political violence. See for example, Leo Hazlewood, "Informal Penetration, Systemic Constraints and Political Violence" (Florida State University, 1971), mimeo.

5. Chadwick F. Alger, "Comparison of Intranational and International Politics," in R. Barry Farrell (ed.), *Approaches to Comparative and International Politics* (Evanston: Northwestern University Press, 1966); Michael Haas, "A Functional Approach to International Organization" in James N. Rosenau (ed.), *International Politics and Foreign Policy,* rev. ed. (New York: Free Press, 1969); and Roger D. Masters, "World Politics as a Primitive Political System," in ibid.

6. See Don Martindale, "The Formation and Destruction of Communities" in George K. Zollschan and Walter Hirsch (eds.), *Explorations in Social Change* (Boston: Houghton Mifflin Co., 1964), p. 71.

7. One sociologist, Talcott Parsons, explicitly calls for a static theory first, as a prerequisite in terms of which dynamic theory can take place. See *The Social System* (New York: Free Press, 1951), esp. pp. 19-20.

8. See Karl W. Deutsch, Lewis J. Edinger, et al., *France, Germany, and the Western Alliance* (New York: Charles Scribner's Sons, 1967); Ronald Inglehart, "An End to European Integration?" *American Political Science Review,* 61 (March 1967), 91-105; and Leon Lindberg, "The European Community as a Political System: Notes toward the Construction of a Model," *Journal of Common Market Studies,* 5 (June 1967), 44-87.

9. See for example, W. Hartley Clark, *The Politics of the Common Market* (Englewood Cliffs, N.J.: Prentice-Hall, 1967), p. 1.

10. Gordon L. Weil, "The European Community: What Lies Beyond the Point of No Return?" *Review of Politics,* 29, 2 (April 1967).

11. John Newhouse, *Collision in Brussels: The Common Market Crisis of 30 June 1965* (London: Faber and Faber, 1967), p. 12.

12. Thomas Kuhn, *The Structure of Scientific Revolutions* (Chicago: University of Chicago Press, 1962).

13. Gabriel Almond, Introduction, in Gabriel A. Almond and James S. Coleman (eds.), *The Politics of the Developing Areas* (Princeton: Princeton University Press), 1960; Almond and Powell, *Comparative Politics: A Developmental Approach.*

14. For a very explicit application of this approach see Lindberg, "The European Community as a Political System."

15. Morton A. Kaplan, *System and Process in International Politics* (New York: John Wiley and Sons, 1957), p. 98.

16. Ernst B. Haas, "International Integration: The European and the Universal Process," in *International Political Communities: An Anthology* (New York: Doubleday and Co., 1966), p. 94.

17. For qualifications to this, especially with reference to specialization in totalitarian systems, see Almond and Powell, *Comparative Politics: A Developmental Approach,* p. 47.

18. Talcott Parsons and Neil J. Smelser, "The Primary Sub-Systems of Society," in Demerath and Peterson (eds.), *System, Change and Conflict,* p. 132.

19. Karl W. Deutsch, Sidney A. Burrell, et al., "Political Community and the North Atlantic Area," in *International Political Communities: An Anthology,* p. 2

20. Talcott Parsons, "On the Concept of Political Power," *Sociological Theory and Modern Society* (New York: Free Press, 1967), p. 308.

21. See especially Parsons, *Sociological Theory and Modern Society*, pp. 337-45.

22. Almond and Powell, *Comparative Politics: A Developmental Approach*, chaps. 2 and 8.

23. Manfred Halpern, "The Revolution of Modernization," in *Comparative Politics: Notes and Readings*, p. 512.

24. Karl von Vorys, "Toward a Concept of Political Development," *Annals of the American Academy of Political and Social Science*, 358 (March 1965), 14-19.

25. Amitai Etzioni describes these two processes as epigenetic and preformist, respectively. This section is particularly indebted to his article, "The Epigenesis of Political Communities at the International Level," *American Journal of Sociology*, 68, 4 (Jan. 1963), 407-422.

26. Almond, "A Developmental Approach to Political Systems," in Finkle and Gable (eds.), *Political Development and Social Change*, esp. pp. 105-111.

27. The strategy here closely follows James N. Rosenau's logic of pre-theories in "Pre-theories and Theories of Foreign Policy" in R. Barry Farrell (ed.), *Approaches to Comparative and International Politics* (Evanston: Northwestern University Press, 1966), pp. 27-93.

28. I hereafter refer to this approach as Almond's approach recognizing that James Coleman, Bingham Powell, Jr., and others played an important part in its development.

29. Alger, in Farrell (ed.), *Approaches to Intranational and International Politics*, esp. pp. 312-19.

30. Almond and Powell, *Comparative Politics: A Developmental Approach*, p. 14.

31. Almond, in Finkle and Gable (eds.), *Political Development and Social Change*, p. 104.

32. Ibid., p. 106.

33. Ibid., p. 102.

34. For a more elaborate discussion of this point see Parsons, *The Social System*, esp. pp. 36-43. This paragraph borrows heavily from the work of Parsons.

35. Werner Feld, "National Economic Interest Groups and Policy Formation in the EEC," *Political Science Quarterly*, 81, 3 (Sept. 1966), 394.

36. Ibid.

37. Werner Feld, *The European Common Market and the World* (Englewood Cliffs, N.J.: Prentice-Hall, 1967), p. 35.

38. Ibid., p. 36.

39. Clark, *The Politics of the Common Market*, p. 40.

40. Ibid., p. 97.

41. Adrien Zeller, *L'Imbroglio Agricole du Marché Commun* (Paris: Calmann-Levy, 1970).

42. E. E. Schattschneider, *The Semi-Sovereign People* (New York: Holt, Rinehart and Winston, 1960), p. 40.

43. Gabriel A. Almond, "Interest Groups and the Political Process," in Macridis and Brown (eds.), *Comparative Politics: Notes and Readings*, p. 231.

44. Lindberg, *The Political Dynamics of European Economic Integration*, p. 252.

45. Ibid., p. 237.

46. "The Agricultural Session of the EEC Council Has Made No More than Modest Progress," *Agence Europe*, Dec. 13, 1963, p. 1.

47. These points, listed as follows, are part of the French document that has come to be known as the decalogue. (1) A rule should be made that the Commission is never to unveil the tenor of its proposals to the Assembly or to the public before they have been officially submitted to the Council. What is more, the Commission should never take the initiative of publishing its proposals in the *Official Community Gazette*. (2) Commission members in their public statements should be required to observe a proper neutrality about the policies pursued by all member governments. (3) Information policy should not be framed and implemented by the Commission alone, but by the Commission and the Council together. Council should exercise an effective supervision of the activities of the Community

Information Service—and not just on the budget side. These were points 2, 8, and 9, respectively, of the decalogue presented by France at the January 17-18, 1966, meeting in Luxembourg.

48. Clark, *The Politics of the Common Market*, p. 107.

49. Ibid., p. 115.

50. Ibid., p. 117.

51. Ibid.

52. Altiero Spinelli, *The Eurocrats: Conflict and Crisis in the European Community* (Baltimore: Johns Hopkins Press, 1966), p. 149.

53. For an excellent analysis of the Commission from the standpoint of its bureaucratic-political role, see David Coombes, *Politics and Bureaucracy in the EEC* (London: George Allen and Unwin, 1970).

54. Louis Cartou, "Le rôle de la Commission," in Pierre Gerbet and Daniel Pepy (eds.), *La Décision dans les Communautés Européennes* (Brussels: University of Brussels Press, 1969), p. 3.

55. Ibid., p. 9.

56. Spinelli, *The Eurocrats*, p. 99.

57. Ibid., p. 56.

58. Lawrence Scheinman, "Some Preliminary Notes on Bureaucratic Relationships in the European Economic Community," *International Organization*, 20, 4 (Autumn 1966), 750-774.

59. Ibid., p. 755.

60. Dusan Sidjanski, *L'Originalité des Communautés Européennes et la Répartition de leurs Pouvoirs* (Paris: Éditions A. Pedone, 1961), pp. 18-19.

61. Werner Feld, *The Court of the European Communities: New Directions in International Adjudication* (The Hague: Martinus Nijhoff, 1964), pp. 34-35.

62. Almond and Powell, *Comparative Politics: A Developmental Approach*, p. 195.

63. Spinelli, *The Eurocrats*, p. 206.

64. Newhouse, *Collision in Brussels*, p. 45.

65. Weil, "The European Community," p. 165.

66. Spinelli, *The Eurocrats*, pp. 207-208.

67. Almond and Powell, *Comparative Politics: A Developmental Approach*, p. 196.

68. Spinelli, *The Eurocrats*, p. 13.

69. Etzioni, *Studies in Social Change*, p. 5

70. Almond and Powell, *Comparative Politics: A Developmental Approach*, p. 198.

71. Clark, *The Politics of the Common Market*, p. 106.

72. See Ronald Inglehart, "An End to European Integration," *American Political Science Review*, 61, 1 (1967), 91-105; Dusan Sidjanski and David Handley, "Aperçu des Sondages d'Opinion sur l'Intégration Européenne, 1945-1969," *Méthodes Quantitatives et Intégration Européenne*, 13, 3 and 4 (Autumn 1970), 118-139; M. Jacques-René Rabier, *L'Opinion Publique et l'Europe* (Brussels: Free University of Brussels Press, 1966), pp. 1-37; and M. Jacques-René Rabier, *L'Information des Européens et l'Intégration de l'Europe* (Brussels: Free University of Brussels Press, 1965), pp. 1-70.

73. Rabier, *L'Opinion Publique et l'Europe*, p. 15.

74. Ibid., p. 11.

75. "Unity: A Probe of European Attitudes," *European Community* (Washington, D.C.), 139 (Oct. 1970), 16.

76. Inglehart, "An End to European Integration?"

77. These figures refer to the composition of Parliamentary membership before Great Britain, Denmark, and Ireland joined the EC on January 1, 1973.

CHAPTER TWO

1. See Gabriel A. Almond, "A Comparative Study of Interest Groups and the Political Process," in David Apter and Harry Eckstein (eds.), *Comparative Politics: A Reader* (New York: Free Press, 1963), pp. 397-408.

2. See for example, Robert Dahl, *Who Governs?* (New Haven: Yale University Press, 1961).

3. Peter Bachrach and Morton S. Baratz, "Decisions and Nondecisions: An Analytical Framework," *American Political Science Review,* 57 (Sept. 1963), 632-642.

4. Emile Durkheim, *The Division of Labor in Society,* trans. George Simpson (New York: Free Press, 1933).

5. Ibid., p. 17; and Gabriel Almond, *The Politics of the Developing Areas* (Princeton: Princeton University Press, 1960), Introduction.

6. Eric A. Nordlinger, "Political Sociology: Marx and Weber," in Eric A. Nordlinger (ed.), *Politics and Society* (Englewood Cliffs, N.J.: Prentice-Hall, 1970), pp. 7, 15.

7. By 1965 there were 350 associational interest groups specifically organized at the Community level. See Jean Meynaud and Dusan Sidjanski, *Les Groupes de Pression et Coopération Européenne,* Récherches no. 14 (Paris: Fondation Nationale des Sciences Politiques, 1968), p. 15. For a breakdown of these groups, by area of specialization as well as by general *vs.* limited purposes of groups, see Fritz Fischer, *Die Institutionalisierte Vertretung der Verbände in der Europäischen Wirtschaftsgemeinschaft* (Hamburg: Hansischer Gildenverlag, 1965), chap. 2, pp. 40-69.

8. Dusan Sidjanski, "Pressure Groups and the EEC," *Government and Opposition,* 1, 3 (April-July 1967), 398-399.

9. Carl J. Friedrich, *Europe: An Emergent Nation?* (New York and Evanston: Harper and Row, 1969), p. 139.

10. Jean Meynaud and Dusan Sidjanski, "L'Action des Groupes de Pression," in Pierre Gerbet and Daniel Pepy (eds.), *La Décision dans les Communautés Européennes* (Brussels: University of Brussels Press, 1969), p. 133.

11. Fritz Fischer, *The Development of Interest Groups in the European Economic Community,* Memoire presented for the Diploma of the College of Europe (Bruges, Belgium, July, 1963), p. 2.

12. Ibid.

13. Jean Meynaud, *Les Groupes de Pression Internationaux,* no. 3, Études de Science Politique (Lausanne, M. Meynaud, 1961), p. 41.

14. Meynaud and Sidjanski, *Groupes de Pression,* p. 14.

15. Chadwick F. Alger, "Problems in Global Organization," *International Social Science Journal,* 22, 4 (1970), 691-709.

16. "Les Entreprises Américaines Installées en Europe Jouissent Souvent de Privilèges Fiscaux Exorbitants," *Le Monde,* June 23, 1970, p. 1. The harmful effect of American business presence in Europe was most effectively vocalized by Servan-Schreiber.

17. "State Offices in Brussels: Two-Way Traffic," *The Bulletin: The Belgian Weekly in English,* July 1, 1970, p. 16.

18. Meynaud and Sidjanski, *Groupes de Pression,* p. 14.

19. Ibid., p. 15, translation mine.

20. For a discussion of the general phenomenon of growth of international organizations and transnational contact, see Robert C. Angell, *Peace on the March: Transnational Participation* (New York: Van Nostrand Reinhold Co., 1969); and Alger, "Problems in Global Organization," p. 22.

21. Dusan Sidjanski, *Dimensions Européennes de la Science Politique* (Paris: Librairie Générale de Droit et de Jurisprudence, 1963), pp. 22-23.

22. Meynaud and Sidjanski, "L'Action des Groupes," p. 134, translation mine.

23. "Die Auf der Ebene der Sechs Zusammengefassten Berufsverbände und die Gemeinschaft," *Bulletin der Europäischen Wirtschaftsgemeinschaft* (Brussels, Commission Secretariat), 4 (April 1961), 14.

24. Fischer, *Development of Interest Groups,* p. 10.

25. *First General Report on the Activities of the Community* (Brussels and Luxembourg: Commission of the European Communities, 1959).

26. See especially "Le Marché Commun et l'Agriculture," *Livre Blanc des Organisations Professionnelles Agricoles* (October 1965), the document produced by COPA during the crisis.

27. See "Les Organisations Professionnelles Agricoles et la CEE," *Documentation Européenne,* (n.p. 1969).

28. See Friedrich, *Europe: An Emergent Nation?* p. 70; and "Le Marché Commun et L'Agriculture," p. 2.

29. Meynaud and Sidjanski, "L'Action des Groupes," p. 146.

30. "Die Auf der Ebene . . . ," p. 12.

31. Fischer, *Development of Interest Groups,* p. 14.

32. Friedrich, *Europe: An Emergent Nation?* p. 80.

33. "Les Organisations Professionnelles Agricoles de la CEE," p. 2.

34. Ibid.

35. Meynaud and Sidjanski, "L'Action des Groupes," p. 146.

36. "Les Organisations Professionnelles Agricoles et la CEE," p. 1.

37. Fischer, *Development of Interest Groups,* p. 26.

38. Dusan Sidjanski, "The European Pressure Groups," *Government and Opposition,* 2, (April-July 1967), 414.

39. "Les Organisations Professionnelles Agricoles et la CEE," p. 2.

40. Sidjanski, "European Pressure Groups," p. 409.

41. Ibid.

42. Ibid.

43. Ibid., p. 414.

44. Meynaud and Sidjanski, "L'Action des Groupes," p. 144.

45. Friedrich, *Europe: An Emergent Nation?* p. 77.

46. Meynaud and Sidjanski, "L'Action des Groupes," pp. 134-35.

47. "Le Marché Commun et l'Agriculture," p. 3, translation mine.

48. J. Pertejo, "Le Thème Européen dans les Élections Présidentielles Françaises des 5 et 19 Décembre 1965," paper presented to a seminar conducted by Professor Sidjanski (Geneva: Institut D'Études Europeennes, May, 1967), p. 17.

49. Perhaps the figures in table 2.1 should be interpreted with great caution. Pertejo has this to say in ibid., p. 16n: "L'enchantillon ne saurait être considéré comme satisfaisant du fait que les personnes consultées le furent 'un peu au hasard!'"

50. Fischer, *Development of Interest Groups,* p. 34.

51. Ibid.

52. Emile Noel, "Comment Fonctionnent les Institutions de la Communauté Européenne," *Les Documents Communauté Européenne* (Paris: Bureau of Information des Communautés Européennes), 51 (Dec. 1968), 13.

53. Fischer, *Development of Interest Groups,* p. 41.

54. Meynaud and Sidjanski, "L'Action des Groupes," p. 137.

55. *Treaty Establishing the European Economic Community and Connected Documents* (Brussels: Publishing Services of the European Communities, n.d.).

56. Edmund Rehwinkel, "Das Misstrauen der Westdeutschen Landwirtschaft gegen der Wirtschaftspolitik der heutigen Bundersregierung," *Agrarpolitik in Umbruch der Zeit* (1966).

57. *Les Groupes de Pression dans la CEE* (Amsterdam: Europa Institut, 1965), p. 16.

58. Leon N. Lindberg and Stuart A. Scheingold. *Europe's Would-Be Polity* (Englewood Cliffs, N.J.: Prentice-Hall, 1970), p. 80.

59. *Les Groupes de Pression,* p. 18.

60. Ibid., p. 22.

61. Werner Feld, "External Relations of the Common Market and Group Leadership Attitudes in the Member States," *ORBIS,* 10, 2 (Summer 1966), 56.

62. Ibid., pp. 568-569.

63. Pierre Gerbet, "La Préparation de la Décision Communautaire au Niveau National Français," in Gerbet and Pepy (eds.), *La Décision dans les Communautés Européennes,* p. 207.

64. Marco M. Olivetti, "La Préparation de la Décision Communautaire au Niveau National Italien," in ibid., p. 217. EC refers to the European Community, including EURATOM, ECSC, and EEC after the merger of the three separate insitutions in 1968. There was a transitional period (July 1, 1967, to July 1, 1970), during which it was referred to in the plural as European Communities. After this period it is simply referred to as European Community (EC).

65. Ibid., p. 219.

66. Ibid., pp. 220-222.

67. John Lambert, *Britain in a Federal Europe* (London: Chatto and Windus, 1968), p. 21.

68. "Position du COPA sur les Propositions de la Commission Concernant la Fixation des Prix pour les Produits Agricoles" COPA Assembly (Brussels, July 22, 1969), Doc. A (69), p. 4.

69. Communication à la Presse (Brussels, July 28, 1965), Doc. 969/65 (Ag 272), p. 1.

70. Meynaud and Sidjanski, ""Action des Groupes," p. 141.

71. Gabriel A. Almond and Sidney Verba. *The Civic Culture* (Boston: Little, Brown and Co., 1965), p. 191.

72. Lindberg and Scheingold, *Europe's Would-Be Polity*, p. 162.

73. Examples cf marathon sessions are provided by agricultural negotiations in January 1962, December 1963, and December 1964.

74. "The Agricultural Session of the EEC Council Has Made No More than Modest Progress," *Agence Europe*, Dec. 13, 1963, p. 1.

75. Hans Wimmer, "Must the Ministers Endure Those All-Night Marathons?" *European Community* (London), 1 (Jan. 1970), 9.

76. Ernst B. Haas, "Technocracy, Pluralism and the New Europe," in Stephen Graubard (ed.), *A New Europe* (Boston: Houghton Mifflin, 1964), and Talcott Parsons, "Polarization of the World and International Order," in Talcott Parsons, *Sociological Theory and Modern Society* (New York: Free Press, 1967), pp. 466-489.

77. Zeller, *L'Imbroglio Agricole du Marché Commun* (Paris: Calmann-Levy, 1970), p. 72, translation mine.

78. "The Righteous Dumpers," *Agenor*, 16 (March 1970), 55-56.

79. Zeller, *L'Imbroglio*, p. 53.

80. See Philippe C. Schmitter, "Three Neo-Functional Hypotheses about International Integration," *International Organization*, 23 (Winter 1969), 162-163.

81. Gabriel A. Almond, "Political Development: Analytical and Normative Perspectives," *Comparative Political Studies*, 1, 4 (Jan. 1969), 447-469.

CHAPTER THREE

1. Norman MacRae, "How the EEC Makes Decisions," *Atlantic Community Quarterly*, 8, 3 (Fall 1970), 363.

2. The umbrella interest groups play a role here, although it is limited for the most part to "finding" preexisting areas of agreement rather than creating them. There are also a number of different groups and practices, most of which have emerged after the problem of quantity of detail appeared, which serve to screen out detail before it reaches the higher decision-making levels. Among these are the Committee of Permanent Representatives and the practices of "written procedure" and "Points A." The written procedure is the process by which the Commission circulates copies of proposals among various Commission members. If the proposal is not questioned within a week, it is deemed acceptable by all members. The "Points A" procedure refers to a practice adopted in 1962 by which the CPR designates certain noncontroversial issues as such. These become "Points A" and when they are passed along to the Council of Ministers they are generally accepted without discussion.

3. Rajni Kothari, *Politics in India* (Boston: Little, Brown and Co., 1970), pp. 216-218.

4. See Johan Galtung, "On the Future of the International System," *Journal of Peace Research*, 4 (1967), 305-333, and James N. Rosenau (ed.), *Linkage Politics* (New York: Free Press, 1969).

5. John Lambert, *Britain in a Federal Europe* (London: Chatto and Windus, 1968), p. 19.

6. In this section I rely heavily upon Leon Lindberg's article, "The European Community as a Political System: Notes toward the Construction of a Model," *Journal of Common Market Studies*, 5, 4 (June 1967), 344-387.

7. See especially Peter Bachrach and Morton S. Baratz, "Two Faces of Power," and by the same authors, "Decisions and Nondecisions: An Analytical Framework," both in Roderick Bell, David V. Edwards, and R. Harrison Wagner (eds.), *Political Power* (New York: Free Press, 1969), pp. 94-110 and pp. 632-642.

8. Werner Feld, "National Economic Interest Groups and Policy Formation in the EEC," *Political Science Quarterly*, 81, 3 (Sept. 1966), 394.

9. Ibid., p. 396.

10. For an excellent and detailed treatment of the CPR see Emile Noel, "The Committee of Permanent Representatives," *Journal of Common Market Studies*, 5, 3 (March 1967), 219-251.

11. The Federal Republic of Germany is an exception.

12. Lambert, *Britain in a Federal Europe*, p. 26.

13. John Newhouse, *Collision in Brussels: The Common Market Crisis of 30 June 1965* (London: Faber and Faber, 1967), p. 82.

14. The Kennedy Round refers to an extended period of multilateral tariff negotiations which began in May 1963 and ended on June 15, 1967. Although the negotiations involved many countries the chief participants were the United States, Japan, England, and the EEC.

15. David Coombes, *Politics and Bureaucracy in the European Community* (London: George Allen and Unwin, 1970), p. 178.

16. "Preparation for Entry Talks," *European Community*, 132 (March 1970), 16.

17. "The European Tour by Mr. Geoffrey Rippon: The New British Negotiator with the EEC," *Agence Europe*, Aug. 24 and 25, 1970, p. 2.

18. Gabriel A. Almond and James S. Coleman (eds.), *The Politics of the Developing Areas* (Princeton: Princeton University Press, 1960), pp. 33-34.

19. *Treaty Establishing the European Economic Community and Connected Documents* (Brussels, Publishing Services of the European Communities, n.d.), pp. 129-130.

20. Ibid., p. 130.

21. Emile Noel, "How the European Economic Community's Institutions Work," Document 8 in Howard Bliss (ed.), *The Political Development of the European Community: A Documentary Collection* (Waltham, Mass.: Blaisdell Publishing Co., 1970).

22. Between July 1, 1967, and July 1, 1970, a Commission of fourteen members sat in Brussels. This was a transitional phenomenon which resulted from the merger of the EEC, ECSC, and EURATOM. On July 1, 1970, the original nine-member Commission returned headed by Franco Malfatti.

23. David Coombes, *Towards a European Civil Service*, Political and Economic Planning Publication, European Ser. 7 (London: Chatham House, March 1968), p. 7.

24. Lambert, *Britain in a Federal Europe*, p. 17.

25. Coombes, *Politics and Bureaucracy*, p. 103.

26. Godfrey Wilson and Monica Wilson, *The Analysis of Social Change* (Cambridge: Cambridge University Press, 1968), p. 52.

27. Leon N. Lindberg, *The Political Dynamics of European Economic Integration* (Stanford: Stanford University Press, 1963), pp. 235-236.

28. *La Politique Industrielle de la Communauté*, Memorandum de la Commission au Conseil (Brussels: Commission des Communautés Européennes, 1970), p. 3, translation mine.

29. *Memorandum on the Reform of Agriculture in the European Economic Community.* Supplement 1. (Brussels: Commission of the European Communities, 1969), p. 3.

30. Fritz Fischer, *Die Institutionalisierte Vertretung Der Verbände in der Europäischen Wirtschaftsgemeinschaft* (Hamburg: Hansischer Gildenverlag, 1965), p. 72.

31. *Memorandum of the Commission on the Action Programme of the Community for the Second Stage* (Brussels, Oct. 1962).

32. Louis Cartou, "Le Rôle de la Commission," in Pierre Gerbert and Daniel Pepy (eds.), *La Décision dans les Communautés Européennes* (Brussels: University of Brussels Press, 1969), p. 5.

33. Ibid., p. 6.

34. Leon N. Lindberg and Stuart Scheingold, *Europe's Would-Be Polity* (Englewood Cliffs, N.J.: Prentice-Hall, 1970), p. 173.

35. See for example Carol Ann Cosgrove and Kenneth J. Twitchett, "Merging the Communities: A Milestone in West European Integration," *ORBIS*, 13, 3 (Fall 1969), 864.

36. Coombes, *Politics and Bureaucracy*, p. 279.

37. Ibid., pp. 242-243.

38. "Summit Revives European Spirit," *European Community*, 130 (Jan. 1970), 3.

39. Macrae, "How the EEC Makes Decisions," p. 368.

40. E. E. Schattschneider, *The Semi-Sovereign People* (New York: Holt, Rinehart and Winston, 1960), p. 35.

41. Ibid.

42. Kothari, *Politics in India*, pp. 216-218.

CHAPTER FOUR

1. For example see Myron Weiner, "The Politics of South Asia," in Gabriel A. Almond and James S. Coleman (eds.), *The Politics of the Developing Areas* (Princeton: Princeton University Press, 1960); and Lloyd Rudolph, *The Modernity of Tradition* (Chicago: University of Chicago Press, 1967).

2. H. Vredeling, "The Common Market of Political Parties," *Government and Opposition*, 6, 4 (Autumn 1971), 448-461.

3. Stanley Henig and John Pinder (eds.), *European Political Parties*, Political and Economic Planning Publication (London: George Allen and Unwin, 1969), 483-484.

4. Terkel T. Nielsen, "Aspects of the EEC Influence of European Groups in the Decision-Making Processes: The Common Agricultural Policy," *Government and Opposition*, 6, 4 (Autumn 1971), 548.

5. Ibid., p. 542.

6. "Les Organisations Professionnelles Agricoles et la CEE," *Documentation Européenne* (1969), p. 1, translation mine.

7. This finding has been loosely confirmed by my own conversations with officials working for these umbrella groups. In particular, COPA officials felt that Feld was correct in his basic position and attributed this to the modifying and compromising aspects involved in the umbrella group route. Feld's findings are reported in "National Economic Interest Groups and Policy-Formation in the EEC," *Political Science Quarterly*, 81, 3 (Sept. 1966), 392-411.

8. Nielsen, "Aspects of the EEC Influence," p. 544.

9. Emile Noel, "How the European Economic Community's Institutions Work," in Howard Bliss (ed.), *The Political Development of the European Community* (Waltham, Mass.: Blaisdell Publishing Co., 1970), document 8.

10. Kenneth Dahlberg, "The Common Market Commission and the Politics of Integration," Ph.D. dissertation (University of Michigan, Ann Arbor: University Microfilms, 1966).

11. Ibid., p. 93.

12. Talcott Parsons, *The Structure of Social Action*, vol. 1 (New York: Free Press, 1937), p. 313.

13. Theodore Lowi, "The Public Philosophy: Interest Group Liberalism," in Edward V. Schneier (ed.), *Policy-Making in American Government* (New York: Basic Books, 1969), p. 335.

14. Ibid.

15. This has been one of the chief arguments in favor of party government in the United States especially as advocated by E. E. Schattschneider. The party provided a stable institution whose concerns cut across the gamut of society, which could be called to account for its actions.

16. Ghita Ionescu, "The New Politics of European Integration," *Government and Opposition*, 6, 4 (1971), 417-421.

17. Emile Noel and Henri Etienne, "Quelques Aspects des Rapports et de la Collaboration entre le Conseil et la Commission," in Pierre Gerbet and Daniel Pepy (eds.), *La Décision dans les Communautés Européennes* (Brussels: University of Brussels Press, 1969), p. 44.

18. Emile Noel and Henri Etienne, "The Permanent Representative Committee and the 'Deepening' of the Communities," *Government and Opposition*, 6, 4 (Autumn 1971), 432.

19. Noel and Etienne, "Quelques Aspects des Rapports," p. 44.

20. Noel and Etienne, "The Permanent Representative," p. 433.

21. Richard Mayne, *The Institutions of the European Community*, Political and Economic Planning, European Ser. 8 (London: Chatham House, 1968), p. 30.

22. Noel, "How the European Community's Institutions Work," pp. 82-83.

23. Ibid., p. 83.

24. *Les Groupes de Pression dans la C.E.E.* (Amsterdam: Europa Institut, 1965), p. 16.

25. Leon N. Lindberg and Stuart A. Scheingold, *Europe's Would-Be Polity: Patterns of Change in the European Community* (Englewood Cliffs, N.J.: Prentice-Hall, 1970), p. 173.

26. These were December-January 1961-62, December 1963, December 1964, May-June 1965, and May-July 1966. These sessions are reported in Frans A. M. Alting von Geusau, "Les Sessions Marathon du Conseil des Ministres," in Pierre Gerbet and Daniel Pepy (eds.), *La Décision dans les Communautés Européennes* (Brussels: University of Brussels Press, 1969), p. 99.

27. Ibid.

28. Ibid., p. 103.

29. "Agriculture," *Bulletin of the European Economic Community*, 2 (Feb. 1960), 38.

30. Michael Shanks and John Lambert, *Britain and the New Europe: The Future of the Common Market* (London: Chatto and Windus, 1962), p. 88.

31. "The Common Agricultural Policy," *Community Topics* (EEC Information Service), 28 (July 1967), 14.

32. Leon N. Lindberg, *The Political Dynamics of European Economic Integration* (Stanford: Stanford University Press, 1963), p. 238.

33. Ibid., p. 279.

34. Ibid., p. 252.

35. Ibid., p. 273.

36. *Seventh General Report on the Activities of the Community*, vol. 7 (Brussels and Luxembourg, 1964), p. 150.

37. "The Agricultural Session of the EEC Council Has Made No More than Modest Progress," *Agence Europe*, Dec. 13, 1963, p. 1.

38. Noel and Etienne, "The Permanent Representative," p. 430.

39. In this section my argument is heavily influenced by the perceptive analysis of David Coombes in *Politics and Bureaucracy in the European Community* (London: George Allen and Unwin, 1970),

40. Ibid., p. 258.

CHAPTER FIVE

1. Philip E. Jacob and Henry Teune, "The Integrative Process: Guidelines for Analysis of the Bases of Political Community," in Philip E. Jacob and James V. Toscano (eds.), *The Integration of Political Communities* (Philadelphia: J. B. Lippincott Co., 1964), p. 5.

2. Gabriel Almond and James S. Coleman (eds.), *The Politics of the Developing Areas* (Princeton: Princeton University Press, 1960), p. 7.

3. "Economic Advance—Political Retreat," *Common Market*, 3, 6 (June 1963), 105.

4. An articulate advocate of this school of thought is Stanley Hoffman, especially "Obstinate or Obsolete? The Fate of the Nation-State and the Case of Western Europe," in Joseph S. Nye, Jr. (ed.), *International Regionalism* (Boston: Little, Brown and Co., 1968).

5. "Unintended consequences" refers to all those areas where policy makers become boxed in or committed to new policy directions because of previous engagement in narrowly defined tasks.

6. This of course changed to a nine-member body once England, Ireland, and Denmark became formal members.

7. W. Hartley Clark, *The Politics of the Common Market* (Englewood Cliffs, N.J.: Prentice-Hall, 1967), p. 20.

8. Emile Noel, "How the European Economic Community's Institutions Work," *Community Topics* (European Community Information Service), 27 (Dec. 1966), 11.

9. Leon N. Lindberg, *The Political Dynamics of European Economic Integration* (Stanford: Stanford University Press, 1963), p. 55.

10. Stephen Holt, *The Common Market: The Conflict between Theory and Practice* (London: Hamish Hamilton, 1967), p. 54.

11. Ibid.

12. Ibid., p. 65.

13. Noel, "How the European Community's Institutions Work," p. 4.

14. Ibid., p. 5

15. Altiero Spinelli, *The Eurocrats: Conflict and Crisis in the European Community* (Baltimore: Johns Hopkins Press, 1966), p. 75.

16. Lindberg, *Political Dynamics*, p. 77.

17. Spinelli, *The Eurocrats*, p. 75.

18. Noel, "How the European Community's Institutions Work," p. 7.

19. Lindberg, *Political Dynamics*, p. 52.

20. Noel, "How the European Community's Institutions Work," p. 7.

21. *Treaty Establishing the European Economic Community and Connected Documents* (Brussels: Publishing Services of the European Communities, n.d.), p. 128.

22. The phrase is Ernst Haas's. See his "International Integration: The European and the Universal Process," in *International Political Communities: An Anthology* (New York: Doubleday and Co., 1966), p. 95.

23. Holt, *The Common Market*, p. 60.

24. Ibid.

25. Ibid., p. 63.

26. Lindberg, *Political Dynamics*, p. 79.

27. John Newhouse, *Collision in Brussels: The Common Market Crisis of 30 June 1965* (London: Faber and Faber, 1967), p. 81-82.

28. Holt, *The Common Market*, p. 65.

29. "The European Community Has Carried Out the Main Part of Its 'Synchronized Working Programme' within the Time Limit which Had Been Laid Down," *Agence Europe*, Dec. 30, 1963, pp. 1-2.

30. Leon N. Lindberg, "The European Community as a Political System: Notes toward the Construction of a Model," *Journal of Common Market Studies*, 5, 4 (June 1967), 344-387.

31. Joseph S. Nye, "Comparative Regional Integration: Concept and Measurement," *International Organization*, 22, 4 (Autumn 1968), esp. pp. 864-871.

32. Since this chapter was written an important article on the multidimensional nature of integration has appeared. See Barry B. Hughes and John E. Schwarz, "Dimensions of Political Integration and the Experience of the European Community," *International Studies Quarterly*, 16, 3 (Sept. 1972), 263-294.

33. Hubert M. Blalock, *Social Statistics* (New York: McGraw-Hill Book Co., 1960), p. 383.

34. On this point see the discussion by Benjamin Fruchter, *Introduction to Factor Analysis* (Princeton: D. Van Nostrand Co., 1954), pp. 5-6.

36. The rotated factors are shown—not the principal components. Basically, factors produced by the principal component solution are derived according to the criterion of what factor explains the most variance, whereas rotated factors represent the most homogeneous clusters.

37. Clark, *Politics of the Common Market*, p. 73.

38. Four indexes of political integration were formed: a general political integration measure, an adjudicative-implementative one, a rule-making one, and one for external affairs.

39. K. E. Boulding, "Toward a General Theory of Growth," *Canadian Journal of Economic and Political Science*, 19, 3 (Aug. 1953), 326.

40. This dimension was based on the first factor of table 5.5.

41. For extensive treatment of the spillover proposition see David Mitrany, *A Working Peace System* (Chicago: Quadrangle Books, 1966), and Ernst B. Haas, *Beyond the Nation State* (Stanford: Stanford University Press, 1964).

42. Philippe C. Schmitter has already suggested that the polarization process ("the process whereby the controversiality of decision-making goes up") is heightened in societies with a low level of structural differentiation. See his "The Process of Central American Integration: Spill-Over or Spill-Around, or Encapsulation?" *Journal of Common Market Studies*, 9, 1 (1971), 1-48.

43. This is given by the formula:

$$ t = \frac{(r12 - r13)\sqrt{(n-3)(1+r23)}}{\sqrt{2(1 - r^2_{12} - r^2_{13} - r^2_{23} + 2r_{12}r_{13}r_{23})}} $$

In Quinn McNemar, *Psychological Statistics* (3d ed.; New York: John Wiley and Sons, 1962), p. 140.

CHAPTER SIX

1. Altiero Spinelli, *The Eurocrats* (Baltimore: Johns Hopkins Press, 1966).

2. Karl Deutsch, Sidney Burrell, et al., "Political Community and the North Atlantic Area," in *International Political Communities: An Anthology* (New York: Anchor Books, 1966).

3. Ronald Inglehart, "An End to European Integration?" *American Political Science Review*, 61, 1 (March 1967), 91-105.

4. Howard Bliss, Introduction in Howard Bliss (ed.), *The Political Development of the European Community* (Waltham, Mass.: Blaisdell Publishing Co., 1970).

5. Leon N. Lindberg and Stuart A. Scheingold, *Europe's Would-Be Polity* (Englewood Cliffs, N.J.: Prentice-Hall, 1970).

6. Barry B. Hughes and John E. Schwarz, "Dimensions of Political Integration and the Experience of the European Community," *International Studies Quarterly*, 16, 3 (Sept. 1972), 264-266.

7. To some extent this is of course necessary. One could illustrate simply by asking how it is possible to coordinate components that are not yet in existence. The focus is therefore not on which process comes into existence first but on the pattern of asymmetries that exist once the original structures come into existence.

8. Howard J. Brickman, "Conceptual Frameworks for the Study of Integration" (Evanston: Northwestern University, May 1969), 2, mimeo.

9. For example see Ernst B. Haas, *Beyond the Nation-State: Functionalism and International Integration* (Stanford: Stanford University Press, 1964); Philippe C. Schmitter, "Central American Integration: Spill-Over, Spill-Around or Encapsulation?" *Journal of Common Market Studies*, 9, 1 (1971), 1-48; and Donald Puchala, "International Transactions and Regional Integration," *International Organization*, 24, 4 (Autumn 1970), 732-763.

10. Morton Kaplan, *System and Process in International Politics* (New York: John Wiley and Sons, 1957), p. 98.

11. Donald T. Campbell, "Common Fate, Similarity, and Other Indices of the Status of Aggregates of Persons as Social Entities," in David Singer (ed.), *Human Behavior and International Politics* (Chicago: Rand McNally and Co., 1965), pp. 85-95.

12. J. David Singer, *A General Systems Taxonomy for Political Science* (New York: General Learning Press, 1971), p. 9.

13. James G. Miller, "The Nature of Living Systems," *Behavioral Science*, 16, 4 (July 1971), 281.

14. Walter Buckley, *Sociology and Modern Systems Theory* (Englewood Cliffs, N.J.: Prentice-Hall, 1967), p. 9.

15. Henry Teune, "Integration of Political Systems," Paper prepared for delivery at 1971 Annual Meeting of the International Studies Association (San Juan, Puerto Rico, 1971), p. 7.

16. "The Nature of Living Systems," p. 292.

17. The following is an example of a multiple-bonded relationship. Suppose A and B are two variables that are unrelated. However, A and C are related and B and C are related. This is a case where the system itself may be characterized as interdependent, irrespective of the lack of relationships among some of the component parts. Another way to express it is to say that this represents a higher-order relationship, where the relationships themselves are related.

18. This design was originally set forth by Donald T. Campbell and Julian C. Stanley, *Experimental and Quasi-Experimental Designs for Research* (Chicago: Rand McNally and Co., 1966).

19. See Adam Przeworski and Henry Teune, *The Logic of Comparative Social Inquiry* (New York: John Wiley, 1970); and Raoul Naroll, "Some Thoughts on Comparative Method in Cultural Anthropology," in Hubert M. Blalock and Anne Blalock (eds.), *Methodology in Social Research* (New York: McGraw-Hill, 1968), pp. 236-277.

20. Donald T. Campbell and Julian C. Stanley, *Experimental and Quasi-Experimental Designs*; and D. Kahneman, "Control of Spurious Association and the Reliability of the Controlled Variable," *Psychological Bulletin*, 64 (1965), 326-329.

21. Paul F. Meehl, "Nuisance Variables and the Ex Post Facto Design," in Michael Radner and Stephen Winokur (eds.), *Analysis of Theories and Methods of Physics and Psychology*, Minnesota Studies in the Philosophy of Science, vol. 4 (Minneapolis: University of Minnesota Press, 1970), pp. 373-402.

22. James A Caporaso and Alan Pelowski, "Economic and Political Integration in Europe: A Time-Series Quasi-Experimental Analysis," *American Political Science Review*, 65, 2 (June 1971), 420-421.

23. Trend-removal techniques are discussed by George E. P. Box and George C. Tiao, "A Change in Level of Non-Stationary Time Series," *Biometrika*, 52, 1 and 2 (1965), 181-192; and by Paul Smoker, "A Time-Series Analysis of Sino-Indian Relations," *Journal of Conflict Resolution*, 13, 2 (June 1969), 172-191.

24. Joyce Sween and Donald T. Campbell, "A Study of the Effect of Proximally Autocorrelated Error on Tests of Significance for the Interrupted Time-Series Quasi-Experimental Design" (Northwestern University, 1965), mimeo.

25. Maurice H. Quenouille, *Associated Measurements* (New York: Academic Press, 1952).

26. Campbell and Stanley, *Experimental and Quasi-Experimental Design,* pp. 42-43.

27. Donald L. Thistlethwaite and Donald T. Campbell, "Regression-Discontinuity Analysis: An Alternative to Ex Post Facto Experiment," *Journal of Educational Psychology,* 51, 6 (Dec. 1960), 314.

28. Caporaso and Pelowski, "Economic and Political Integration in Europe," pp. 418-433.

29. Sween and Campbell, "A Study of the Effects of Proximally Autocorrelated Error," p. 6.

30. All values are expressed quarterly, i.e., four times a year at three-month intervals. Generally, observations run from 1958 to 1967-69, though not always.

31. A T score is a simple linear transformation of a standard score. The following formula is utilized to compute it: $T = 10(Z) + 50$, where Z is the standard score. In a normal distribution with standard scores ranging from +3 to −3, this formula will yield values ranging from +80 to +20.

32. See Dusan Sidjanski, *L'Originalité des Communautés Européennes et la Répartition de Leurs Pouvoirs* (Paris: Éditions A. Pedone, 1961), p. 25.

33. Leon N. Lindberg, "Interest Group Activities in the EEC," in Paul A. Tharp, Jr. (ed.), *Regional International Organizations: Structures and Functions* (New York: St. Martin's Press, 1971), p. 13.

34. "Die Auf der Ebene der Sechs Zusammengefassten Berufsverbände und die Gemeinschaft," *Bulletin der Europäischen Wirtschaftsgemeinschaft,* 4 (April 1961), 11, no author cited, translation mine.

35. The data were compiled from *Répertoire des Organismes dans le Cadre des Communautés Européennes* (Brussels: Services des Publications des Communautés Européennes, 1969).

36. "Agricultural Marathon Well on Way to Compromise Based on Commission's Proposals," *Agence Europe,* Dec. 14, 1964, p. 1.

37. Ibid.

38. Cited in *Germany in Europe* (New York: German Information Center, n.d.), p. 13.

39. Kenneth E. Boulding, "Toward a General Theory of Growth," *Canadian Journal of Economics and Political Science,* 19, 3 (Aug. 1953), 326-340.

40. Of course one way out of this difficulty is simply to adopt an extreme operationalist posture and say that export integration is one concept and import integration another. While one is free to adopt this position it seems to me to have two defects. By making a concept coterminous with its indicator a great deal of the concept's theoretical power is drained away. Since in this context indicators do not really indicate (they define), it becomes impossible to assess the error involved; it thus becomes impossible to assess the discrepancy between a pointer and an underlying concept. Also, if all there is to concepts are their indicators, it appears nonsensical to attempt to deal with these problems in a comparative framework. Indicators are often peculiar to given social settings. The view here is that indicators are incomplete and fallible attempts to catch a concept. It is possible to assess how well this is done by referring to standards of reliability and validity, that is, by the language of measurement.

41. Miriam Camps, *European Unification in the Sixties* (New York: McGraw-Hill Book Co., 1966), p. 115.

42. Norman Macrae, "How the EEC Makes Decisions," *Atlantic Community Quarterly,* 8, 3 (Fall 1972), 363-371.

43. A wearing-off effect is where the causal event actually weakens (and gradually extinguishes) with the passage of time. Since the event is conceptualized as a discrete occurrence it is assumed that its continued influence is a function of some trace or residue it deposits in the system, such traces becoming increasingly less operant with the passage of time. An erosion effect, by contrast, retains its full (absolute) force over time but its causal impact is decreased because of the incorporation of additional variables.

44. The results presented by Caporaso and Pelowski in "Economic and Political Integration in Europe," justifies the conclusion that the EEC was only a "weakly integrating system." The differences are admittedly those of degree and are probably attributable to the presence of more stable, composite indexes here. The analysis in the article cited was carried out with single indicators as dependent variables.

45. G. E. P. Box and George C. Tiao, "A Change in Level of a Non-Stationary Time Series," *Biometrika*, 52, 1 and 2 (1965), 181-192.

46. Ibid., p. 182.

47. Ibid., p. 188.

48. Kenneth E. Boulding, *A Primer on Social Dynamics* (New York: Free Press, 1970), pp. 14-15.

CHAPTER SEVEN

1. For a systematic treatment of some of these changes see Andrew M. Scott, *The Revolution in Statecraft: Informal Penetration* (New York: Random House, 1965); and James N. Rosenau (ed.), *Linkage Politics* (New York: Free Press, 1969).

2. "Two-Way Traffic: State Offices in Brussels," in *The Bulletin: The Belgian Weekly in English*, 26 (July 1970), 16.

3. Henry A. Kissinger, *American Foreign Policy* (New York: W. W. Norton and Co., 1969).

4. Talcott Parsons, "A Functional Theory of Change," in Amitai Etzioni and Eva Etzioni (eds.), *Social Change: Sources, Patterns and Consequences* (New York: Basic Books, 1964).

5. Werner Feld, "The Association Agreements of the European Communities: A Comparative Analysis," in Carol Ann Cosgrove and Kenneth J. Twitchett (eds.), *The New International Actors: The United Nations and the European Economic Community* (London: Macmillan and Co., 1970), p. 237.

6. Ralf Dahrendorf, "Possibilities and Limits of a European Communities Foreign Policy," *World Today*, 27, 4 (April 1971), 149-150.

7. J. F. Deniau, "The External Policy of the European Economic Community," *Law and Contemporary Problems*, 26, 3 (Summer 1961), 366-367.

8. W. Hartley Clark, *The Politics of the Common Market* (Englewood Cliffs, N.J.: Prentice-Hall, 1967), p. 130.

9. Werner Feld, "External Relations of the Common Market and Group Leadership Attitudes in the Member States," *ORBIS*, 10, 2 (Summer 1966), 564.

10. Gordon L. Weil, "From External Relations to Foreign Policy: The Community and the World," *European Community*, 9 (Sept. 1968), 8.

11. Frans A. M. Alting von Geusau, *Beyond the European Community: The Case of Political Unification* (Belgium: Heule Publishers, 1968), esp. pp. 16-17.

12. Stanley Hoffman, *Gulliver's Troubles, or the Setting of American Foreign Policy* (New York: McGraw-Hill Book Co., 1968).

13. Walter F. Buckley, *Sociology and Modern Systems Theory* (Englewood Cliffs, N.J.: Prentice-Hall, 1967); Ludwig von Bertalanffy, *General Systems Theory* (New York: George Braziller, 1968); E. C. Tolman and E. Brunswick, "The Organism and the Causal Texture of the Environment," *Psychological Review*, 42 (1935), 43-77; and Donald T. Campbell, "Pattern-Matching as Essential to Distal Knowing," in K. R. Hammond (ed.), *The Psychology of Egon Brunswick* (New York: Holt, Rinehart and Winson, 1966), pp. 81-106.

14. W. R. Ashby, "Self-Regulation and Requisite Variety," in F. E. Emery (ed.), *Systems Thinking* (Middlesex, England: Penguin Books, 1969), p. 110.

15. Herbert Simon, *The Sciences of the Artificial* (Cambridge: Massachusetts Institute of Technology Press, 1969).

16. Buckley, *Sociology and Modern Systems Theory*, p. 62.

17. Werner J. Feld, "National-International Linkage Theory: The East European Communist System and the EEC," *Journal of International Affairs*, 22, 1 (1968), 107-120.

18. Von Geusau, *Beyond the European Community*, p. 17.

19. Ibid.

20. Ronald Steel, *Pax Americana*, rev. ed. (New York: Viking Press, 1970), p. 99.

21. Ibid., p. 100.

22. Jeffrey Hertzfeld, "COMECON and the Western Trade of COMECON Countries," *Common Market*, 8, 1 (Jan. 1968), 309-312.

23. Albania and East Germany joined later in February 1949 and September 1950, respectively.

24. Andrez Korbonski, "COMECON," *International Conciliation*, 549 (Sept. 1964), 10.

25. Ibid., p. 11.

26. Marshall D. Shulman, "The Communist States and Western Integration," in Francis O. Wilcox and H. Field Haviland, Jr. (eds.), *The Atlantic Community: Progress and Prospects* (New York: Praeger, 1963), p. 133.

27. Feld, "National-International Linkage Theory," p. 111.

28. Shulman, *The Atlantic Community: Progress and Prospects*, p. 131.

29. David Coombes, *Politics and Bureaucracy in the European Community* (London: George Allen and Unwin, 1970), p. 168.

30. Werner Feld, *The European Common Market and the World* (Englewood Cliffs, N.J.: Prentice-Hall, 1967), p. 102.

31. Frans A. M. Alting von Geusau (ed.), *Economic Relations after the Kennedy Round* (Leiden: A. W. Sijthoff, 1969), p. 36.

32. Ibid., p. 37.

33. The disparities issue refers to the fact that the U.S. tariffs included a substantial proportion of items that had very high tariffs and a large number that were very low while the EC countries had tariffs concentrated mostly in the range of 10 to 25 percent. The Community argument was that in cases where these inequalities were great the principle of a linear tariff reduction would not be applied. See Feld, *The European Common Market and the World*, pp. 94-95.

34. Coombes, *Politics and Bureaucracy in the European Community*, p. 193.

35. Ibid., pp. 193-194.

36. L'Europe Européenne: Est-Elle Née à Genève?" *Revue du Marché Commun*, 102 (May 1969), 283-284.

37. In this section I rely heavily on chapter 1 of my *Functionalism and Regional Integration: A Logical and Empirical Assessment*, Sage Professional Papers, International Studies Series, vol. 1 (Beverly Hills, Calif.: Sage Publications, 1972).

38. David Mitrany, quoted in Cosgrove and Twitchett (eds.), *The New International Actors*, p. 51. The original source in which Mitrany's quote appeared is not given.

39. E. H. Carr, *Nationalism and After* (London: Macmillan and Co., 1945), p. 45.

40. David Mitrany, "Delusions of Regional Unity," in Bart Landheer (ed.), *Limits and Problems of European Integration* (The Hague; Martinus Nijhoff, 1965), p. 45.

41. For an elaboration of this point see Donald J. Puchala, "International Transactions and Regional Integration," *International Organization*, 24, 4 (Autumn 1970), 732-763; James A. Caporaso, "Theory and Method in the Study of International Integration," *International Organization*, 25, 2 (Spring 1971), 228-253; and Barry B. Hughes, "Transaction Data and Analysis: In Search of Concepts," *International Organization*, 26, 4 (Autumn 1972), 659-680.

42. *Treaty of Rome*, Part 4, Article 131, cited in P. N. C. Okigbo, *Africa and the Common Market* (Evanston: Northwestern University Press, 1967), p. 26.

43. Okigbo, *Africa and the Common Market*, p. 46.

44. Pierre Jalée, *The Pillage of the Third World* (New York: Modern Reader Paperbacks, 1968), p. 96.

45. Feld, *The European Common Market and the World*, p. 121.

46. Jalée, *Pillage of the Third World*, p. 88.

47. Ibid., p. 89.

48. Gunnar Myrdal, *The Challenge of World Poverty* (New York: Vintage Books, 1971), p. 286.

49. Feld, *The European Common Market and the World*, p. 116.

50. Rupert Emerson, "The Atlantic Community and the Emerging Countries," in Francis O. Wilcox and H. Field Haviland, Jr. (eds.), *The Atlantic Community: Progress and Prospects* (New York: Praeger, 1963), p. 119.

51. "Common Market Curb on Produce Angers 18 African Countries," *New York Times*, Oct. 18, 1972, p. 10.

52. Ali A. Mazrui, "African Attitudes to the European Economic Community," in Lawrence B. Krause (ed.), *The Common Market: Progress and Controversy* (Englewood Cliffs, N.J.: Prentice-Hall, 1964), p. 126.

53. Shulman, "The Communist States and Western Integration," p. 132.

54. Ibid., p 133.

55. Ibid., p. 142.

56. David Mitrany, "The Prospect of Integration: Federal or Functional?" in Joseph S. Nye, Jr. (ed.), *International Regionalism: Readings* (Boston: Little, Brown and Co., 1968), p. 47.

57. Ronald Inglehart, "The New Europeans: Inward or Outward-Looking?" *International Organization*, 24, 1 (Winter 1970), 129-139.

58. Ronald Inglehart, "Cognitive Mobilization and European Identity," *Comparative Politics*, 3, 1 (Oct. 1970), 45-70.

59. Inis Claude, Jr., "European Organization in the Global Context," Lectures given on March 15-17, 1965, Free University of Brussels, no. 12, p. 3.

60. Ibid., p. 18.

61. Technically, GATT is not a global (in the sense of universal) organization although its membership is sufficiently large to make it more than a regional organization. Basically GATT is a multilateral trade agreement whose members include all of the major free-world trading nations. These member nations are responsible for over 80 percent of world trade.

62. James Jay Allen, "The European Common Market and General Agreement on Tariffs and Trade: A Study in Compatibility," *Law and Contemporary Problems*, 26, 3 (Summer 1961), 564.

63. In actual practice a simple arithmetic mean would have resulted in a customs tariff that might have been unacceptable to GATT since it would have ignored the volume of trade of the member countries. To remedy this a series of exception lists were drawn up and treated distinctly.

64. M. E. Kreinin, "The 'Outer Seven' and European Integration," *American Economic Review*, 50, 3 (June 1960), 372.

65. Jacob Viner, *The Customs Union Issue* (London: Carnegie Endowment for International Peace, 1950), p. 54.

66. Kreinin, "The 'Outer Seven' and European Integration," p. 373.

67. Denis de Rougement, "Man's Western Quest," cited in W. Warren Wagar, *The City of Man* (Baltimore: Penguin Books, 1963), p. 234.

68. Robert Tucker, *Nation or Empire* (Baltimore: Johns Hopkins Press, 1968).

69. Mancur Olson, Jr. and Richard Zeckhauser, "An Economic Theory of Alliances," in Bruce M. Russett (ed.), *Economic Theories of International Politics* (Chicago: Markham Publishing Co., 1968).

70. Charles E. Lindbloom, *The Intelligence of Democracy: Decion-Making Through Mutual Adjustment* (New York: Free Press, 1965).

71. Henry A. Kissinger, *The Troubled Partnership* (New York: Anchor Books, 1966).

72. John Pinder and Roy Pryce, *Europe after de Gaulle* (Middlesex, England: Penguin Books, 1969), p. 134.

73. Ibid., p. 135.

208   THE STRUCTURE AND FUNCTION OF EUROPEAN INTEGRATION

74. Ibid., p. 136.
75. Johan Galtung, "On the Future of the International System," *Journal of Peace Research*, 4 (1967), p. 306.
76. Kenneth Waltz, "The Stability of a Bipolar World," in David V. Edwards (ed.), *International Political Analysis: Readings* (New York: Holt, Rinehart and Winston, 1970), pp. 318-342.
77. Morton Kaplan, *Macropolitics* (Chicago: Aldine Publishing Co., 1969).
78. Karl W. Deutsch and J. David Singer, "Multipolar Power Systems and International Stability," in David V. Edwards (ed.), *International Political Analysis: Readings* (New York: Holt, Rinehart and Winston, 1970), p. 348.
79. Johan Galtung, "Entropy and the General Theory of Peace," *Proceedings of the International Peace Research Association: Second Conference* (Oslo, 1967), p. 23.
80. Morton A. Kaplan, "International Politics and International Security," Paper delivered at the Midwest Workshop on National Security Education (Spring 1971), p. 4.
81. Richard A. Brody, "Some Systemic Effects of the Spread of Nuclear Weapons Technology: A Study through Simulation of a Multi-Nuclear Future," *Journal of Conflict Resolutions*, 7 (Dec. 1963), 633-753.
82. Leo. A. Hazlewood, "Informal Penetration, Systemic Constraints and Political Violence" (Florida State University, 1971), mimeo.
83. The normative implications of a multiunit system are explicit in Galtung's writings. To the best of my knowledge, Galtung is responsible for the distinction between associative and dissociative policies as two ways of constituting relationships among nations.
84. Jalée, *Pillage of the Third World*, p. 85.
85. Ashby, "Self-Regulation and Requisite Variety," p. 110.
86. Buckley, *Sociology and Modern Systems Theory*, p. 58.
87. Although relying on the Emery-Trist article for the original insight I have departed considerably from their formulation in some aspects. See F. E. Emery and E. L. Trist, "The Causal Texture of Organizational Environments," in F. E. Emery (ed.), *Systems Thinking* (Baltimore: Penguin Books, 1969), pp. 241-257.
88. M. P. Schutzenburger, "A Tentative Classification of Goal-Seeking Behaviors," ibid., p. 246.
89. Morton Grodzins, "Centralization and Decentralization in the American Federal System," in Robert A. Goldwin (ed.), *A Nation of States* (Chicago: Rand McNally and Co., 1961).

CONCLUSION

1. Leon N. Lindberg and Stuart A. Scheingold, *Europe's Would-Be Polity: Patterns of Change in the European Community* (Englewood Cliffs, N.J.: Prentice-Hall, 1970), p. 261.
2. Donald J. Puchala, "Of Blind Men, Elephants, and International Integration," *Journal of Common Market Studies*, 10, 3 (1972), 277.
3. Ibid., pp. 277-283.
4. Hans Kohn, *Nationalism: Its Meaning and History*, Rev. ed. (Princeton: D. Van Nostrand Co., 1965), p. 26.

Index

209